Level 2 • Part 1
Integrated Chinese

中文听说读写
中文聽説讀寫

TEXTBOOK

Simplified and Traditional Characters

Third Edition

THIRD EDITION BY

Yuehua Liu and Tao-chung Yao
Nyan-Ping Bi, Yaohua Shi, Liangyan Ge

ORIGINAL EDITION BY

Yuehua Liu and Tao-chung Yao
Yaohua Shi and Nyan-Ping Bi

CHENG & TSUI COMPANY

Boston

22 21 20 19 18   8 9 10 11 12

Published by
Cheng & Tsui Company, Inc.
25 West Street
Boston, MA 02111-1213 USA
Fax (617) 426-3669
www.cheng-tsui.com
"Bringing Asia to the World"™

ISBN 978-0-88727-680-4— ISBN 978-0-88727-679-8 (pbk.)

Cover Design: studioradia.com

Cover Photographs: Man with map © Getty Images; Shanghai skyline © David Pedre/iStockphoto; Building with masks © Wu Jie; Night market © Andrew Buko. Used by permission.

Interior Design: Wanda España, Wee Design

Illustrations: 洋洋兔动漫

Dim Sum photo (p. 82): Victoria E. Kichuk
Food photos (p. 94–95): Andrew Buko
Map of China (p. 325): Mapping Specialists, Inc.
Map of China (p. 334): exxorian / iStockphoto
Yunnan photo (p. 338): Julian Damashek
Harbin Ice Festival photo (p. 339): Harry Alverson / Flickr
Snow sculpture at Harbin Ice Festival photo (p. 339): www.flickr.com/photos/emmajg
Jinsha Jiang photo (p. 339): Chen Ying / Flickr
Cube photo (p. 341): Allen Li / Flickr
Bird's Nest photo (p. 341): Curt Smith / Flickr
Shanghai photo (p. 341): Jakob Montrasio / Flickr
Hangzhou photo (p. 347): Gustavo Madico / Flickr
Nanjing photo (p. 353): Liang Wang / Flickr

Library of Congress Cataloging-in-Publication Data

Integrated Chinese = [Zhong wen ting shuo du xie]. Level 2, part 1 / third ed. by Yuehua Liu ... [et al.] ; original ed. by Yuehua Liu ... [et al.] -- 3d ed.
    <v. 1> cm.
  Chinese and English.
  Parallel title in Chinese characters.
  Includes index.
  Contents: [1]. Textbook --
  ISBN 978-0-88727-680-4 -- ISBN 978-0-88727-679-8 (pbk.)
  1. Chinese language--Textbooks for foreign speakers--English. I. Liu, Yuehua. II. Title: Zhong wen ting shuo du xie.

PL1129.E5I683 2009
495.1'82421--dc22

                    2009075151

Printed in the United States of America

Contents

Lesson 1: 開學/开学   1

Lesson 4: 買東西/买东西   105

Lesson 5: 選課/选课   **137**

Let's Review! (Lessons 1–5)   **175**

Lesson 8: 打工   255

A. 壓力／压力 (pressure)

B. 受到 (to receive)

C. 減輕／减轻 (to lessen)

D. 適合／适合 (to suit) and 合適／合适 (suitable)

E. 影響／影响 (to influence or affect; influence)

F. 取得 (to obtain)

G. 說到／说到 (speaking of)

H. 嫌 (to dislike)

I. 不是A,就是B (if it's not A, it's B; either A or B)

J. 多 (How…it is!)

Lesson 9: 教育   291

1 Adverb 才

2 Descriptive Complements

3 Adverb 並／并

4 Adjectives as Predicates

5 不是A,而是B

A. 一直 (all along; continuously)

B. 好(不)容易 (with a lot of difficulty)

C. 像…一樣／像…一样 (as if)

D. 可以說／可以说 (you could say)

E. 這麼說／这么说 (so that means)

F. 最好 (had better; it's best)

Lesson 10: 中國地理/中国地理   **325**

Let's Review! (Lessons 6–10)   **365**

Indexes   **371**

Publisher's Note

When *Integrated Chinese* was first published in 1997, it set a new standard with its focus on the development and integration of the four language skills (listening, speaking, reading, and writing). Today, to further enrich the learning experience of the many users of *Integrated Chinese* worldwide, Cheng & Tsui is pleased to offer this revised and updated third edition of *Integrated Chinese*. We would like to thank the many teachers and students who, by offering their valuable insights and suggestions, have helped *Integrated Chinese* evolve and keep pace with the many positive changes in the field of Chinese language instruction. *Integrated Chinese* continues to offer comprehensive language instruction, with many new features and useful shared resources available on our website at **www.cheng-tsui.com**.

The Cheng & Tsui Chinese Language Series is designed to publish and widely distribute quality language learning materials created by leading instructors from around the world. We welcome readers' comments and suggestions concerning the publications in this series. Please contact the following members of our Editorial Board, in care of our Editorial Department (e-mail: editor@cheng-tsui.com).

Preface to the Third Edition

It has been over ten years since *Integrated Chinese* (*IC*) came into existence in 1997. During these years, amid all the historical changes that took place in China and the rest of the world, the demand for Chinese language teaching-learning materials has been growing dramatically. We are greatly encouraged by the fact that *IC* not only has been a widely used textbook at the college level all over the United States and beyond, but also has become increasingly popular with advanced language students at the high school level. Over the years, regular feedback from the users of *IC*, both students and teachers, has greatly facilitated our repeated revisions of the series. Following its second edition published in 2006 that featured relatively minor changes and adjustments, this third edition of Level 2 is the result of a much more extensive revision.

Changes in the Third Edition

Revised Storyline

In the present edition, a new, connected storyline about a diverse group of characters strings together all the lessons in Level 2. The relationships among the main characters are carefully scripted. We hope students will get to know the characters well and will enjoy following their life stories, and by doing so will feel more of a personal involvement in the process of learning the language.

Current Vocabulary

In Level 2, we have made a special effort to recycle many of the vocabulary items from Level 1. At the same time, we have accelerated the pace at which new vocabulary items and expressions are introduced, in the hope of enhancing students' ability to communicate. However, we are mindful of the number of vocabulary items introduced in this level and have tried to keep it manageable. Excluding proper nouns, there are about 350 vocabulary items introduced in Level 2, Part 1. Most of the *pinyin* renderings and parts of speech of the vocabulary items are based on the 5th Edition of the *Modern Chinese Dictionary* (現代漢語詞典第五版/现代汉语词典第五版) published by the Commercial Press (商務印書館/商务印书馆). For easy referencing, we have appended to the Level 2 textbook the Chinese-English Vocabulary Index from Level 1.

More Accessible Grammar and Usage Explanations

Apart from adding new grammar points, we have made the following important changes in the grammar explanations in Level 2:

- We have further expanded explanations of some of the grammatical concepts that are first introduced in Level 1 and offered detailed, contrastive discussions of some of the language structures that are similar in some way, to help students differentiate among them.
- As Level 2 is intended for students at the intermediate level, we have emphasized the use of linking words and phrases in order to improve students' ability to express themselves coherently in a series of sentences.
- The usage of some of the more difficult but common words and phrases is discussed in a new section, "Words & Phrases." Those items are highlighted in green in the main text of each lesson.

Clear Learning Objectives and an Engaging Learner-Centered Approach

Ever since its inception in 1997, *IC* has been a communication-oriented language textbook which also aims at laying a solid foundation in language form and accuracy for students. The third edition holds fast to that pedagogic philosophy. It has adopted a task-based teaching approach, which is intended to intensify students' motivation and heighten their awareness of the learning objectives in each chapter. Each lesson includes "Learning Objectives" and "Relate and Get Ready" sections at the beginning to help students prepare and concentrate. At the end of each lesson, questions in "Self-Assessment" are to be used by students in self-testing their achievement of the learning objectives.

Additionally, we have introduced in Level 2 another set of new features, which delineates successive steps in building effective learning strategies: the section "Before You Study" helps students focus on the theme of the lesson and gives them opportunities to make predictions based on their own experience; the section "When You Study" encourages students to skim or scan the lesson for the main ideas or specific information; and the section "After You Study" allows the students to confirm their predictions, to recap what happens in the lesson, or to understand the organization of the text. These guidelines are student-centered and designed to be done independently by the students themselves. But they can also be carried out in Chinese as part of the in-class activities if the instructor considers it appropriate to do so and if the students are linguistically ready.

Contextualized and Interactive Language Practice

The section "Language Practice" highlights the functions of the expressions in the current lesson and provides task-oriented classroom activities centered on those expressions. In particular, we have increased the number of interactive exercises as well as exercises that were designed for enhancing students' skills in oral communication and discourse formation. In at least one of such exercises, students are invited to link up a group of individual sentences and organize them in a coherent passage.

Similar changes are also present in the *Integrated Chinese* workbook, which offers new exercises that are more distinctly communication-oriented and more closely aligned with the learning objectives of each chapter. The exercises in the workbook cover the three modes of communication as explained in the "Standards for Foreign Language Learning in the 21st Century": interpretive, interpersonal and presentational. To help the user locate different types of exercises, we have labeled the workbook exercises in terms of the three communication modes.

Linguistically and Thematically Appropriate Cultural Information and Authentic Materials

In comparison with the earlier editions, there is more cultural information in the third edition. The revised texts provide a broader perspective on Chinese culture, and important cultural features and topics are discussed in the "Culture Highlights." In the meantime, more up-to-date language ingredients, such as authentic linguistic materials, new realia, and new illustrations, are introduced with a view towards reflecting cultural life in the dynamic and rapidly changing contemporary China. We believe that language is a carrier of culture and a second/foreign language is acquired most efficiently in its native cultural setting. Based on that conviction, we have attempted to offer both linguistic and cultural information in a coherent, consistent manner and simulate a Chinese cultural environment in our texts, especially those that are set in China.

A New, Colorful, and User-Friendly Design

Where design and layout are concerned, the third edition represents a significant improvement over the previous editions. We have taken full advantage of colors to highlight different components of each chapter, and have brought in brand-new illustrations and photos to complement the content of the text. The book has also been thoroughly redesigned for optimal ease of use.

Updated Audio Recordings

Throughout this book, an audio CD icon 💿 appears next to the main texts and vocabulary. This symbol indicates the presence of audio recordings, which are available on the companion audio CD set and as MP3 downloads.

It is our hope that these changes will enable students to learn Chinese in a more efficient and pragmatic way. By making these changes, we have attempted to place language acquisition in a real-world context and make *IC* all the more conducive to active use of the language, not only in the classroom, but more importantly, beyond it.

Acknowledgments

During the course of preparing for the third edition, we accumulated more academic and intellectual debts than any acknowledgment can possibly repay. We wish to express our deep gratitude to all those who helped us in so many different ways. In particular, our heartfelt thanks go to Professor Zheng-sheng Zhang of San Diego State University; Ms. Kristen Wanner; colleagues and friends at Beijing Language and Culture University; and Ms. Laurel Damashek at Cheng & Tsui.

As authors, we take great pleasure in the contributions that *IC* has made to Chinese teaching and learning over the past ten years, and we also feel the weight of responsibility to constantly improve on what has been done before. In retrospect, *IC* has traversed a long way since its earliest incarnation, yet we know its improvement will not end with the present edition. We promise to renew our efforts in the future, and we expect to continue to benefit from the invaluable comments and suggestions we receive from *IC* users.

An Overview of the New Features of the Third Edition

Chapter Opener

Each lesson opens with an illustration that highlights the theme for the lesson.

Learning Objectives for every lesson help students focus their study and envision what they will have accomplished at the end of the lesson. The self-reflective questions in **Relate and Get Ready** help students analyze similarities and differences between their native language and culture and Chinese language and culture.

LEARNING OBJECTIVES

In this lesson, you will learn to use Chinese to

1. Name basic clothing, bedding, and bath items;
2. Describe your shopping preferences and criteria;
3. Disagree with others tactfully;
4. Present your arguments with rhetorical questions.

RELATE AND GET READY

In your own culture/community—

- Can you purchase clothing and other necessities all in one shopping area?
- Do people usually pay for their purchases in cash, with checks, or with credit cards?
- Is there a sales tax?

Before, When, and After You Study

Before You Study

Check the statements that apply to you.

☐ 1. I have already declared my major.
☐ 2. I plan to double major.
☐ 3. I have an academic advisor.

When You Study

Listen to the audio recording and scan the text. Ask yourself the following questions before you begin a close reading of the text.

1. Where does the conversation take place?
2. Do the two characters know what courses they are going to take next semester?

New in Level 2, **Before You Study** and **When You Study** are placed before the main text, whereas **After You Study** appears at the end of the main text. The trio assists students to use various strategies when studying.

Text Design

Each text begins with two illustrations depicting the scene, with traditional text on the left page and simplified text mirrored on the right.

Language Notes, Grammar Callouts, Words & Phrases

In the text, words or expressions with corresponding **Language Notes** are clearly marked and numbered in green circles, and the notes are placed at the bottom of the page for ease of reference. The **Grammar Points** are highlighted and numbered in red to draw students' attention to the language forms covered in the grammar section of each lesson. Words that are explained in more details in the **Words & Phrases** section are highlighted in green for ease of reference.

張天明從家裏來的時候，媽媽給他買了一些衣服，像T恤衫❶、毛衣、牛仔褲❷什麼的，可是他覺得無論是樣子還是顏色都不太好①。今天是星期日，正好林雪梅和麗莎

LANGUAGE NOTES

❶ T恤衫 is a portmanteau word formed by combining the sounds and meanings of the Cantonese transliteration of the English "T-shirt" T恤 (pronounced *tiseot* in Cantonese) and the Mandarin morpheme 衫 "shirt." Modern Standard Chinese is based on the speech of Beijing and the vocabulary and syntax of the modern Chinese literary canon. Contributions from various dialects

Culture Highlights

Culture Highlights

❶ Harbin is the capital of Heilongjiang Province, which borders Russia. The city is well known for its long winters and historic Russian-style architecture. Since 1963, Harbin has hosted an annual ice and snow festival which draws many tourists from near and far. The festival includes an ice sculpting contest and numerous colorful ice lanterns.

哈爾濱的冰燈
哈尔滨的冰灯

❷ The Yellow River is historically considered the cradle of Chinese civilization. Its middle reach is heavily silted with loess soil from the Yellow Earth Plateau, which elevates the riverbed far above ground.

Photos or other authentic materials accompany the culture notes.

Language Practice

In addition to role plays and partner activities, this section also includes contextualized drill practice with the help of visual cues, as well as exercises to practice how to build a discourse. New sentence patterns are highlighted in blue.

E. It's Good for You!

a. Your friend Mr. Sickly is recovering from a debilitating illness. Offer him some health advice.

EXAMPLE:

 → 喝水對身體有好處。
喝水对身体有好处。

1.

2. X

3.

English Text

English Text

Before Zhang Tianming came to school, his mom bought him some clothes such as T-shirts, sweaters, jeans, and so on, but he doesn't think they are very good either in terms of style or color. Today is Sunday, and it just so happens that Lin Xuemei and Lisa need to buy some daily necessities such as toilet paper, toothpaste, towels, and laundry detergent, so Ke Lin takes them to the biggest shopping center nearby.

Ke Lin:	What clothes do you want to buy?
Zhang Tianming:	I'd like to buy a sweatsuit set.
Ke Lin:	Here they are. Look at this one. The style, size, and length are all very suitable. Plus, it's 20 percent off.
Zhang Tianming:	The color isn't bad, either. How much money? What's the brand?
Lin Xuemei:	The price is not expensive. I've never heard of the brand.
Lisa:	But it's pure cotton.
Zhang Tianming:	It won't do if it's not a good brand. I want name brand.
Ke Lin:	You're really fashionable, wearing name brands! That one looks like it's name brand. Oh my, way too expensive.
Zhang Tianming:	When it comes to shopping, I only buy name brand or I won't buy, because name-brand clothes are better quality.
Lisa:	That's right. Some clothes are inexpensive, but they are not good brands. After you've worn them once or twice, you don't want to wear them

The English translation of each text is added for students' reference at the end of the chapter, away from the main text, so that students will not be distracted when studying the main character text.

Self-Assessment

It is important for students to feel engaged and responsible for their own learning. At the end of each lesson, students are asked to check on their learning progress and evaluate whether they have achieved the learning objectives.

SELF-ASSESSMENT

How well can you do these things? Check (✔) the boxes to evaluate your progress and see which areas you may need to practice more.

I can	Very Well	OK	A Little
Name my major and other required courses	☐	☐	☐
Talk about my plans for after graduation	☐	☐	☐
Talk about ways to enhance my future job prospects	☐	☐	☐
Discuss whether my parents have a say in choosing my major and career path	☐	☐	☐
List ways to save money for school	☐	☐	☐

Let's Review

Let's Review! (Lessons 1-5)

I. Chinese Character Crossword Puzzles

You have learned many vocabulary items from Lessons 1–5. You may have noticed that some words/phrases share the same characters. Let's see whether you can recall these characters. The common character is positioned in the center of the cluster of rings. The block arrows indicate which way you should read the words. Work with a partner and see how many association rings you can complete. Of course, you may add more rings if you can think of additional words/phrases sharing the same characters or you may create your own clusters of rings.

EXAMPLE:

子 → 毯 / 被 子 牌 / 椅

After every five lessons, there is a section to help the students review the language forms and language functions introduced.

Preface to the Second Edition

The *Integrated Chinese* series is an acclaimed, best-selling introductory course in Mandarin Chinese. With its holistic, integrated focus on the four language skills of listening, speaking, reading, and writing, it teaches all of the basics that are needed by beginning and intermediate students to function in Chinese. *Integrated Chinese* helps students understand how the Chinese language works syntactically and semantically, and how to use Chinese functionally in real life.

The Chinese title of *Integrated Chinese*, which is simply 中文聽説讀寫/中文听说读写 (Zhōngwén Tīng Shuō Dú Xiě), reflects our belief that a healthy language program should be a well-balanced one. To ensure that students will be strong in all skills, and because we believe that each of the four skills needs special training, the exercises in the *Integrated Chinese* Workbooks are divided into four sections: listening, speaking, reading, and writing. Within each section, there are two types of exercises, namely, traditional exercises (such as fill-in-the-blank, sentence completion, translation, etc.) to help students build a solid foundation, and communication-oriented exercises to prepare students to face the real world.

How Integrated Chinese Has Evolved

Integrated Chinese (IC) began in 1993 as a set of course materials for beginning and intermediate Chinese courses at the East Asian Summer Language Institute's Chinese School, at Indiana University. Since that time, it has become a widely used series of Chinese language textbooks in the United States and beyond. Teachers and students appreciate the fact that *IC*, with its focus on practical, everyday topics and its numerous and varied exercises, helps learners build a solid foundation in the Chinese language.

What's New in the Second Edition

Thanks to all those who have used *Integrated Chinese* and given us the benefit of their suggestions and comments, we have been able to produce a second edition that includes the following improvements:

☐ **Level 2 offers full text in simplified and traditional characters.** The original Level 2 Textbook and Workbook, although geared toward both traditional- and simplified-character learners, contained sections in which only the traditional characters were given. This was of course problematic for students who were principally interested in learning simplified characters. This difficulty has been resolved in the new edition, as we now provide both traditional and simplified characters throughout both the Textbook and the Workbook. Wherever simplified and traditional character versions of a phrase or sentence fit on the same line, they are separated by a slash (/). Wherever simplified and traditional character versions do not fit on the same line, they appear one after another on separate lines. When only one version is given, the reader is to assume that the traditional and simplified characters are the same. For the **authentic materials** and for some photos that contain Chinese characters, we present them in their original forms to preserve their authenticity. An appendix containing alternate character versions is provided as a learning tool for those interested in reading both forms.

☐ A copy of the **pinyin text** is added at the end of each lesson for easy reference.

☐ Many **examples cited in the Grammar Notes section** have been revised to recycle vocabulary learned in previous levels. When words that have not been taught are introduced, glosses are provided. Grammatically incorrect sentences used in the grammar explanations are marked with an asterisk*.

☐ Typographical errors present in the first edition have been corrected, and the content has been carefully edited to ensure accuracy and minimize errors.

☐ The design has been revised and improved for easier use, and the Textbooks feature two colors.

☐ **New photos** provide the reader with visual interest and relevant cultural information.

☐ The Textbook contains a **new appendix of measure words.** This appendix includes all of the measure words introduced in Integrated Chinese as well as some additional, useful measure words.

☐ The original **Chinese-English vocabulary index** has been revised, and an **English-Chinese vocabulary index** has been added to the Textbook.

☐ In the Workbook, there is a **new index of vocabulary words** that are glossed in the workbook exercises.

☐ **The Workbook has been extensively revised.** New and different varieties of exercises have been added. Teachers can choose those that best suit their needs. To help students complete some assignments, visual clues are provided in addition to written instructions. More authentic materials are included. The materials are presented in their original characters to preserve their authenticity.

A Note about Vocabulary Lists

In the vocabulary lists, we indicate the part of speech for each vocabulary item. Four-character phrases, idiomatic expressions, and other phrases that cannot be classified by part of speech are left unmarked.

Vocabulary introduced in Integrated Chinese, Level 1, and glossed again in Integrated Chinese, Level 2, is marked with an asterisk *. Students who have studied the Level 1 text may refer to the first book if needed.

In the vocabulary lists and pinyin texts, we mark the **tone changes** that sometimes occur when a syllable is juxtaposed with another. But in the indices, we give the base tones for easy viewing.

Basic Organizational Principles

The field of language teaching has increasingly held it self-evident that the ultimate goal of learning a language is to communicate in that language. *Integrated Chinese* is a set of materials that gives students grammatical tools and also prepares them to function in a Chinese language environment. The materials cover two years of instruction, with smooth transitions from one level to the next. They first deal with topics of everyday life and gradually move to more abstract subject matter. The materials are not limited to one method or one approach, but instead they blend several teaching approaches that can produce good results. Here are some of the features of *Integrated Chinese* that distinguish it from other Chinese language textbooks:

Integrating Pedagogical and Authentic Materials

All of the materials in *Integrated Chinese* are graded. We believe that students can grasp the materials better if they learn simple and easy-to-control language items before the more difficult or complicated ones. We also believe that students should be taught some authentic materials even in the early stage of their language instruction. Therefore, most of the pedagogical materials are actually simulated authentic materials. Real authentic materials (written by native Chinese speakers for native Chinese speakers) are incorporated in the lessons when appropriate.

Integrating Written Style and Spoken Style

One way to measure a person's Chinese proficiency is to see if she or he can handle the "written style" (書面語/书面语, shūmiànyǔ) with ease. The "written style" language is more formal and literary than the "spoken style" (口語/口语, kǒuyǔ); however, it is also widely used in news broadcasts and formal speeches. In addition to "spoken style" Chinese, basic "written style" expressions are gradually introduced in Integrated Chinese, Level 2. Although we try to make the dialogues sound as natural as possible, we have avoided using expressions that are excessively colloquial or clearly reflective of regional usages. Where relevant, we have noted lexical differences between mainland China and Taiwan. In principle, we maintain a course that steers between extreme colloquialism and stilted textbook Chinese, between PRC-inflected and ROC-sounding phraseologies. We think this is the right decision for beginning students.

Integrating Traditional and Simplified Characters

We believe that by the second year of studying Chinese, all students should be taught to read both traditional and simplified characters. Therefore, the text of each lesson in *Integrated Chinese*, Level 2 is shown in both forms, and the vocabulary list in each lesson also contains both forms. Considering that students in a second-year Chinese language class might come from different backgrounds and that some may have learned the traditional form and others the simplified form, students should be allowed to write in either traditional or simplified form. It is important that the learner write in one form only, and not a hybrid of both forms. In the Character Workbook, each of the characters is given a frequency indicator based on the Xiàndài Hànyǔ Pínlǜ Dà Cídiǎn 《現代漢語頻率詞典/现代汉语频率词典》, published in 1986 by the Beijing Language Institute.

Integrating Teaching Approaches

Realizing that there is no single teaching method that is adequate in training a student to be proficient in all four language skills, we employ a variety of teaching methods and approaches in *Integrated Chinese* to maximize the teaching results. In addition to the communicative approach, we also use traditional methods such as grammar-translation and direct method. Users of *Integrated Chinese* appreciate that a major strength of the textbooks is their functional orientation. The focus of each lesson of *Integrated Chinese*, Level 2 is not on discrete grammatical points, but rather, we take a holistic approach to language teaching. Vocabulary, grammar, and discursive strategies are integrated in order to facilitate the learner's ability to function appropriately in different sociolinguistic environments. In short, our aim is not the compilation of a grammar manual but rather the presentation of grammar in a way that will allow learners to use the language in context accurately and appropriately.

Reinforcing Grammar Points Introduced in Integrated Chinese Level 1

Integrated Chinese was conceived and designed as a complete series for beginning and intermediate learners. *Integrated Chinese* Level 2 builds on *Integrated Chinese* Level 1, and the basic grammar introduced in Level 1 is reinforced in Level 2. But rather than simply regurgitate Level 1, we focus on some of the most important and complex grammatical phenomena in Level 2. In many instances, our approach is to zero in on the structures (numbering around 40) that are confusing to non-native learners, e.g., the difference between 了 and 過/过, or between 了 and 是…的 . Our treatment of grammar is systematically built and spirals upon the foundation of Level 1. (For instance, there is more analysis on various kinds of complements in Level 2.)

Furthermore, we have added grammar notes on topicalization and cohesion—subjects seldom if ever covered in intermediate level textbooks—to help students achieve greater fluency and proficiency at the discourse level. Users of Level 2 will find that many of the grammatical items are presented in a series—Cohesion (I) and (II), Word Order (I), (II), and (III), for instance. In the revised edition, we have also adjusted the numbering of the structures so that they follow the order of their appearance in the texts.

Online Supplements to Integrated Chinese

Integrated Chinese is not a set of course materials that employs printed volumes only. It is, rather, a network of teaching materials that exist in many forms. Resources are posted for *Integrated Chinese* users at **my.cheng-tsui.com**, Cheng & Tsui Company's online site for downloadable and web-based resources. Please visit this site often for new offerings.

Other materials are available at the *IC* website http://eall.hawaii.edu/yao/icusers/, which was set up by Ted Yao, one of the principal *Integrated Chinese* authors, when the original edition of *Integrated Chinese* was published. Thanks to the generosity of teachers and students who are willing to share their materials with other *Integrated Chinese* users, this website is constantly growing, and has many useful links and resources, such as links to resources that show how to write Chinese characters, provide vocabulary practice, and more.

Acknowledgments

Since publication of the first edition of *Integrated Chinese*, in 1997, many teachers and students have given us helpful comments and suggestions. We cannot list all of these individuals here, but we would like to reiterate our genuine appreciation for their help. We do wish to recognize the following individuals who have made recent contributions to the *Integrated Chinese* revision. We are indebted to Tim Richardson, Jeffrey Hayden, Ying Wang, and Xianmin Liu for field-testing the new edition and sending us their comments and corrections. We would also like to thank Chengzhi Chu for letting us try out his "Chinese TA," a computer program designed for Chinese teachers to create and edit teaching materials. This software saved us many hours of work during the revision. Last, but not least, we want to thank James Dew for his superb, professional editorial job, which enhanced both the content and the style of the new edition. We are also grateful to our editors at Cheng & Tsui, Sandra Korinchak and Kristen Wanner, for their painstaking work throughout the editing and production process. Naturally, the authors assume full responsibility for what appears between the covers of the *IC* series.

As much as we would like to eradicate all errors in the new edition, some will undoubtedly remain, so please continue to send your comments and corrections to editor@cheng-tsui.com, and accept our sincere thanks for your help.

Scope and Sequence

Lessons	Topics & Themes	Learning Objectives & Functions	Culture Highlights
1	開學/开学	1. Explain how to write your Chinese name 2. Say where you were born and grew up 3. Discuss the pros and cons of living on and off campus 4. Express politely a dissenting opinion	1. Housing for undergraduate students in China 2. Disambiguating homophones in Chinese
2	宿舍	1. Name basic pieces of furniture in a house 2. Describe your living quarters 3. Comment on someone's living quarters 4. Disagree tactfully	1. Housing for graduate students in China 2. Housing for international students in China
3	在飯館兒/ 在饭馆儿	1. Name four principal regional Chinese cuisines 2. Order food and drinks 3. Talk about what flavors you like or dislike 4. Make your dietary restrictions or preferences known	1. Settling a bill and tipping in Chinese restaurants 2. Private banquet rooms in restaurants in China 3. Basic Chinese cooking techniques 4. Major culinary styles in China
4	買東西/ 买东西	1. Name basic clothing, bedding, and bath items 2. Describe your shopping preferences and criteria 3. Disagree with others tactfully 4. Present your arguments with rhetorical questions	1. Knowing when to bargain 2. Cash, credit card, or personal check

Forms & Accuracy	Words & Phrases
1. The Dynamic Particle 了 (I) 2. The 是…的… Construction 3. 除了…以外 4. 再説/再说 5. Connecting Sentences (I)	A. 覺得/觉得 (to feel) B. 方便 (convenient) C. 安全 (safe) D. 省錢/省钱 (to save money; to economize) E. 自由 (free; unconstrained) F. 不見得/不见得 (not necessarily) G. 好處/好处 (advantage; benefit) H. 適應/适应 (to adapt; to become accustomed to)
1. Existential Sentences 2. Adverb 真 3. 比較/比较 4. 得很 5. 那(麼)/那(么) 6. Conjunctions	A. 恐怕 (I'm afraid; I think perhaps) B. 差不多 (about; roughly) C. 吵 (noisy; to quarrel) D. 安靜/安静 (quiet) E. 一般 (generally speaking) F. 不怎麼樣/不怎么样 (not that great; just so-so) G. 地道 (authentic; genuine; pure)
1. Topic-Comment Sentence Structure 2. 一 + V 3. 又 Adj/Verb, 又 Adj/Verb 4. The Emphatic 是 5. 不如	A. 正好 (coincidentally) B. 特別是 (especially) C. 麻煩/麻烦 ([may I] trouble [you]; troublesome) D. 這(就)要看…(了)/这(就)要看…(了) (that depends on…) E. 比如(説)/比如(说) (for example)
1. 無論…, 都…/无论…, 都… 2. Conjunction 於是/于是 3. Adj/V+是+Adj/V, 可是/但是… 4. Adverb 難道/难道	A. …什麼的/…什么的 (…etc.) B. 大小, 長短/长短, 寬窄/宽窄… (size, length, width…) C. 打折 (to discount; to sell at a discount) D. (要) 不然 (otherwise) E. 非…不可 (have to; must) F. 標準/标准 (criterion; standard) G. 在乎 (to mind; to care)

Lessons	Topics & Themes	Learning Objectives & Functions	Culture Highlights
5	選課/选课	1. State your major area of study/academic department and some required general courses you have taken 2. Talk about what you plan to do after graduating 3. Explore what will enhance your future job opportunities 4. Explain whether your family members have an influence on your choice of major and career path 5. Share tips on how to save money for your education	1. The compartmentalized educational system in China 2. Graduate school or research institute
Let's Review		Review Lessons 1–5	
6	男朋友 女朋友	1. Say if you have an upbeat personality 2. State if you share your interests or hobbies with others 3. Inquire if everything is OK and find out what has happened 4. Describe typical behaviors of a forgetful person 5. Give a simple description of what you look for in a boyfriend/girlfriend 6. Tell what makes you anxious or angry	1. Dating and marriage in China 2. Chinese Valentine's Day

Forms & Accuracy	Words & Phrases
1. 對⋯來説/对⋯来说	A. 只是 or 就是 (it's just that)
2. Resultative Complements	B. 受不了 (unable to bear)
3. Preposition 至於/至于	C. 肯定 (definitely)
4. 另外	D. 跟⋯打交道 (to deal with…)
5. 再, 又, and 還/还 Compared	E. 這樣/这样 (in this way)
6. 要麽⋯, 要麽⋯/要么⋯, 要么⋯	F. 不過/不过 (but)
1. Chinese Character Crossword Puzzles	
2. Make a Word List	
3. Organize Your Thoughts	
4. Let Me Explain Myself	
1. (在)⋯上	A. 到底 (what on earth; what in the world; in the end)
2. V來V去/V来V去	B. 根本 (at all, simply)
3. Adverbials and 地 (de)	C. 一乾二淨/一干二净 (completely, thoroughly, spotless)
4. 的, 得, and 地 Compared	D. 難怪/难怪 (no wonder)
5. 原來/原来 as Adverb and Adjective	E. 實際上/实际上 (actually; in fact; in reality)
6. Set Phrases	F. 丟三拉四 (scatterbrained; forgetful)
	G. 一會兒⋯, 一會兒⋯, 一會兒又⋯/一会儿⋯, 一会儿⋯, 一会儿又⋯ (one minute…, the next minute…)

Lessons	Topics & Themes	Learning Objectives & Functions	Culture Highlights
7	電腦和網絡/ 电脑和网络	1. Find out if others are angry with you and apologize if so 2. Reduce potential tension in a conversation by changing the subject 3. Let people know about the trouble you had to go through because of their thoughtlessness or carelessness 4. Name your activities on the internet and discuss how you make use of the internet 5. Discuss the pros and the cons of using the internet	1. Trendy new words in China 2. Instant messaging in China
8	打工	1. Review your monthly income and spending patterns 2. Talk about how you balance your personal budget 3. Name some possible reasons to work part-time while in school 4. Discuss the pros and cons of working part-time while in school 5. Describe what you dislike or what bothers you	1. Educational expenses in China 2. Part-time jobs for college students in China
9	教育	1. Comment if you had a stress-free childhood 2. Name some typical classes offered in after-school programs 3. Indicate agreement or disagreement 4. Present your opinions 5. Talk about parents' aspirations for their children	1. A Chinese model for friendship and mutual appreciation 2. Dragon and phoenix as metaphors

Forms & Accuracy	Words & Phrases
1. Conjunction 甚至 2. Potential Complements 3. 好 as a Resultative Complement 4. Connecting Sentences (II)	A. 從…到…/从…到… (from…to…) B. 結果/结果 (as a result) C. 或者 (or) D. 害(得) (to cause trouble [so that]); to do harm [so that]) E. 幾乎/几乎 (almost) F. 看起來/看起来 (it seems) G. 聽起來/听起来 (it sounds)
1. Directional Complements Suggesting Result 2. 來/来 Connecting Two Verb Phrases 3. The Dynamic Particle 了 (II) 4. Rhetorical Questions 5. Adverb 可	A. 壓力/压力 (pressure) B. 受到 (to receive) C. 減輕/减轻 (to lessen) D. 適合/适合 (to suit) and 合適/合适 (suitable) E. 影響/影响 (to influence or affect; influence) F. 取得 (to obtain) G. 說到/说到 (speaking of) H. 嫌 (to dislike) I. 不是A,就是B (if it's not A, it's B; either A or B): J. 多 (How…it is!)
1. Adverb 才 2. Descriptive Complements 3. Adverb 並/并 4. Adjectives as Predicates 5. 不是A,而是B	A. 一直 (all along; continuously) B. 好(不)容易 (with a lot of difficulty) C. 像…一樣/像…一样 (as if) D. 可以說/可以说 (you could say) E. 這麼說/这么说 (so that means) F. 最好 (had better; it's best)

Lessons	Topics & Themes	Learning Objectives & Functions	Culture Highlights
10	中國地理/ 中国地理	1. Locate major Chinese cities, provinces, and rivers on the map 2. Give a brief introduction to the geographic features of China 3. Compare some basic geographic aspects of China and the United States 4. Describe features that may attract you to or deter you from visiting a tourist site 5. Plan a trip to China	1. The City of Harbin 2. The Yellow River 3. The Yangtze River 4. Yunnan Province 5. Nationalities in China 6. Administrative divisions in China
Let's Review		Review Lessons 6-10	

Forms & Accuracy	Words & Phrases
1. 起來/起来 Indicating the Beginning of an Action 2. Conjunction 而 3. 最Adj不過了/最Adj不过了 4. 過/过 Indicating Experience	A. 為了/为了 (in order to) and 因為/因为 (because) B. 一下子 (in an instant) C. 大多 (mostly) D. 呢 (indicating a pause in speech)
1. Chinese Character Crossword Puzzles 2. Matching Words 3. Make a Word List 4. Organize Your Thoughts 5. Are You a Fluent Speaker?	

Abbreviations of Grammatical Terms

adj	Adjective
adv	Adverb
conj	Conjunction
interj	Interjection
m	Measure word
mv	Modal verb
n	Noun
nu	Numeral
ono	Onomatopoeia
p	Particle
pr	Pronoun
prefix	Prefix
prep	Preposition
pn	Proper noun
qp	Question particle
qpr	Question pronoun
t	Time word
v	Verb
vc	Verb plus complement
vo	Verb plus object

Cast of Characters

Zhang Tianming
張天明/张天明
is an American-born Chinese. His parents immigrated to the United States from Nanjing, China. He is a rabid sports fan and a computer whiz. He is very outgoing and has many friends, but his girlfriend thinks he spends too much time online. He is a college freshman.

Lisha
麗莎/丽莎
Lisa Cohen
is also a college freshman. She and Zhang Tianming were high school sweethearts. Lisa loves music and is interested in all things Chinese.

Li Zhe
李哲
Zack Ruiz
is a senior and a good friend of Zhang Tianming's. He and Zhang Tianming like to hang out together and talk or play basketball. Li Zhe's older brother is an information technology specialist. His sister-in-law is originally from Hong Kong. Li Zhe has an eight-year old niece.

Lin Xuemei
林雪梅
is a graduate student from Hangzhou, China. She and Ke Lin are about four or five years older than Zhang Tianming and Lisa. Lin Xuemei and Lisa quickly became good friends.

Ke Lin
柯林
Al Collins
is Lin Xuemei's boyfriend. He is also a graduate student. He wants to study in China after he receives his master's degree. He is very warm and loves to help others.

第一课　第一课
開學　开学

 LEARNING OBJECTIVES

In this lesson, you will learn to use Chinese to

1. Explain how to write your Chinese name;
2. Say where you were born and grew up;
3. Discuss the pros and cons of living on and off campus;
4. Express politely a dissenting opinion.

 RELATE AND GET READY

In your own culture/community—

- How do people talk about the origins of their names?
- Do students prefer on-campus or off-campus housing?
- What services are provided for first-year students when they arrive on campus?

Before You Study

Check the statements that apply to you.

☐ 1. I am a first-year student.

☐ 2. I flew in before the beginning of this new school year.

When You Study

Listen to the audio recording and scan the text. Ask yourself the following questions before you begin a close reading of the text.

1. When and where does the conversation take place?

張天明是大學一年級的新生❶。快開學了，他家離大學很遠，得坐飛機去學校。他坐飛機坐了兩個多小時。下飛機以後，他馬上叫了一輛出租汽車，很快就到了學校宿舍①。

LANGUAGE NOTES

❶ 新生 (xīnshēng, new student) is the Chinese term for students in an incoming school class. College freshmen are also known as 新鮮人／新鲜人 (xīnxiānrén) in Taiwan, a (perhaps initially facetious) translation from English that may raise an eyebrow or two in mainland since the adjective

☐ 3. I am used to campus life.
☐ 4. I live in a student dorm.
☐ 5. I know the meaning of the characters of my Chinese name.

2. What do the two characters have in common?
3. What is the main topic of the conversation?

张天明是大学一年级的新生❶。快开学了，他家离大学很远，得坐飞机去学校。他坐飞机坐了两个多小时。下飞机以后，他马上叫了一辆出租汽车，很快就到了学校宿舍①。

新鲜/新鲜 (xīnxian, fresh) is associated with food or events where the word means "novel" or "unusual." Returning students are called 老生 (lǎoshēng, old students) in Chinese.

張天明：　人真多！

柯林：　　你是新生吧？

張天明：　是，我是新生。你呢？

柯林：　　我是研究生。在這兒幫新生搬東西。請問，你叫什麼名字？

張天明：　我叫張天明。

柯林：　　張天明？是中文名字嗎？

張天明：　對，我爸爸媽媽是從中國來的。可是我是在美國出生，在美國長大的②。請問你的名字是…

柯林：　　我正在學中文，我的中文名字是柯林。你的名字是哪三個字？

張天明：　張是弓長張，就是一張紙的張，天是天氣的天，明是明天的明。

柯林：　　你是怎麼來學校的？

張天明：　我先坐飛機，從機場到學校坐出租汽車。柯林，你也住在這兒嗎？

柯林：　　不，這是新生宿舍，我住在校外。

張天明：　是嗎？你為什麼住校外？你覺得住在校內好，還是住在校外好？

柯林：　　有的人喜歡住學校宿舍，覺得又方便又安全，有的人喜歡住在校外，因為校外的房子比較便宜。我住在校外，除了想省點兒錢以外③，還為了自由。再說④，住在校內也不見得很方便。

張天明：　真的嗎？那我以後也搬到校外去。

张天明：人真多！

柯林：　你是新生吧？

张天明：是，我是新生。你呢？

柯林：　我是研究生。在这儿帮新生搬东西。请问，你叫什么名字？

张天明：我叫张天明。

柯林：　张天明？是中文名字吗？

张天明：对，我爸爸妈妈是从中国来的。可是我是在美国出生，在美国长大的^②。请问你的名字是…

柯林：　我正在学中文，我的中文名字是柯林。你的名字是哪三个字？

张天明：张是弓长张，就是一张纸的张，天是天气的天，明是明天的明。

柯林：　你是怎么来学校的？

张天明：我先坐飞机，从机场到学校坐出租汽车。柯林，你也住在这儿吗？

柯林：　不，这是新生宿舍，我住在校外。

张天明：是吗？你为什么住校外？你觉得住在校内好，还是住在校外好？

柯林：　有的人喜欢住学校宿舍，觉得又方便又安全，有的人喜欢住在校外，因为校外的房子比较便宜。我住在校外，除了想省点儿钱以外^③，还为了自由。再说^④，住在校内也不见得很方便。

张天明：真的吗？那我以后也搬到校外去。

柯林：　　你剛來，在學校住對你有好處❷，可以適應一下學校
　　　　　的生活。要是你以後想搬家，我可以幫你找房子。

張天明：　好吧，我以後要是搬家，一定請你幫忙。

柯林：　　天明，前邊沒人了，我幫你把行李搬進去吧。

張天明：　好，謝謝。哎，我的電腦呢？…糟糕，電腦可能
　　　　　拉❸在出租車上了！

After You Study

Challenge yourself to complete the following tasks in Chinese.

1. Describe briefly who the two characters are.

誰住在這兒?
谁住在这儿?

LANGUAGE NOTES

❷ The opposite of 好處/好处 (advantage; benefit) is 壞處/坏处, (huàichu, disadvantage; harm).

❸ In this text, 拉 (là) meaning "to leave something behind" is used colloquially. 拉 (là) and 落/落 (là)

柯林：　　你刚来，在学校住对你有好处❷，可以适应一下学校的生活。要是你以后想搬家，我可以帮你找房子。

张天明：　好吧，我以后要是搬家，一定请你帮忙。

柯林：　　天明，前边没人了，我帮你把行李搬进去吧。

张天明：　好，谢谢。哎，我的电脑呢？…糟糕，电脑可能拉❸在出租车上了！

2. List any similarities that you share with either of the two characters regarding your background and school life.

3. Name your criteria for choosing a place to live.

誰住在這兒?
谁住在这儿?

are both used to represent the sound. Note also that in this context both characters deviate from their normal pronunciation and meaning (拉, lā, to pull, and 落/落, luò, to fall.)

VOCABULARY

1.	開學	开学	kāi xué	vo	to begin a new semester
2.	新生		xīnshēng	n	new student
3.	輛	辆	liàng	m	(measure word for vehicles)
4.	研究生		yánjiūshēng	n	graduate student
5.	出生		chūshēng	v	to be born
6.	弓		gōng	n	bow
7.	長	长	cháng	adj	long
8.	校外		xiào wài		off campus
9.	校內		xiào nèi		on campus
10.	安全		ānquán	adj	safe
11.	比較	比较	bǐjiào	adv/v	relatively; comparatively; rather; to compare
12.	省錢	省钱	shěng qián	vo	to save money; to economize
13.	自由		zìyóu	adj	free; unconstrained
14.	不見得	不见得	bú jiàn de		not necessarily
15.	好處	好处	hǎochu	n	advantage; benefit
16.	適應	适应	shìyìng	v	to adapt; to become accustomed to
17.	生活		shēnghuó	n/v	life; livelihood; to live
18.	搬家		bān jiā	vo	to move (one's residence)
19.	幫忙	帮忙	bāng máng	vo	to help

Parts of speech are indicated for most vocabulary items. Detachable compounds are marked as "vo." Four-character phrases, idiomatic expressions, and other phrases that cannot be categorized by part of speech are left unmarked.

| 20. | 拉 | | là | v | (colloq.) to leave (something) behind |

Proper Nouns

| 21. | 張天明　张天明 | Zhāng Tiānmíng | Zhang Tianming (a personal name) |
| 22. | 柯林 | Kē Lín | Ke Lin (a personal name) |

Enlarged Characters

機　搬　離　邊　遠　處
机　搬　离　边　远　处

住宿費就是住在學校宿舍裏得付的錢。
住宿费就是住在学校宿舍里得付的钱。

Culture Highlights

1   Most college students in China live in on-campus dormitories,
typically with four students to a room. To alleviate crowding, many
universities have invested in off-campus "student apartments"
學生公寓/学生公寓 (xuéshēng gōngyù) in recent years.
Municipally-funded colleges may have students who commute. Government-supported
boarding schools for elementary, middle, and
high school students can be found in remote
rural areas. There are also private and
expensive boarding schools. Living conditions
at these schools vary. Coed dormitories are
uncommon, if not unheard of.

A student apartment number plate

2   Because homonyms abound in Chinese, there is sometimes a need to
disambiguate. For instance, Zhang Tianming's family name
張/张 (Zhāng) sounds the same as another family name 章 (Zhāng).
Therefore, to distinguish one from the other, it is necessary to explain how
to write the character. One common way to do that is to take the character
apart, so Zhang Tianming's family name is said to be 弓長張/弓长张
(gōng cháng Zhāng) as opposed to 立早章 (lì zǎo Zhāng), with 張/张
(zhāng) being made up of 弓 (gōng) and 長/长 (cháng), and 章 (zhāng)
being made up of 立 (lì) and 早 (zǎo). Another method of disambiguation
is to use the family name in a disyllabic context or reference the same last
name from a famous Chinese person. For instance, to differentiate the
surname 江 (Jiāng) from another with an identical pronunciation
姜 (Jiāng), one may say, 長江的江/长江的江 (Chángjiāng de
Jiāng), 不是姜太公的姜 (bú shì Jiāng Tàigōng de Jiāng), [it's] the
Jiang in Changjiang, (the Yangtze River), not the Jiang in Jiang Taigong
(a famous historical figure).

Zhāng	张/張	弓长张
	章	立早章

Hú	斛	角落的角右加北斗的斗
	胡	古月胡
	湖	江湖的湖
	壶/壺	茶壶的壶
	弧	括弧的弧
	狐	犬犹旁右加西瓜的瓜

According to this chart, how many of these six family names can be introduced by taking apart their character components?

Grammar

1. The Dynamic Particle 了 (I)

The dynamic particle 了 indicates that an action has occurred. It can appear either after a verb or at the end of a sentence. When 了 appears after a verb, it signals the occurrence of an action. There is usually a time phrase in the sentence.

❶   昨天晚上我看了一個電影。
      昨天晚上我看了一个电影。
(Last night I saw a movie.)

❷   去年我媽媽去了一次北京，在那兒住了很長時間。
      去年我妈妈去了一次北京，在那儿住了很长时间。
(Last year my mother went to Beijing and stayed there for a long time.)

❸ A: 這本書你看了嗎?

這本书你看了吗?

(Did you read this book?)

B: 我看了。

我看了。

(Yes, I read it.)

Notice that 了 is not the equivalent of the past tense. The action can take place in the future as in ❹.

❹ 明天我吃了早飯去飛機場。

明天我吃了早饭去飞机场。

(Tomorrow I'll go to the airport after breakfast.)

Sometimes when 了 appears after the object it also indicates occurrence of an action.

❺ A: 你昨天做什麼了?

你昨天做什么了?

(What did you do yesterday?)

B: 我搬家了。

我搬家了。

(I moved.)

Sometimes there isn't a time phrase in the sentence. The time implied is "just now" or "up till now":

❻ A: 你買明天的電影票了嗎?

你买明天的电影票了吗?

(Did you buy the ticket for tomorrow's movie?)

B: 買了。

买了。

(Yes, I did.)

A: 等了多長時間？
等了多长时间？
(How long did you wait?)

B: 人不多，只等了五分鐘。
人不多，只等了五分钟。
(There weren't many people. I only waited five minutes.)

If there is an object after the verb and 了, the object is usually quantified, as in ❶ and the first clause of ❷. Under certain circumstances, the object need not be quantified in any way:

a. If the object is followed by another 了:
我給小李打了電話了。
我给小李打了电话了。
(I called Little Li.)

b. If the object is followed by another clause:
張天明買了機票就回家了。
张天明买了机票就回家了。
(Zhang Tianming went home right after he bought the plane ticket.)

c. If the object refers to a definite person or thing:
昨天我在學校裏看見了小王。
昨天我在学校里看见了小王。
(Yesterday I saw Little Wang at school.)

When 了 occurs at the end of a sentence, it may signify a new situation, some kind of change, or the occurrence or realization of an event or state:

❼ 十月了，天氣慢慢冷了。
十月了，天气慢慢冷了。
(It's October. The weather is gradually turning cold.)

❽   我想今天晚上看電影，可是明天要考試，所以不看了。
我想今天晚上看电影，可是明天要考试，所以不看了。

(I wanted to go see a movie tonight, but I have an exam tomorrow, so I won't be going.)

When there are two verb phrases in a sentence and the first verb phrase is followed by the particle 了, the two actions denoted by the verbs are consecutive. The second action begins when the first one is completed.

❾   我下了課再去找你。
我下了课再去找你。

(I'll go look for you after my class.)

❿   昨天我搬進了宿舍就去餐廳吃飯了。
昨天我搬进了宿舍就去餐厅吃饭了。

(Yesterday as soon I finished moving into the dorm, I went to eat at the cafeteria.)

In ❾, the time of 去 is 下了課/下了课, or after the speaker finishes his/her class. In ❿, the time of 去餐廳吃飯/餐厅吃饭 is 搬進了宿舍/搬进了宿舍, i.e., immediately after moving into the dorm.

2. The 是…的… Construction

When both the speaker and the listener know that an action or event has occurred and the speaker wants to draw attention to the time, place, manner, purpose, or agent of the action, the 是…的… construction is required. Although we call it the 是…的… construction, 是 is, in fact, often optional:

❶   A: 柯先生來了嗎？
柯先生来了吗？

(Did Mr. Ke come?)

B: 來了。
来了。

(Yes, he did.)

A: (是)什麼時候來的?

(是)什么时候来的?

(When did he come?)

B: (是)昨天晚上來的。

(是)昨天晚上来的。

(Yesterday evening.)

A: (是)跟誰一起來的?

(是)跟谁一起来的?

(Whom did he come with?)

B: (是)跟他姐姐一起來的。

(是)跟他姐姐一起来的。

(With his older sister.)

A: (是)坐飛機來的還是開車來的?

(是)坐飞机来的还是开车来的?

(Did they come by plane or by car?)

B: 開車來的。

开车来的。

(By car.)

❷　張天明(是)在美國出生的。

張天明(是)在美国出生的。

(Zhang Tianming was born in America.)

That Zhang Tianming was already born is a given. The point of the statement is *where* he was born.

❸ **A:** 你是大學生嗎?

你是大学生吗?

(Are you an undergrad?)

B: 不，我是研究生。
不，我是研究生。
(No, I am a graduate student.)

A: 你是在哪兒上的大學？
你是在哪儿上的大学？
(Where did you go to college?)

B: 我是在紐約上的大學。
我是在纽约上的大学。
(I went to college in New York.)

To recapitulate, when it is a known fact that an action already took place, in order to inquire about or explain the particulars of the action, one should use 是…的… instead of 了.

3. 除了…以外

除了…以外,還/还… is an inclusive pattern. The English equivalent is "besides" or "in addition to."

❶ 他除了學中文以外，還學日文。
他除了学中文以外，还学日文。
(=他學中文，也學日文。)
(=他学中文，也学日文。)
(Besides Chinese, he's also studying Japanese.)

❷ 我們班除了小王以外，還有小林去過中國。
我们班除了小王以外，还有小林去过中国。
(=小王和小林都去過中國。)
(=小王和小林都去过中国。)
(In our class, besides Little Wang, Little Lin has also been to China.)

❸　昨天張天明除了搬家以外，還買東西了。
昨天张天明除了搬家以外，还买东西了。
(=昨天張天明搬家、買東西。)
(=昨天张天明搬家、买东西。)
(In addition to moving, Zhang Tianming also went shopping yesterday.)

除了…以外，都…, on the other hand, is an exclusive pattern. The English equivalent is "except for":

❹　除了小柯以外，我們班的同學都去過中國。
除了小柯以外，我们班的同学都去过中国。
(=小柯沒去過中國。)
(=小柯没去过中国。)
(Except for Little Ke, every student in our class has been to China.)
[Little Ke is the only one who has not been to China.]

❺　除了看書以外，晚上什麼事我都願意做。
除了看书以外，晚上什么事我都愿意做。
(=我晚上不願意看書。)
(=我晚上不愿意看书。)
(Except for reading, I am willing to do anything in the evening.)
[Reading is the only thing that I am not willing to do in the evening.]

4. 再說/再说

再說/再说 is used to provide additional reasons.

❶　你別走了，天太晚了，再說我們要說的事還沒說完呢。
你别走了，天太晚了，再说我们要说的事还没说完呢。
(Please stay. It's getting late. Besides, we haven't finished discussing everything that we need to discuss.)

❷ 我不打算去日本旅行，日本東西太貴，再說我以前去
過日本。

我不打算去日本旅行，日本东西太贵，再说我以前去
过日本。

(I'm not planning on traveling to Japan. Things in Japan are too expensive.
Besides, I've already been to Japan.)

❸ 她不應該找那樣的人做男朋友，那個人不太聰明，
再說對她也不好。

她不应该找那样的人做男朋友，那个人不太聪明，
再说对她也不好。

(She shouldn't be dating someone like him. He isn't very bright. Besides, he isn't
nice to her.)

而且 also means "besides" or "in addition." But unlike 再說/再说, it is not always
explanatory. Consider the use of 而且 in the 不但…而且… (not only...but also...)
structure:

❹ 我這個學期不但上英文課，而且還上中文課。

我这个学期不但上英文课，而且还上中文课。

(Besides English, I'm also taking Chinese this semester.)

❺ 我妹妹不但喜歡唱歌，而且也喜歡跳舞。

我妹妹不但喜欢唱歌，而且也喜欢跳舞。

(My younger sister not only likes to sing but also likes to dance.)

In ❶, ❷, and ❸, 再說/再说 is interchangeable with 而且, but in ❹ and ❺,
而且 cannot be replaced by 再說/再说.

5. Connecting Sentences (I)

We often speak in multiple sentences and need to connect them. In this lesson we have this example:

❶ 張天明: 是嗎？你為什麼住校外？你覺得住在校內好，還
　　　　是住在校外好？

張天明: 是吗？你为什么住校外？你觉得住在校内好，还
　　　　是住在校外好？

(Zhang Tianming: Is that so? Why do you live off campus? Do you think it's better to live on or off campus?)

柯林: 有的人喜歡住學校宿舍，覺得又方便又安全，有的人
　　　喜歡住在校外，因為校外的房子比較便宜。我住在校
　　　外，除了想省點兒錢以外，還為了自由。再説，住在
　　　校內也不見得很方便。

柯林: 有的人喜欢住学校宿舍，觉得又方便又安全，有的人
　　　喜欢住在校外，因为校外的房子比较便宜。我住在校
　　　外，除了想省点儿钱以外，还为了自由。再说，住在
　　　校内也不见得很方便。

(Ke Lin: Some people like to live on campus. They think it's both convenient and safe. Some people like to live off campus because off-campus housing is relatively inexpensive. I live off campus. Besides wanting to save some money, I also want freedom. On top of that, it's not necessarily so convenient to live on campus.)

This exchange begins with Zhang Tianming asking Ke Lin, "Why do you live off campus?" Ke Lin mentions three reasons in his answer and uses 因為/因为…, 除了…以外, 還/还…, and 再説/再说… to connect them. Another way to connect the reasons is to use 第一…, 第二…, 第三… (first...second...third...).

❷ 柯林: 有的人喜歡住學校宿舍，覺得又方便又安全，有的人喜歡住在校外，因為，第一，校外的房子比較便宜，第二，住校外比較自由，第三，住在校內不見得很方便。

柯林: 有的人喜欢住学校宿舍，觉得又方便又安全，有的人喜欢住在校外，因为，第一，校外的房子比较便宜，第二，住校外比较自由，第三，住在校内不见得很方便。

學生還沒搬進來。
学生还没搬进来。

Words & Phrases

> ### A. 覺得/觉得 (to feel; to think)

覺得/觉得 can express a feeling as well as an opinion.

❶ 我今天覺得有點不舒服，不能跟你一起去游泳了。
[feeling]
我今天觉得有点不舒服，不能跟你一起去游泳了。
(I don't feel very well today. I can't go swimming with you.)

❷ 大家都説那個電影好看，可是我看了以後覺得不怎麼樣。[opinion]
大家都说那个电影好看，可是我看了以后觉得不怎么样。
(Everybody says that's a very interesting film, but I didn't think it was all that great after seeing it.)

❸ 很多美國人認為 (rènwéi) 十八歲以後就應該離開家搬到別的地方住，我覺得不一定。[opinion]
很多美国人认为 (rènwéi) 十八岁以后就应该离开家搬到别的地方住，我觉得不一定。
(Many Americans think that you should leave home and live somewhere else after you turn eighteen. I don't necessarily agree.)

When expressing an opinion, 覺得/觉得 is less formal than 認為/认为.

> ### B. 方便 (convenient)

As an adjective, 方便 can appear in a sentence either as a predicate or an attributive.

❶ 住在城裏買東西很方便。[predicate]
住在城里买东西很方便。
(It's very convenient to shop in a city.)

❷   我想問您一個問題，您現在方便嗎？ [predicate]

我想问您一个问题，您现在方便吗？

(I'd like to ask you a question. Is it convenient for you now?)

❸   方便的時候，請給我打個電話。 [attributive]

方便的时候，请给我打个电话。

(Please give me a call whenever it's convenient for you.)

C. 安全 (safe)

安全 is an adjective. It can be used as a predicate as well as an attributive.

❶   這棟樓很安全。 [predicate]

这栋楼很安全。

(This building is very safe.)

❷   你不必擔心，她現在很安全。 [predicate]

你不必担心，她现在很安全。

(You don't have to worry. She's very safe now.)

❸   我們宿舍的安全問題很大。 [attributive]

我们宿舍的安全问题很大。

(Our dorm has a big problem with safety.)

❹   最安全的辦法是下午五點以後不准人進公司。
[attributive]

最安全的办法是下午五点以后不准人进公司。

(The safest solution is to not allow people to come into the company's building after 5:00 p.m.)

D. 省錢/省钱 (to save money; to economize)

省錢/省钱 means "to economize." It is a verb-object compound. Numerals and particles such as 了 can be inserted between the verb and the object.

❶ 每個星期少開一天車，一年可以省不少錢。

每个星期少开一天车，一年可以省不少钱。

(If you refrain from driving once a week, you'll save a lot of money over a year.)

❷ 這件襯衫週末打五折，可以省三十塊錢。

这件衬衫周末打五折，可以省三十块钱。

(This shirt is half off this weekend. You can save \$30/¥30.)

❸ 我去年住在中國，吃飯很便宜，省了很多錢。

我去年住在中国，吃饭很便宜，省了很多钱。

(I lived in China last year. Food was very inexpensive. I saved a lot of money.)

E. 自由 (free; unconstrained)

自由 can be either a noun or an adjective.

❶ A: 在那個國家，你覺得人們有自由嗎？ [noun]

在那个国家，你觉得人们有自由吗？

(In that country do you think people have freedom?)

B: 我在那兒住了半年，覺得很自由。 [adjective]

我在那儿住了半年，觉得很自由。

(I lived there for half a year. I found it very free.)

❷ 我妹妹住在表姐家裏，她覺得很不自由。 [adjective]

我妹妹住在表姐家里，她觉得很不自由。

(My younger sister lives with my cousin. She finds it very restrictive.)

❸   那個孩子快兩歲了，可以在地上自由地走來走去。

[adjective + 地 = adverbial]

那个孩子快两岁了，可以在地上自由地走来走去。

(That child is almost two. He can walk around freely.)

F. 不見得／不见得 (not necessarily)

An adverb, 不見得／不见得 can be used to express a dissenting opinion politely.

❶ **A:** 她是在中國出生的，中文一定很好吧？

她是在中国出生的，中文一定很好吧？

(She was born in China. Her Chinese must be very good.)

B: 在中國出生的人，中文不見得好。

在中国出生的人，中文不见得好。

(People who were born in China don't necessarily speak good Chinese.)

❷   報上說的不見得對。

报上说的不见得对。

(They don't necessarily have it right in the papers.)

❸   這個城市路上車多，人多，開車不見得比走快。

这个城市路上车多，人多，开车不见得比走快。

(This city's streets are full of people and cars. Driving is not necessarily faster than walking.)

G. 好處／好处 (advantage; benefit)

好處／好处 is a noun. It can be used as a subject or an object.

❶   坐飛機的好處是很快。 [subject]

坐飞机的好处是很快。

(The advantage of flying is speed.)

❷   請你說說這樣做的好處。 [object]

請你说说这样做的好处。

(Please tell us the advantage of doing it this way.)

好處/好处 often occurs in this construction:

A 對/对 **B** 有好處/有好处 (**A is advantageous for B**)

❸   聽錄音對學中文有好處。

听录音对学中文有好处。

(Listening to recordings is good for learning Chinese.)

❹   這樣做對你沒有好處。

这样做对你没有好处。

(Doing this has no advantage for you.)

❺   在中國，上過大學、會用電腦、會說外語，對找工作
有好處。

在中国，上过大学、会用电脑、会说外语，对找工作
有好处。

(In China, having a college degree, knowing how to use a computer, and being able
to speak a foreign language are advantages when it comes to looking for a job.)

H. 適應/适应 (to adapt; to become accustomed to)

適應/适应 is a verb. It takes a direct object.

❶   你適應大學的生活了嗎？

你适应大学的生活了吗？

(Are you accustomed to college life now?)

❷   我來了兩年了，到現在還不適應這裏的生活。

我来了两年了，到现在还不适应这里的生活。

(I've been here for two years, but I'm still not used to life here.)

The object can be introduced by the preposition 對/对 and be placed before the verb 適應/适应.

❸ 你對這裏的天氣已經適應了嗎？

你对这里的天气已经适应了吗？

(Are you already used to the weather here?)

❹ 我們剛來美國，對美國的天氣還不適應。

我们刚来美国，对美国的天气还不适应。

(We've just arrived in the United States. We're not used to American weather yet.)

在這兒可以找到人幫你搬行李。

在这儿可以找到人帮你搬行李。

Language Practice

A. What's Your Name?

Go around the class and introduce yourself. Explain your Chinese name so that your classmates will know which characters it uses. Ask your classmates to explain how to write their Chinese names. Ask your teacher to give you a Chinese name if you don't already have one.

B. So You Are Back!

Now that both you and your partner are back from summer break, ask and answer questions about your trips back to school by using the 是⋯的 construction.

EXAMPLE:

What date?

A: 你是幾號回學校來的？   A: 你是几号回学校来的？

→ B: 我是二十三號回學校   B: 我是二十三号回学校
　　 來的。　　　　　　　　　　 来的。

What day of the week?

How?

With whom?

C. What Else?

a. You know that your partner is taking Chinese this semester. Find out what other courses he or she is taking using 除了⋯以外, 還/还⋯. You may use English to name the courses if you don't know how to say them in Chinese.

b. You know your partner can speak Chinese. Find out what other languages he or she can speak using 除了⋯以外, 還/还⋯.

D. Not Necessarily!

You are in a contrarian mood today. Using 不見得/不见得, disagree with everything that your partner says.

EXAMPLE: student dorm   convenient

A: 住在學生宿舍很方便。   **A:** 住在学生宿舍很方便。

→ **B:** 住在學生宿舍不見得很方便。   **B:** 住在学生宿舍不见得很方便。

what the teacher says	correct
living off campus	more freedom
writing English	easier than writing Chinese
airplane tickets	most expensive in August
people born in China	cook delicious Chinese food

E. It's Good for You!

a. Your friend is recovering from a debilitating illness. Offer him some health advice.

EXAMPLE:

    →   喝水對身體有好處。
喝水对身体有好处。

1.

2.

3.

b. Your friend Mr. Sinophilic is starting to learn Chinese by himself. Offer him some advice on Chinese study.

EXAMPLE:

 → 聽錄音對學中文有好處。
听录音对学中文有好处。

First piece of advice

Second piece of advice

Third piece of advice

F. Shoot! I Left It Behind!

EXAMPLE:

 → 糟糕，我把書拉在宿舍了。
糟糕，我把书拉在宿舍了。

1.

2.

3.

4.

G. Helping the Newcomers

Work with a partner to brainstorm a list of things you can do to help a first-year student feel more at ease when he or she first arrives on campus.

H. Pros and Cons

a. List the pros and cons of living on campus in a dorm.

Pros

_____

_____

_____

...

Cons

_____

_____

_____

b. List the pros and cons of living off campus in an apartment or a house.

Pros

_____

_____

_____

...

Cons

_____

_____

_____

c. Survey three of your classmates and see who prefers living on campus or off campus. Record their reasons and report back to the class.

Classmate #1　　覺得住在校外比住在　　　　觉得住在校外比住在
　　　　　　　　校內好。因為⋯　　　　　　校内好。因为⋯

Classmate #2

_____ 。

Classmate #3

_____ 。

I. Should I Move?

Have a discussion about the pros and cons of living on campus compared to living off campus, and then summarize the group members' opinions by using the expression 有的⋯, 有的⋯. Possible points for discussion include: safety, doing laundry, use of the internet, shopping, expenses, dating, freedom…

EXAMPLE: close to classrooms

有的同學覺得住在校內,　　　　有的同学觉得住在校内,
離教室近, 上課很方便。　　　　离教室近, 上课很方便。
有的同學覺得⋯　　　　　　　　有的同学觉得⋯

J. I Live Where I Live Because…

a. Your partner will ask you the following questions. First answer them according to your own situation. Make sure to incorporate the expressions or constructions you have learned in this lesson.

1. Where do you live, on campus or off campus?
2. When did you move into the dorm/off campus?
3. What can you say to support your choice of living on/off campus?
4. Do all your friends live on/off campus as you do?
5. What would you say to those who have made a different choice?
6. Will you continue to live on/off campus next year?

b. Then, based on your answers to the questions above, can you now explain your choice of living on/off campus in a short but coherent paragraph? Don't forget to incorporate 因為/因为, 除了⋯以外, 還/还⋯, 再說/再说 and/or 第一,第二,第三 in order to connect the sentences.

Pinyin Text

Zhāng Tiānmíng shì dàxué yì niánjí de xīnshēng❶. Kuài kāi xué le, tā jiā lí dàxué hěn yuǎn, děi zuò fēijī qù xuéxiào. Tā zuò fēijī zuò le liǎng ge duō xiǎoshí. Xià fēijī yǐhòu, tā mǎshàng jiào le yí liàng chūzū qìchē, hěn kuài jiù dào le xuéxiào sùshè①.

Zhāng Tiānmíng:	Rén zhēn duō!
Kē Lín:	Nǐ shì xīnshēng ba?
Zhāng Tiānmíng:	Shì, wǒ shì xīnshēng. Nǐ ne?
Kē Lín:	Wǒ shì yánjiūshēng. Zài zhèr bāng xīnshēng bān dōngxi. Qǐng wèn, nǐ jiào shénme míngzi?
Zhāng Tiānmíng:	Wǒ jiào Zhāng Tiānmíng.
Kē Lín:	Zhāng Tiānmíng? Shì Zhōngwén míngzi ma?
Zhāng Tiānmíng:	Duì, wǒ bàba māma shì cóng Zhōngguó lái de. Kěshì wǒ shì zài Měiguó chūshēng, zài Měiguó zhǎng dà de②. Qǐng wèn nǐ de míngzi shì...
Kē Lín:	Wǒ zhèng zài xué Zhōngwén, wǒ de Zhōngwén míngzi shì Kē Lín. Nǐ de míngzi shì nǎ sān ge zì?
Zhāng Tiānmíng:	Zhāng shì gōng cháng zhāng, jiù shì yì zhāng zhǐ de zhāng, Tiān shì tiānqì de tiān, Míng shì míngtiān de míng.
Kē Lín:	Nǐ shì zěnme lái xuéxiào de?
Zhāng Tiānmíng:	Wǒ xiān zuò fēijī, cóng jīchǎng dào xuéxiào zuò chūzū qìchē. Kē Lín, nǐ yě zhù zài zhèr ma?
Kē Lín:	Bù, zhè shì xīnshēng sùshè, wǒ zhù zài xiào wài.
Zhāng Tiānmíng:	Shì ma? Nǐ wèishénme zhù xiào wài? Nǐ juéde zhù zài xiào nèi hǎo, háishi zhù zài xiào wài hǎo?
Kē Lín:	Yǒude rén xǐhuan zhù xuéxiào sùshè, juéde yòu fāngbiàn yòu ānquán, yǒude rén xǐhuan zhù zài xiào wài, yīnwèi xiào wài de fángzi bǐjiào piányi. Wǒ zhù zài xiào wài, chúle xiǎng shěng diǎnr qián yǐwài③, hái wèile zìyóu. Zàishuō④, zhù zài xiào nèi yě bú jiàn de hěn fāngbiàn.
Zhāng Tiānmíng:	Zhēn de ma? Nà wǒ yǐhòu yě bān dào xiào wài qù.
Kē Lín:	Nǐ gāng lái, zài xuéxiào zhù duì nǐ yǒu hǎochu❷, kěyǐ shìyìng yí xià xuéxiào de shēnghuó. Yàoshi nǐ yǐhòu xiǎng bān jiā, wǒ kěyǐ bāng nǐ zhǎo fángzi.

Zhāng Tiānmíng: Hǎo ba, wǒ yǐhòu yàoshi bān jiā, yídìng qǐng nǐ bāng máng.

Kē Lín: Tiānmíng, qiánbian méi rén le, wǒ bāng nǐ bǎ xíngli bān jin qu ba.

Zhāng Tiānmíng: Hǎo, xièxie. Āi, wǒ de diànnǎo ne? … Zāogāo, diànnǎo kěnéng là ❸ zài chūzū chē shang le!

English Text

Zhang Tianming is a college freshman. School is about to start. His home is very far from the university, so he has to take a plane to get to school. He is on the plane for more than two hours. After he gets off the plane, he hails a cab immediately. In no time he arrives at his school dormitory.

Zhang Tianming: There are a lot of people here!

Ke Lin: You must be a freshman.

Zhang Tianming: Yes, I am a freshman. How about you?

Ke Lin: I'm a graduate student. I'm here to help the freshmen move. What's your name?

Zhang Tianming: My name is Zhang Tianming.

Ke Lin: Zhang Tianming? Is that a Chinese name?

Zhang Tianming: That's right. My mom and dad are from China, but I was born and grew up in America. Your name is…?

Ke Lin: I'm studying Chinese. My Chinese name is Ke Lin. What are the Chinese characters for your name?

Zhang Tianming: Zhang with *gong* (bow) [on the left] and *chang* (long) [on the right], same character as the one for "piece" as in "a piece of paper," *Tian* as in "weather," *Ming* as in "tomorrow."

Ke Lin: How did you get to school?

Zhang Tianming: I flew. From the airport I took a taxi. Ke Lin, do you also live here?

Ke Lin: No, this is the freshmen's dorm. I live off campus.

Zhang Tianming: Is that so? Why do you live off campus? Do you think it's better to live on or off campus?

Ke Lin:	Some people like to live on campus. They think it's both convenient and safe. Some people like to live off campus because off-campus housing is cheaper. I live off campus. Besides wanting to save some money, I also want my freedom. On top of that, it's not necessarily so convenient to live on campus.
Zhang Tianming:	Really? Then I'll move off campus, too, in the future.
Ke Lin:	You've just arrived, so it's good for you to live on campus and get used to school life. If you want to live off campus later, I can help you find a place.
Zhang Tianming:	OK. If I want to move later, I'll definitely ask for your help.
Ke Lin:	There's no one in front of you now. I'll help you move your baggage into your room.
Zhang Tianming:	OK. Thank you. Hey, where's my computer? Shoot, I might have left it in the cab!

SELF-ASSESSMENT

How well can you do these things? Check (✔) the boxes to evaluate your progress and see which areas you may need to practice more.

I can	Very Well	OK	A Little
Explain how to write my Chinese name	☐	☐	☐
Ask and answer questions about where I was born and grew up	☐	☐	☐
Discuss my preferences for living on or off campus	☐	☐	☐
Express a contrary view politely	☐	☐	☐

第二课　第二课
宿舍　宿舍

2

 LEARNING OBJECTIVES

In this lesson, you will learn to use Chinese to

1. Name basic pieces of furniture in a house;
2. Describe your living quarters;
3. Comment on someone's living quarters;
4. Disagree tactfully.

 RELATE AND GET READY

In your own culture/community—

- Do student dormitories and apartments usually come furnished or unfurnished?
- What facilities and services do student dormitories offer?
- Are student dormitories usually air-conditioned?

Before You Study

Check the statements that apply to you.

☐ 1. I live in a student dormitory.

☐ 2. The student dormitories on my campus have great amenities.

When You Study

Listen to the audio recording and scan the text. Ask yourself the following questions before you begin a close reading of the text.

1. What is the text preceding the conversation about?

張天明宿舍的房間不太大，住兩個人。他的同屋❶已經來了。房間裏傢具不多，靠窗戶擺著兩張書桌，每張桌子的前邊有一把椅子。書桌的旁邊是床①，床上有被子❷和毯子。床前有兩個衣櫃，櫃子裏掛著一些衣服。門旁邊放著兩個書架，書架還是空的。

LANGUAGE NOTES

❶ Another word for "roommate" is 室友 (shìyǒu, literally, "friend who shares a room").

3. I eat at the student cafeteria.

4. The food served in the student cafeteria is good.

2. Where does the conversation take place?

3. What is the one concern that both people share?

4. Will the two meet again soon? Why or why not?

张天明宿舍的房间不太大，住两个人。他的同屋❶已经来了。房间里家具不多，靠窗户摆着两张书桌，每张桌子的前边有一把椅子。书桌的旁边是床①，床上有被子❷和毯子。床前有两个衣柜，柜子里挂着一些衣服。门旁边放着两个书架，书架还是空的。

---

❷ In northern spoken Chinese, the word for a quilt is 被 instead of 被子.

張天明：真②熱，房間裏怎麼沒有空調❸？

柯　林：這棟樓比較③舊，我大一④的時候在這兒住過。

張天明：衛生間也比較小。住在這兒恐怕很不方便吧？

柯　林：不，這兒很方便。學生餐廳❺就在樓下，餐廳旁邊有一個小商店，賣日用品和文具。教室離這兒不遠，走路差不多五、六分鐘。

張天明：洗衣服方便嗎？

柯　林：方便得很④。這層樓有三台洗衣機和三台烘乾機。

張天明：這兒吵不吵？

柯　林：不吵，這兒離大馬路很遠，很安靜。

張天明：聽說學校餐廳的飯一般都不太好。這兒的呢？

柯　林：你說對了，餐廳的飯真的②不怎麼樣。

張天明：真的？那怎麼辦？

柯　林：你別着急。附近有很多飯館兒，還有一家中國餐館兒呢。

張天明：我覺得美國的中國餐館兒，好吃的不多。

柯　林：那也不見得。附近那家中國餐館兒的菜就很地道。我和我的女朋友常去。

張天明：真的嗎？那麼⑤過幾天你帶我去那兒看看，好嗎？

柯　林：好，沒問題。

LANGUAGE NOTES

❸ 空調/空调 is short for 空氣調節器/空气调节器 (kōngqì tiáojié qì, air control or air adjustment machine), although the long term is almost never used. It can have a dual heating and cooling function whereas a 冷氣機/冷气机 (lěngqì jī) by definition has only a cooling function. In Taiwan, 空調/空调 is called 冷氣/冷气.

张天明：　真②热！房间里怎么没有空调❸？

柯林：　　这栋楼比较③旧，我大一❹的时候在这儿住过。

张天明：　卫生间也比较小。住在这儿恐怕很不方便吧？

柯林：　　不，这儿很方便。学生餐厅❺就在楼下，餐厅旁边有一个小商店，卖日用品和文具。教室离这儿不远，走路差不多五、六分钟。

张天明：　洗衣服方便吗？

柯林：　　方便得很④。这层楼有三台洗衣机和三台烘干机。

张天明：　这儿吵不吵？

柯林：　　不吵，这儿离大马路很远，很安静。

张天明：　听说学校餐厅的饭一般都不太好。这儿的呢？

柯林：　　你说对了，餐厅的饭真的②不怎么样。

张天明：　真的？那怎么办？

柯林：　　你别着急。附近有很多饭馆儿，还有一家中国餐馆儿呢。

张天明：　我觉得美国的中国餐馆儿，好吃的不多。

柯林：　　那也不见得。附近那家中国餐馆儿的菜就很地道。我和我的女朋友常去。

张天明：　真的吗？那么⑤过几天你带我去那儿看看，好吗？

柯林：　　好，没问题。

---

❹ Both 我是大學一年級的學生/我是大学一年级的学生 and 我大一 mean "I am a first-year college student."

❺ The word 餐廳/餐厅 can mean either a cafeteria, i.e., a company or school cafeteria, or a small independent restaurant. Canteens in China are 食堂 (shítáng), which are generally not open to the general public. They are often subsidized by schools or companies to exclusively serve their respective students or employees, and may take meal cards instead of cash.

After You Study

Challenge yourself to complete the following tasks in Chinese.

1. List the furniture in Zhang Tianming's room.
2. Describe Zhang Tianming's room.

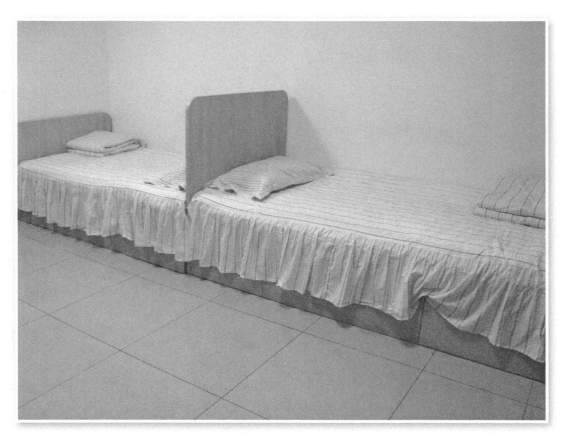

床上有枕頭 (zhěntou) 和被子。
床上有枕头 (zhěntou) 和被子。

3. List the facilities and amenities that Zhang Tianming's dormitory has.
4. Recap what Zhang Tianming likes and doesn't like about his dormitory.

這個房間有什麼？書架是空的嗎？
这个房间有什么？书架是空的吗？

VOCABULARY

1.	同屋		tóngwū	n	roommate
2.	擺	摆	bǎi	v	to put; to place
3.	被子		bèizi	n	comforter; quilt
4.	毯子		tǎnzi	n	blanket
5.	衣櫃	衣柜	yīguì	n	wardrobe
6.	櫃子	柜子	guìzi	n	cabinet; cupboard
7.	掛	挂	guà	v	to hang; to hang up
8.	門	门	mén	n	door
9.	空		kōng	adj	empty
10.	空調	空调	kōngtiáo	n	air conditioning
11.	棟	栋	dòng	m	(measure word for buildings)
12.	舊	旧	jiù	adj	(of things) old
13.	恐怕		kǒngpà	adv	I'm afraid that; I think perhaps; probably
14.	日用品		rìyòngpǐn	n	daily necessities
15.	文具		wénjù	n	stationery; writing supplies
16.	洗		xǐ	v	to wash
17.	層	层	céng	m	(measure word for stories of a building)
18.	台		tái	m	(measure word for machines)
19.	洗衣機	洗衣机	xǐyījī	n	washing machine
20.	烘乾機	烘干机	hōnggānjī	n	(clothes) dryer
21.	馬路	马路	mǎlù	n	road
22.	一般		yìbān	adv	generally

23.	真的		zhēn de		really; truly
24.	着急		zháojí	v	to worry
25.	餐館兒	餐馆儿	cānguǎnr	n	restaurant
26.	地道		dìdao	adj	authentic; genuine; pure
27.	過幾天	过几天	guò jǐ tiān		in a few days

Enlarged Characters

窗　擺　櫃　舊　餐　廳
窗　摆　柜　旧　餐　厅

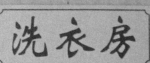

什麼時候可以洗衣服？
什么时候可以洗衣服？

學生在學生餐廳吃飯。
学生在学生餐厅吃饭。

Culture Highlights

❶ Chinese graduate students have many more housing options than undergraduates. Besides campus housing, graduate students can also rent apartments off campus. Married and part-time graduate students can live at home.

❷ Chinese universities' accommodations for international students 留學生/留学生 (liúxuéshēng) vary. Typically, international students live in designated buildings. Some share a communal bathroom, but most have private bathrooms. In general, amenities are comparable to what students may be accustomed to at home. Both single rooms and double rooms are available. In some programs, international students can share a room with a Chinese roommate. Each floor has a laundry room with clotheslines and drying racks; dryers are not common. Neither are communal kitchens. Internet access is often available for a fee. Universities with a sizeable international student population tend to have many stores and restaurants that cater to them. Food is relatively inexpensive and variety endless in big cities such as Beijing and Shanghai.

兩台洗衣機，沒有烘乾機。
两台洗衣机，没有烘干机。

Grammar

1. Existential Sentences

The word order of an existential sentence is somewhat different from that of a typical Chinese sentence. The structure of an existential sentences is as follows:

place word/phrase + verb + (了 or 著/着) + numeral + measure word + noun

Existential sentences indicate that something exists at a certain place.

❶ 桌子上放著一本書。
桌子上放着一本书。
(There is a book lying on the desk.)

❷ 床前有一把椅子。
(There is a chair in front of the bed.)

❸ 書桌的旁邊是衣櫃。
书桌的旁边是衣柜。
(Next to the desk there is a wardrobe.)

There are three kinds of verbs in existential sentences: 有, 是, and verbs signifying bodily actions such as 站, 坐, 躺, 拿, 放, and 擺/摆.

❹ 教室裏有一些學生。
教室里有一些学生。
(There are some students in the classroom.)

❺ 桌子上是一張地圖。
桌子上是一张地图。
(On the desk is a map.)

❻ 書架上擺著三張照片。
书架上摆着三张照片。
(There are three photos on the bookshelf.)

❼ 那個男孩子手裏拿了一個小飛機。
那个男孩子手里拿了一个小飞机。
(That boy is holding a model plane in his hand.)

Existential sentences are used to describe someone's appearance or the surroundings of a place.

❽ 床上坐著一個人。
床上坐着一个人。
(Someone is sitting on the bed.)

When denoting existence, 有 and 是 differ from each other in that 是 suggests that there is only one, or one type of, object or person at a particular place, whereas 有 can refer to multiple objects or types of objects/people. Compare:

❾ 桌子上有一枝筆，一份報和一些紙。
桌子上有一枝笔，一份报和一些纸。
(There's a pen, a newspaper, and some paper on the desk.)
[There may be other items on the desk as well.]

❿ **A:** 你看，桌子上放著什麼？
你看，桌子上放着什么？
(Look, what's on the table?)

B: 桌子上是一枝筆。
桌子上是一枝笔。
(A pen is on the table.)
[There's nothing else on the table.]

⓫ 這個時候從前邊走來一個人，他身上穿
著一件白襯衫，手裏拿著一條紅毯子。
这个时候从前边走来一个人，他身上穿
着一件白衬衫，手里拿着一条红毯子。
(At that moment a man walked over from the front. He was wearing a white shirt and carrying a red blanket in his hand.)

⑫ 我住的地方非常漂亮，也非常安靜。房子前邊有很多
花，房子後邊是一個小山，山上有很多樹。左邊有一个
小公園，右邊有一條小路，從那條小路可以去學校。

我住的地方非常漂亮，也非常安静。房子前边有很多
花，房子后边是一个小山，山上有很多树。左边有一个
小公园，右边有一条小路，从那条小路可以去学校。

(The place where I live is very pretty and very quiet. There are many flowers in front
of the house. Behind the house is a small hill, and on this hill there are many trees.
To the left is a small park, and to the right is a small road from which I can go to the
school.)

2. Adverb 真

真 is used to convey an affirmative, exclamatory tone of voice. It is used before adjectives
and before verbs that denote thoughts or feelings.

❶ 今天真冷，穿三件毛衣都不行。
今天真冷，穿三件毛衣都不行。
(It's really cold today. You could be wearing three sweaters, and you would still be
cold.)

❷ 這條褲子樣子真好，我想給哥哥買一條。
这条裤子样子真好，我想给哥哥买一条。
(This pair of pants looks great. I am thinking about getting a pair for my older
brother.)

❸ 我們老師給的功課真多，我做了三個鐘頭了還沒做完。

我们老师给的功课真多，我做了三个钟头了还没做完。

(My teacher really assigned a lot of homework. I've been at it for three hours, and I still haven't finished it.)

❹ 這台烘乾機真吵，你應該買一台新的。

这台烘干机真吵，你应该买一台新的。

(This dryer is really noisy. You should get a new one.)

Like 很, 非常, and 特別, 真 also suggests an extreme degree. However, it appears in exclamatory sentences. It is used to indicate an emphatic tone of voice, rather than to provide new information. Therefore, avoid using 真 in ordinary descriptive sentences, e.g.,

❺ **A:** 小張，你看天氣預報了嗎？明天的天氣怎麼樣？

小张，你看天气预报了吗？明天的天气怎么样？

(Little Zhang, did you watch the weather forecast? What's the weather going to be like tomorrow?)

B: 天氣預報說明天會下雪，很冷。

天气预报说明天会下雪，很冷。

(According to the weather forecast, it's going to snow tomorrow. It'll be very cold.)

Compared to

天氣預報說明天會下雪，*真冷。

天气预报说明天会下雪，*真冷。

真 can sometimes mean "truly, honestly." When used in this way, it is often followed by the particle 的.

❻ 這碗酸辣湯真的又酸又辣。

这碗酸辣汤真的又酸又辣。

(This bowl of hot and sour soup is truly hot and sour.)

❼ **A:** 學校的宿舍真的太貴了，我想搬到校外去住。

學校的宿舍真的太贵了，我想搬到校外去住。

(It's really too expensive to live in the dorm. I plan to move off campus.)

B: 校外沒有校内方便，你真的想搬出去嗎？

校外没有校内方便，你真的想搬出去吗？

(Living off campus is not as convenient as living on campus. Do you honestly want to move out?)

3. 比較/比较

The word 比較/比较 (relatively, comparatively, rather) is not used to make explicit comparisons such as "A is more/less than B" where the terms of comparison are clearly articulated, but rather to make general statements about a *relative* degree or extent.

❶ 這把椅子比較貴，你別買了。

这把椅子比较贵，你别买了。

(This chair is rather expensive. Don't buy it.)

❷ 今天比較冷，你多穿點衣服吧。

今天比较冷，你多穿点衣服吧。

(It's pretty cold today. You'd better put on more clothes.)

❸ **A:** 你喜歡什麼運動？

你喜欢什么运动？

(What kind of sports do you like?)

B: 我比較喜歡打網球。

我比较喜欢打网球。

([Generally speaking,] I prefer playing tennis.)

4 A: 聽說你這兩天不太舒服，今天覺得怎麼樣？
　　听说你这两天不太舒服，今天觉得怎么样？
(I heard that you were sick the last couple of days. How are you feeling today?)

　B: 好一點兒了。
　　好一点儿了。
(A bit better.)

Because B's condition now is specifically being compared to that of "the last couple of days," it's incorrect to say in this context

*比較好。
*比较好。

5 我很高，我哥哥更高。
(I'm very tall. My older brother is even taller.)

It's incorrect to say

*我很高，我哥哥比較高。
*我很高，我哥哥比较高。

4. 得很

得很 can be used after adjectives and certain verbs that denote thoughts or feelings to suggest an extreme extent. For instance, 冷得很 suggests a much more intense degree of cold than 很冷.

1 學校剛開學，大家都忙得很。
　　学校刚开学，大家都忙得很。
(School just started. Everyone has been extremely busy.)

2 今天搬進宿舍的新生多得很，我們明天再搬吧。
　　今天搬进宿舍的新生多得很，我们明天再搬吧。
(There are way too many freshmen moving into the dorm today. Let's move tomorrow.)

❸   我們的宿舍安靜得很，大家都很喜歡。

我们的宿舍安静得很，大家都很喜欢。

(Our dorms are very quiet. Everyone likes them a lot.)

❹   來學校一個多星期了，張天明想家得很。

来学校一个多星期了，张天明想家得很。

(It has been over a week since Zhang Tianming arrived on campus. He is really homesick.)

5. 那(麼)/那(么)

那(麼)/那(么) connects two sentences. The second sentence is a conclusion or judgment that derives from the preceding sentence. 那麼/那么 can be abbreviated as 那.

❶ **A:** 晚上去買洗衣機，好嗎？

晚上去买洗衣机，好吗？

(Let's go shopping for a washing machine tonight, OK?)

B: 可是今天晚上我沒有空兒。

可是今天晚上我没有空儿。

(But I don't have time tonight.)

A: 那(麼)就明天吧。

那(么)就明天吧。

(Tomorrow then.)

B: 好吧。

(OK.)

❷ **A:** 媽媽，我不想當醫生。

妈妈，我不想当医生。

(Mom, I don't want to be a doctor.)

B: 那(麼)學電腦怎麼樣？

那(么)学电脑怎么样？

(Then how about studying computer science?)

A: 我也沒興趣。

我也没兴趣。

(I'm not interested in that, either.)

B: 那就什麼都不學，在家裏做飯、洗衣服吧。

那就什么都不学，在家里做饭、洗衣服吧。

(Then don't study anything. Stay home, cook and do laundry.)

A: 媽，看您說的！

妈，看您说的！

(Mom, listen to you!)

6. Conjunctions

Conjunctions are often omitted in spoken Chinese, e.g.,

❶ 張天明：真熱！房間裏怎麼沒有空調？

張天明：真热！房间里怎么没有空调？

(Zhang Tianming: It's so hot! How come there's no air conditioning in this room?)

柯林：(因為)這棟樓比較舊…

柯林：(因为)这栋楼比较旧…

(Ke Lin: [Because] this building is relatively old...)

❷ 張天明：這兒吵不吵？

張天明：这儿吵不吵？

(Zhang Tianming: Is it noisy here?)

柯林: 不吵，(因為)這兒離大馬路很遠，(所以)很安靜。

柯林: 不吵，(因为)这儿离大马路很远，(所以)很安静。

(Ke Lin: No, it's not noisy here. [Because] it's far from the major roads, [that's why] it's very quiet here.)

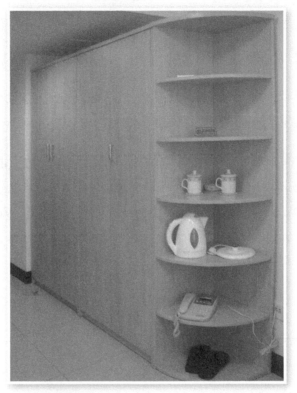

架子上有什麼?

架子上有什么?

Words & Phrases

A. 恐怕 (I'm afraid; I think perhaps)

The adverb 恐怕 is used to express the speaker's assessment of or concern about a particular situation.

❶   下雨了，恐怕我們不能打球了。

下雨了，恐怕我们不能打球了。

(It's raining. I'm afraid we can't play ball.)

❷ 十一點了，現在給他打電話恐怕太晚了。

   十一点了，现在给他打电话恐怕太晚了。

   (It's eleven o'clock already. I'm afraid it's too late to call him now.)

❸ 這兒沒空調，恐怕夏天很熱吧?

   这儿没空调，恐怕夏天很热吧?

   (There's no air conditioning here. It's probably very hot in the summer, isn't it?)

❹ 窗戶外有一條馬路，這兒恐怕很吵吧?

   窗户外有一条马路，这儿恐怕很吵吧?

   (There's a street outside the window. It must be very noisy here, right?)

We do not usually say 我恐怕. For instance, we do not normally say 我恐怕他不能去. If someone says 我恐怕不能去了, what he or she really means is, (我)恐怕我不能去了 (I'm afraid I won't be able to go). We can also say 他恐怕不能去了 meaning (我)恐怕他不能去了 (I'm afraid he won't be able to go). In other words, the implied subject is 我. In 他恐怕不能去了, 他 functions as the topic of the sentence.

B. 差不多 (about; roughly)

差不多 means "roughly" or "approximately," and can be used as an adverbial.

❶ 我跟姐姐差不多高。 [adverbial]

   (I'm about the same height as my older sister.)

❷ 教室離這兒不遠，走路差不多五、六分鐘。 [adverbial]

   教室离这儿不远，走路差不多五、六分钟。

   (The classroom isn't far from here. It's about a five or six-minute walk.)

❸ A: 你同屋的書架上一共有幾本書?

   你同屋的书架上一共有几本书?

   (How many books are on your roommate's bookshelves?)

   B: 差不多有一百本。 [adverbial]

   (About a hundred.)

❹ 電影兩點開始，現在差不多一點半了，快走吧。 [adverbial]
電影兩点开始，现在差不多一点半了，快走吧。
(The film starts at 2:00. It's almost 1:30. We'd better go now.)

❺ A: 你多長時間給你母親打一次電話？
你多长时间给你母亲打一次电话？
(How often do you call your mom?)

B: 我差不多一個星期打一次。 [adverbial]
我差不多一个星期打一次。
(About once a week.)

差不多 can also be an adjective, meaning "almost the same." In this sense, it can be used as a predicate.

❻ A: 你弟弟長得什麼樣？
你弟弟长得什么样？
(What does your younger brother look like?)

B: 跟我差不多，好多人看見我常常叫他的名字。 [predicate]
跟我差不多，好多人看见我常常叫他的名字。
(Very much like me. Many people call me by his name when they see me.)

❼ 今天的天氣跟昨天差不多，不冷不熱，很舒服。 [predicate]
今天的天气跟昨天差不多，不冷不热，很舒服。
(Today's weather is very similar to yesterday's—not too cold, not too hot, very comfortable.)

C. 吵 (noisy; to quarrel)

吵 can be used as an adjective, meaning the opposite of "quiet."

❶ 外邊很吵，我不能看書。 [adjective]
外边很吵，我不能看书。
(It's very noisy out. I can't read.)

② 這兒很安靜，一點兒也不吵。 [adjective]

這儿很安静，一点儿也不吵。

(It's very quiet here. Not at all noisy.)

吵 can also be used as a verb meaning "to quarrel."

③ 他們兩個人不知道為什麼，吵起來了。 [verb]

他们两个人不知道为什么，吵起来了。

(The two of them started to quarrel. I don't know why.)

④ 別吵了！有什麼問題，好好說。 [verb]

別吵了！有什么问题，好好说。

(Stop quarreling. If there's a problem, talk it out.)

D. 安靜/安静 (quiet)

安靜/安静 is an adjective. It can be used as a predicate or attributive.

① 我們的宿舍很安靜。 [predicate]

我们的宿舍很安静。

(Our dorms are quiet.)

② 這兒安靜得很，我們就在這兒坐一下吧。 [predicate]

这儿安静得很，我们就在这儿坐一下吧。

(It's very quiet here. Let's sit here for a while.)

③ 安靜點兒，弟弟在睡覺。 [predicate]

安静点儿，弟弟在睡觉。

(Be quiet. Our younger brother is sleeping.)

请保持安静

What does the sign ask people to do?

④ 我們找一個安靜的地方聊聊，好嗎？ [attributive]

我们找一个安静的地方聊聊，好吗？

(Let's find a quiet place to talk, OK?)

> ### E. 一般 (generally speaking)

This is an adjective, often used as an adverbial.

❶　我聽說學校餐廳的飯一般都不太好。[adverbial]
　　我听说学校餐厅的饭一般都不太好。
　　(I hear that the school cafeteria food is generally not very good.)

❷　新生一般都沒有車，差不多都找老生開車帶他們去買
　　東西。[adverbial]
　　新生一般都没有车，差不多都找老生开车带他们去买
　　东西。
　　(Freshmen usually don't have cars. They almost all ask sophomores, juniors, and seniors to take them shopping.)

❸　週末學校宿舍一般都有一點吵，圖書館比較安靜。[adverbial]
　　周末学校宿舍一般都有一点吵，图书馆比较安静。
　　(On weekends the dorms are generally a bit noisy. It's quieter in the library.)

❹　星期一到星期五，她一般都在學校餐廳吃飯，週末常常
　　去飯館。[adverbial]
　　星期一到星期五，她一般都在学校餐厅吃饭，周末常常
　　去饭馆。
　　(Monday through Friday, she usually eats at the school cafeteria. On weekends she often goes out to eat.)

一般 can also be used as a predicate meaning "ordinary," "not that great."

❺　我的中文一般，沒有我哥哥好。[predicate]
　　(My Chinese is nothing special. It's not as good as my older brother's.)

❻　這個學校很一般，不太有名。[predicate]
　　这个学校很一般，不太有名。
　　(This school is very ordinary. It's not very well known.)

F. 不怎麼樣/不怎么样 (not that great; just so-so)

不怎麼樣/不怎么样 is a colloquial expression, usually used as a predicate meaning "not that great."

①   這個圖書館不怎麼樣，書很少。
   这个图书馆不怎么样，书很少。
   (This library is not that great. There are very few books.)

② **A:** 你覺得這棟樓怎麼樣？
   你觉得这栋楼怎么样？
   (What do you think about this building?)

   B: 不怎麼樣，又舊又差。
   不怎么样，又旧又差。
   (Not that great. It is old and inferior.)

③ **A:** 你看，這是我的房間，你覺得傢具擺得怎麼樣？
   你看，这是我的房间，你觉得家具摆得怎么样？
   (Look, this is my room. What do you think about the arrangement of the furniture?)

   B: 不怎麼樣，你的床應該靠右，你的書桌應該靠窗戶。
   不怎么样，你的床应该靠右，你的书桌应该靠窗户。
   (Not so good. Your bed should be on the right, and your desk should be against the window.)

   A: 對，你說得對，我現在就搬。
   对，你说得对，我现在就搬。
   (Yes, you're right. I'll rearrange that now.)

這是一家什麼商店？
这是一家什么商店？

G. 地道 (authentic; genuine; pure)

地道 is an adjective meaning "authentic." It is most often used to describe food or someone's accent.

❶　他説的北京話很地道。 [predicate]
　　他说的北京话很地道。
　　(His Beijing dialect is impeccable.)

❷　這是地道的中國菜。 [attributive]
　　这是地道的中国菜。
　　(This is authentic Chinese food.)

❸　我今天買了一些地道的日本茶。 [attributive]
　　我今天买了一些地道的日本茶。
　　(I bought some authentic Japanese tea today.)

地道 is interchangeable with 道地 as seen in (2a) and (3a). However, 道地 cannot be used as a predicate as seen in (1a):

*(1a)　他説的北京話很道地。 [predicate]
　　　他说的北京话很道地。

(2a)　這是道地的中國菜。 [attributive]
　　　这是道地的中国菜。

(3a)　我今天買了一些道地的日本茶。

[attributive]

　　　我今天买了一些道地的日本茶。

這家飯館的菜應該很地道。
这家饭馆的菜应该很地道。

Language Practice

A. Don't Brag about Your Place!

Role play with a partner. Pretend you have just moved into a new apartment, and your friend asks you how things are. You like your place and would like to be positive about it, but at the same time, you don't want to brag too much. What can you say?

EXAMPLE:

客廳
大

→ **A:** 你的公寓客廳很大吧?
　　B: 客廳比較大。

客厅
大

A: 你的公寓客厅很大吧?
B: 客厅比较大。

1. 傢具
　 新
2. 房租
　 便宜
3. 附近
　 安靜
4. 買東西
　 方便

1. 家具
　 新
2. 房租
　 便宜
3. 附近
　 安静
4. 买东西
　 方便

B. Very Much So!

Work with a partner. Dissuade him or her from doing something by using the expression ...得很.

EXAMPLE:　eat at the cafeteria　　　　　　　　　　awful food

→　A: 我想去學生餐廳吃午飯。　　A: 我想去学生餐厅吃午饭。
　　B: 別去，學生餐廳的飯　　　　B: 别去，学生餐厅的饭
　　　 難吃得很。　　　　　　　　　 难吃得很。

1. go jogging in the park	freezing cold
2. study at the coffee shop	loud and noisy
3. get a part-time job at the bookstore	totally boring
4. go to the new store to shop	incredibly far away

C. I'm Afraid...

a. Your best friend wants to relocate to a different state. You don't want him or her to leave, so you express your disagreement with his or her choice of location in an indirect and polite way.

EXAMPLE:　　Alaska

→　A: 我想搬到Alaska去。　　　A: 我想搬到Alaska去。
　　B: 是嗎？ Alaska恐怕　　　　B: 是吗？ Alaska恐怕
　　　 太冷了吧？　　　　　　　　　太冷了吧？

1. Florida
2. California
3. New York
4. Texas
5. Michigan

b. Your roommate is thinking of moving to a different dorm. You come up with several reasons to convince him or her that the new place is not as good as he or she thinks.

EXAMPLE: small room size

→   **A:** 我想搬到 (name of the dorm) 宿舍去。你覺得怎麼樣?

B: 恐怕那兒的房間 有點兒小吧?

A: 我想搬到 (name of the dorm) 宿舍去。你觉得怎么样?

B: 恐怕那儿的房间 有点儿小吧?

1. old furniture
2. restrictive
3. noise level
4. not convenient to have parties

D. Generally Speaking…

Based on the pictures below, talk about Zhang Tianming's and Ke Lin's weekly schedules.

	星期一	星期二	星期三	星期四	星期五	星期六	星期天

Lesson 2 · 宿舍　　**63**
</header>

EXAMPLE:

→ **A:** 張天明星期幾買菜？ 　　**A:** 张天明星期几买菜？

　　B: 張天明一般星期六買菜。　　**B:** 张天明一般星期六买菜。

1.

2.

3.

4.

...

E. Not a Satisfied Customer!

Take turns with your partner to ask and answer questions about items in a shopping center. Make it clear that you are unimpressed.

EXAMPLE:

→ **A:** 這家店的文具怎麼樣？ 　**A:** 这家店的文具怎么样？

　　B: 這家店的文具不怎麼樣， **B:** 这家店的文具不怎么样，
　　　 又貴又不好。 　　　　　　 又贵又不好。

1.

2.

3.

4.

5.

F. What Is Over There?

a. Name the furniture in the room.

b. Take turns with your classmates to describe the arrangement of the room.

Make your description as logical as you can, e.g., begin with the entrance and describe the objects going from left to right.

G. Campus Tour

Imagine you are helping a group of freshmen get to know the layout of your campus. Bring a map of your campus to class and work with a partner to identify where the main buildings/facilities are on the map. For instance, 運動場的南邊是圖書館/运动场的南边是图书馆.

H. Tell and Draw

a. List the furniture in your bedroom and share the list with your partner.

b. Bring in a picture or a sketch of your room. Work with a partner and describe your picture to him or her using language such as 房間的右邊有一把椅子，椅子上掛著一件衣服/房間的右边有一把椅子，椅子上挂着一件衣服 etc. Have your partner, without looking at your original sketch, draw a picture of your room by following your description. Compare the original picture and your partner's drawing to see whether your descriptions were correct and whether your partner faithfully followed your descriptions.

I. My Dream House

Imagine you are building your dream house and want to describe it to your architect. Your partner will pretend to be your architect and sketch the house based on your description.

Make your description as logical as you can, e.g., begin with the entrance and go from downstairs to upstairs, as well as from left to right.

J. My Own Living Quarters

a. List the things that you like and don't like about your room/building.

喜歡/喜欢	不喜歡/不喜欢
_____	_____
_____	_____
_____	_____
_____	_____
_____	_____

b. Share the lists with your partner and give your reasons.

c. Listen to your partner's list and reasons, and then agree or disagree with him or her politely.

Pinyin Text

Zhāng Tiānmíng sùshè de fángjiān bú tài dà, zhù liǎng ge rén. Tā de tóngwū❶ yǐjīng lái le. Fángjiān li jiājù bù duō, kào chuānghu bǎi zhe liǎng zhāng shūzhuō, měi zhāng zhuōzi de qiánbian yǒu yì bǎ yǐzi. Shūzhuō de pángbiān shì chuáng①, chuáng shang yǒu bèizi② hé tǎnzi. Chuáng qián yǒu liǎng ge yīguì, guìzi li guà zhe yì xiē yīfu. Mén pángbiān fàng zhe liǎng ge shūjià, shūjià hái shì kōng de.

Zhāng Tiānmíng:	Zhēn② rè! Fángjiān li zěnme méiyǒu kōngtiáo❸?
Kē Lín:	Zhè dòng lóu bǐjiào③ jiù, wǒ dà yī④ de shíhou zài zhèr zhù guo.
Zhāng Tiānmíng:	Wèishēngjiān yě bǐjiào xiǎo. Zhù zài zhèr kǒngpà hěn bù fāngbiàn ba?
Kē Lín:	Bù, zhèr hěn fāngbiàn. Xuéshēng cāntīng❺ jiù zài lóu xià, cāntīng pángbiān yǒu yí ge xiǎo shāngdiàn, mài rìyòngpǐn hé wénjù. Jiàoshì lí zhèr bù yuǎn, zǒu lù chàbuduō wǔ, liù fēnzhōng.
Zhāng Tiānmíng:	Xǐ yīfu fāngbiàn ma?
Kē Lín:	Fāngbiàn de hěn④. Zhè céng lóu yǒu sān tái xǐyījī hé sān tái hōnggānjī.
Zhāng Tiānmíng:	Zhèr chǎo bù chǎo?
Kē Lín:	Bù chǎo, zhèr lí dà mǎlù hěn yuǎn, hěn ānjìng.
Zhāng Tiānmíng:	Tīngshuō xuéxiào cāntīng de fàn yìbān dōu bú tài hǎo. Zhèr de ne?
Kē Lín:	Nǐ shuō duì le, cāntīng de fàn zhēn de② bù zěnmeyàng.
Zhāng Tiānmíng:	Zhēn de? Nà zěnme bàn?
Kē Lín:	Nǐ bié zháojí. Fùjìn yǒu hěn duō fànguǎnr, hái yǒu yì jiā Zhōngguó cānguǎnr ne.
Zhāng Tiānmíng:	Wǒ juéde Měiguó de Zhōngguó cānguǎnr, hǎochī de bù duō.
Kē Lín:	Nà yě bú jiàn de. Fùjìn nà jiā Zhōngguó cānguǎnr de cài jiù hěn dìdao. Wǒ hé wǒ de nǚpéngyou cháng qù.
Zhāng Tiānmíng:	Zhēnde ma? Nàme⑤ guò jǐ tiān nǐ dài wǒ qù nàr kàn kan, hǎo ma?
Kē Lín:	Hǎo, méi wèntí.

English Text

Zhang Tianming's room is not very big: two people can live there. His roommate has already arrived. There isn't a lot of furniture in the room. Against the windows are two desks, and in front of each desk there is a chair. Next to the desks are [two] beds, upon which are quilts and blankets. Facing the beds are two wardrobes with some clothes hanging inside. Next to the door are two bookshelves, still empty.

Zhang Tianming: It's so hot. How come there's no air conditioning in the room?

Ke Lin: This building is rather old. I used to live here as a freshman.

Zhang Tianming: The bathroom is pretty small, too. It must be very inconvenient to live here, right?

Ke Lin: No, it's very convenient here. The student cafeteria is right downstairs, and next to it there is a small store selling daily necessities and stationery. The classroom buildings are not far from here, only a five- or six-minute walk.

Zhang Tianming: Is it convenient to do laundry here?

Ke Lin: Extremely convenient. On this floor there are three washing machines and three dryers.

Zhang Tianming: Is it noisy here?

Ke Lin: No, it's not. The major roads are far from here.

Zhang Tianming: I hear that school cafeteria food is, generally speaking, not very good. What about here?

Ke Lin: You're right. The food in the cafeteria is really not that good.

Zhang Tianming: Then what should I do?

Ke Lin: Don't worry. There are many restaurants nearby. There's even a Chinese restaurant.

Zhang Tianming: I think there aren't that many good Chinese restaurants in America.

Ke Lin: That's not necessarily true. The food at that Chinese restaurant nearby is very authentic. My girlfriend and I go there all the time.

Zhang Tianming: Really? Then could you take me there in a few days to check it out?

Ke Lin: Sure. No problem.

SELF-ASSESSMENT

How well can you do these things? Check (✔) the boxes to evaluate your progress and see which areas you may need to practice more.

I can	Very Well	OK	A Little
Name the furniture in my room	☐	☐	☐
Describe my living quarters and where things are placed	☐	☐	☐
Talk about the facilities/amenities in my building	☐	☐	☐
Comment on the quality of food in my school's cafeteria	☐	☐	☑
Give my opinions indirectly and politely	☐	☐	☐

第三课
在飯館兒

第三课
在饭馆儿

3

 LEARNING OBJECTIVES

In this lesson, you will learn to use Chinese to

1. Name four principal regional Chinese cuisines;
2. Order food and drinks;
3. Talk about what flavors you like or dislike;
4. Make your dietary restrictions or preferences known.

 RELATE AND GET READY

In your own culture/community—

- Are there different regional cuisines?
- What seasonings/spices do cooks put in their food?
- Do people usually cook by steaming, stir-frying, grilling, or baking?

Before You Study

Check the statements that apply to you.

☐ 1. I like vegetables.

☐ 2. I can handle spicy food.

When You Study

Listen to the audio recording and scan the text. Ask yourself the following questions before you begin a close reading of the text.

1. How many people went to the restaurant? Who are they? Did they all know each other before?

  今天是週末，功課也做完了①，張天明就給柯林打電話，
說他和他的女朋友麗莎想吃中國飯，問他想不想去。
柯林説正好他也想吃中國飯，就讓張天明在宿舍門口等
著，他開車來接他。

半個鐘頭以後，柯林的汽車到了。張天明和麗莎上
車一看②，車裏還有一個女孩兒，柯林介紹說，她是從
中國來的留學生，叫林雪梅。幾分鐘以後，他們四個人
到了那家中國飯館兒。

3. I like my meat dishes well-done.

4. I have a sweet tooth.

5. I prefer my food light and plain.

2. Are they vegetarian? How do you know?

3. What did Ke Lin suggest right before the food was served?

今天是周末，功课也做完了①，张天明就给柯林打电话，说他和他的女朋友丽莎想吃中国饭，问他想不想去。柯林说正好他也想吃中国饭，就让张天明在宿舍门口等着，他开车来接他。

半个钟头以后，柯林的汽车到了。张天明和丽莎上车一看②，车里还有一个女孩儿，柯林介绍说，她是从中国来的留学生，叫林雪梅。几分钟以后，他们四个人到了那家中国饭馆儿。

(The four of them follow the waitress to their table.)

服務員： 這是菜單。

柯林： 謝謝。麗莎，天明，你們想吃點兒什麼?

張天明： 這兒什麼菜好吃?

柯林： 這兒雞做得不錯，魚也很好，特別是清蒸魚，味道
好極了。

林雪梅： 芥蘭牛肉也挺好，又嫩又香③。

麗莎： 可以點❶一個湯嗎?

柯林： 當然可以，這兒的菠菜豆腐湯做得很好，叫一個吧。

林雪梅： 再來一個青菜吧。

麗莎： 好，好。

服務員： 現在可以點菜了嗎?

柯林： 可以。一個清蒸魚，
一個芥蘭牛肉，一
個菠菜豆腐湯。今
天你們有什麼新鮮
的青菜?

服務員： 小白菜怎麼樣?

柯林： 行。服務員，菜要清淡一點兒，別太鹹，少放油，
別放味精。

張天明： 麻煩先來四杯冰水，再多給我們一些餐巾紙。

服務員： 好，沒問題。對了，您要飯嗎?

林雪梅： 我們不"要飯"❷，我們要四碗米飯。

LANGUAGE NOTES

❶ To order from a menu is 點／点 in Chinese, or more casually, 要, 叫 or 來／来.

(The four of them follow the waitress to their table.)

服务员：　这是菜单。

柯林：　　谢谢。丽莎，天明，你们想吃点儿什么？

张天明：　这儿什么菜好吃？

柯林：　　这儿鸡做得不错，鱼也很好，特别是清蒸鱼，味道
　　　　　好极了。

林雪梅：　芥兰牛肉也挺好，又嫩又香③。

丽莎：　　可以点❶一个汤吗？

柯林：　　当然可以，这儿的菠菜豆腐汤做得很好，叫一个吧。

林雪梅：　再来一个青菜吧。

丽莎：　　好，好。

服务员：　现在可以点菜了吗？

柯林：　　可以。一个清蒸鱼，
　　　　　一个芥兰牛肉，一
　　　　　个菠菜豆腐汤。今
　　　　　天你们有什么新鲜
　　　　　的青菜？

服务员：　小白菜怎么样？

柯林：　　行。服务员，菜要清淡一点儿，别太咸，少放油，
　　　　　别放味精。

张天明：　麻烦先来四杯冰水，再多给我们一些餐巾纸。

服务员：　好，没问题。对了，您要饭吗？

林雪梅：　我们不"要饭"❷，我们要四碗米饭。

---

❷ Beggars are colloquially known as 要饭的/要饭的, and 要饭/要饭 means "to beg." That is
why Lin Xuemei corrects the waitress, who meant, "Do you want any rice?"

服務員：　對、對、對，要四碗米飯。

…

張天明：　林雪梅，柯林說這兒中國菜很地道，是真的嗎？

林雪梅：　這個飯館兒的菜是④不錯，但是不如⑤我們杭州的飯館兒。

張天明：　我聽我父母❸說中國各個地方的菜不一樣，哪兒的菜最好吃？

林雪梅：　這就要看你的口味了。比如我愛吃甜的，就喜歡上海菜；柯林愛吃辣的，就喜歡四川菜、湖南菜。要是喜歡比較清淡的，就吃廣東菜…

柯林：　　雪梅，你別說了，我的口水都快流出來了…我們寒假去中國吧。

林雪梅：　去中國旅行，吃中國菜？可以考慮。

麗莎：　　這個主意❹不錯，我也可以考慮。

張天明：　有吃有玩兒？我當然可以考慮。

林雪梅：　真的？那太好了！大家都去！

麗莎：　　要是能去中國學中文就更好了。

柯林：　　哎，我們的菜來了。

After You Study

Challenge yourself to complete the following tasks in Chinese.

1. List the beverages and dishes these four characters have ordered.

LANGUAGE NOTES

❸ Unlike 爸爸媽媽/爸爸妈妈, the word 父母 is literary and used as a collective noun meaning "parents."

服务员：　对、对、对，要四碗米饭。

…

张天明：　林雪梅，柯林说这儿中国菜很地道，是真的吗？

林雪梅：　这个饭馆儿的菜是④不错，但是不如⑤我们杭州的饭馆儿。

张天明：　我听我父母❸说中国各个地方的菜不一样，哪儿的菜最好吃？

林雪梅：　这就要看你的口味了。比如我爱吃甜的，就喜欢上海菜；柯林爱吃辣的，就喜欢四川菜、湖南菜。要是喜欢比较清淡的，就吃广东菜…

柯林：　雪梅，你别说了，我的口水都快流出来了…我们寒假去中国吧。

林雪梅：　去中国旅行，吃中国菜？可以考虑。

丽莎：　这个主意❹不错，我也可以考虑。

张天明：　有吃有玩儿？我当然可以考虑。

林雪梅：　真的？那太好了！大家都去！

丽莎：　要是能去中国学中文就更好了。

柯林：　哎，我们的菜来了。

---

2. Make a note of who likes which flavors and types of cuisine.
3. List the characters' dietary restrictions.

---

❹ In this word, 意 is in the neutral tone and 主 changes to the second tone from the third.

VOCABULARY

1.	正好		zhènghǎo	adv	coincidentally
2.	門口	门口	ménkǒu	n	doorway; entrance
3.	留學生	留学生	liúxuéshēng	n	student studying abroad
4.	菜單	菜单	càidān	n	menu
5.	雞	鸡	jī	n	chicken
6.	清蒸	清蒸	qīngzhēng	v	to steam (food without heavy sauce)
7.	味道		wèidao	n	taste; flavor
8.	芥蘭	芥兰	jièlán	n	Chinese broccoli
9.	嫩		nèn	adj	tender
10.	香		xiāng	adj	fragrant; pleasant-smelling
11.	菠菜	菠菜	bōcài	n	spinach
12.	叫(菜)	叫(菜)	jiào (cài)	v(o)	to order (food)
13.	新鮮	新鲜	xīnxian	adj	fresh
14.	清淡		qīngdàn	adj	light in flavor
15.	鹹	咸	xián	adj	salty
16.	油		yóu	n/adj	oil; oily
17.	餐巾		cānjīn	n	napkin
18.	不如		bùrú	v	not equal to; inferior to; to not measure up to [See Grammar 5.]
19.	各		gè	pr	each; every
20.	口味		kǒuwèi	n	taste; dietary preference
21.	比如		bǐrú	v	for example

22.	辣		là	adj	spicy
23.	口水		kǒushuǐ	n	saliva
24.	流		liú	v	to flow
25.	考慮	考虑	kǎolǜ	v	to consider
26.	主意		zhúyi	n	idea

Proper Nouns

27.	麗莎	丽莎	Lìshā		Lisa (a personal name)
28.	林雪梅		Lín Xuěméi		Lin Xuemei (a personal name)
29.	四川		Sìchuān		Sichuan (a Chinese province)
30.	湖南		Húnán		Hunan (a Chinese province)
31.	廣東	广东	Guǎngdōng		Guangdong (a Chinese province)

Which dish can be classified as Sichuan cuisine?

Enlarged Characters

蘭	鹹	慮	麗	廣
兰	咸	虑	丽	广

Which sign says that the restaurant/store is closed for a break?

Culture Highlights

❶ To settle the bill in a restaurant is 結賬/结账 (jié zhàng) or more colloquially 買單/买单 (mǎi dān). Some write it as 埋單/埋单 (mái dān). No tips are expected. Very upscale restaurants may charge a service fee, typically around 15 percent.

❷ Although restaurants in China come in all shapes and sizes, many of the more popular establishments tend to be raucous, multistoried affairs. They almost always include private banquet rooms, which may or may not include a 10 to 15 percent service charge or a minimum consumption charge.

❸ The most basic and best-known technique in Chinese cooking is stir-frying (炒, chǎo), which is traditionally done in a heavy cast iron wok. Other common techniques include 紅燒/红烧 (hóngshāo, braising in soy sauce) and 清蒸/清蒸 (qīngzhēng, steaming fresh lightly seasoned food). The three must-haves when cooking Chinese food are green onion (葱/葱, cōng), ginger (薑/姜, jiāng), and garlic (蒜/蒜, suàn).

葱/葱 (cōng)

薑/姜 (jiāng)

蒜/蒜 (suàn)

❹ 川 (Chuān), 粵/粤 (Yuè), 魯/鲁 (Lǔ), and 蘇/苏 (Sū) are the abbreviated names of four Chinese provinces: Sichuan, Guangdong, Shandong, and Jiangsu, famous for their distinct cuisines, collectively called the "Four Great Culinary Schools" (四大菜系/四大菜系, sì dà cài xì). The telltale fiery and tingling taste of Sichuan cooking (川菜, Chuān cài) comes from its two main seasonings: chili pepper and Sichuan peppercorn. Hot bean paste is another common ingredient. Best known outside China is the far milder Cantonese (廣東/广东, Guangdong) cooking (粵菜/粤菜, Yuè cài), which takes advantage of the region's bountiful fresh seasonal produce and seafood. Shandong (山東/山东), with its coastline in the east and mountains in the west, gave rise to a varied cooking tradition 魯菜/鲁菜 (Lǔ cài) emphasizing broths, seafood, and poultry. Because of the region's proximity to the imperial court, Shandong cooking became the favorite of the Manchu aristocracy during the Qing period (1616–1911). The long prosperity and cultural prominence of the lower Yangtze region also made its cuisine influential. 蘇菜/苏菜 (Sū cài) or 淮(揚)菜/淮(扬)菜 (Huái{yáng} cài) makes abundant use of the region's various types of tofu products and freshwater fish. Both 上海菜/上海菜 (Shànghǎi cài) and 杭州菜/杭州菜 (Hángzhōu cài) are subcategories of 蘇菜/苏菜 (Sū cài).

Grammar

1. Topic-Comment Sentence Structure

If someone, something, or some event is already known—in other words, if it is no longer new information to the speaker or the listener—then it should appear at the beginning of a Chinese sentence. The positioning of known information at the beginning of a sentence is an important characteristic of Chinese and is referred to as a "topic-comment" sentence structure in which a "topic" is mentioned in the first part of the sentence and commented on in the latter part of the sentence. Known information can also include information that has already been mentioned or activities that are taken for granted, such as eating, sleeping, or students going to classes, doing homework, etc.

❶   今天是週末，再説功課也做完了…
    今天是周末，再说功课也做完了…

    (Today is a weekend. Besides, [I've] already finished [my] homework...)
    [This is about a student. Everyone knows that students are supposed to have homework, so homework is not new information.]

❷ A: 你知道附近那個鞋店明天要打折嗎？
    你知道附近那个鞋店明天要打折吗？

    (Did you know that there is a sale tomorrow at that shoe store nearby?)

   B: 這件事我早就知道了。
    这件事我早就知道了。

    (I already knew [this].)
    ["This" refers to the shoe store's sale tomorrow that is mentioned in the previous statement.]

❸   你去台北的飛機票買好了嗎？
    你去台北的飞机票买好了吗？

    (The ticket for your flight to Taipei—have you booked it?)
    [The speaker knows that you are going to Taipei and that you need a plane ticket.]

❹ 我們昨天在"小香港"吃了清蒸魚，那個餐館兒的
清蒸魚做得很好。

我们昨天在"小香港"吃了清蒸鱼，那个餐馆儿的
清蒸鱼做得很好。

(Yesterday we had steamed fish at Little Hong Kong.
That restaurant's steamed fish is really good.)

["Steamed fish" appears in the first clause. Therefore,
it's treated as a topic in the second clause.]

This type of "topic-comment" structure differs from the basic Chinese word order:

"subject+verb+object."

❺ 這張碟你看完了嗎？

这张碟你看完了吗？

(Have you finished watching this DVD?)

❻ 功課你做完了嗎？

功课你做完了吗？

(Have you finished your homework?)

❼ 飯要慢慢吃，吃得太快對身體不好。

饭要慢慢吃，吃得太快对身体不好。

(Eat your food [more] slowly. Eating too fast is not good for your health.)

❽ A: 聽說學校商店的東西學生不能買了，是真的嗎？

听说学校商店的东西学生不能买了，是真的吗？

(I hear that students can no longer buy the things in the school store. Is that true?)

B: 誰說的？ 那不是真的。

谁说的？ 那不是真的。

(Who said that? That's not true.)

While many Chinese sentences follow a basic word order that is similar to English, namely
"subject+verb+object," the "topic-comment" structure is also a very important and
distinctive feature of Chinese grammar. It is required in certain circumstances, some of
which are illustrated above.

2. 一 + V

We know that 一 before a verb (usually monosyllabic) expresses the completion of a brief action. It must be followed by a second clause:

❶　外面有人叫我，我開門一看，是送信的。
　　外面有人叫我，我开门一看，是送信的。

(There was someone shouting my name outside. I opened the door and took a look, and it was the letter carrier.)

一…就…, on the other hand, is used to connect two consecutive actions. In this structure, 就 is required in some cases and optional in others.

If the first action is closely followed by the second action, and if there isn't a pause in the sentence, the second verb is usually preceded by 就:

❷　老師剛才説的話，我一聽就懂了。
　　老师刚才说的话，我一听就懂了。

(What the teacher just said—I understood it immediately.)

❸　我同屋每天一回宿舍就做功課。
　　我同屋每天一回宿舍就做功课。

(Every day my roommate does his homework as soon as he comes back to the dorm.)

❹　我一收到你發的短信就跑來了。
　　我一收到你发的短信就跑来了。

(I came as soon as I got your text message.)

If there is a pause in the sentence, and there is an adverbial before the second verb, sometimes 就 can be omitted as seen in ❺ and ❻. But it's also OK to leave it in as seen in (5a) and (6a).

❺　他把毯子往床上一放，很快地跑了出去。

(He put the blanket down on the bed and quickly ran out.)

In the above sentence 跑了出去 happened hard on the heels of the previous action 放.

(5a)　他把毯子往床上一放，就很快地跑了出去。

6 回家以後，我把包往桌子上一放，馬上給小李打了一個
電話。

回家以后，我把包往桌子上一放，马上给小李打了一个
电话。

(After I got back home, I put down my bag on the desk and gave Little Li a call right
away.)

(6a) 回家以後，我把包往桌子上一放，就馬上給小李打了
一個電話。

回家以后，我把包往桌子上一放，就马上给小李打了
一个电话。

If the subjects are different, usually there must be a 就 before the second action:

7 A: 我們什麼時候走？
我们什么时候走？

(When are we leaving?)

B: 你一到，我們就走。
你一到，我们就走。

(We'll leave as soon as you come.)

8 下午我的朋友一來，我們就一起去滑冰了。
下午我的朋友一来，我们就一起去滑冰了。

(This afternoon, as soon as my friend came we went skating together.)

The two actions in the 一···就··· pattern can be identical:

9 那個餐館很容易找，我們一找就找到了。
那个餐馆很容易找，我们一找就找到了。

(That restaurant was really easy to find. As soon as we started looking, we found it.)

Sometimes the first action expresses a condition. If the condition is met, then 就 is needed
before the second verb:

⑩   他病了。一看書就頭疼。
　　　他病了。一看书就头疼。

(He's sick. As soon as he tries to read, he gets a headache.)

⑪   我一吃味精，就得喝很多水。

(I have to drink a lot of water whenever I eat MSG.)

3. 又 Adj/Verb, 又 Adj/Verb

The "又 Adj/Verb, 又 Adj/Verb" pattern can be used to indicate two simultaneous qualities or two concurrent actions.

❶   媽媽做的清蒸魚又嫩又香。
　　　妈妈做的清蒸鱼又嫩又香。

(The steamed fish that my mother makes is tender *and* it smells delicious.)

❷   那個衣櫃又舊又小。
　　　那个衣柜又旧又小。

(That wardrobe is old *and* small.)

❸   孩子們又跑又跳，玩兒得非常高興。
　　　孩子们又跑又跳，玩儿得非常高兴。

(The kids ran *and* jumped. They had a great time.)

❹   那個小孩又哭又吵，我們一點辦法也沒有。
　　　那个小孩又哭又吵，我们一点办法也没有。

(That child cried *and* fussed. We didn't know what to do.)

When two adjectives are used in this way, they must either be both positive or both negative. Furthermore, the adjectives must be related in meaning. For instance, when describing people, we often say, "clever and pretty;" "tall and thin;" "short and overweight." "The weather is hot and stuffy" or "cold and humid." When two verbs are involved, the actions denoted must be concurrent. For example, "talk and laugh," "cry and yell," etc.

4. The Emphatic 是

Used before adjectives and verbs, it reaffirms the validity of a prior statement.

Note that when an adjective is used as a predicate, it generally cannot be preceded by 是. However, this special emphatic usage of 是 before an adjective requires that 是 be stressed, and the adjective should have already been mentioned, as seen in ❶ and ❷.

❶ A: 住在這個宿舍很方便。
住在这个宿舍很方便。
(This dorm is really convenient.)

B: 住在這個宿舍是方便，去上課，去醫院，去餐廳都不遠。
住在这个宿舍是方便，去上课，去医院，去餐厅都不远。
(This dorm is very convenient. It's not far from school, the hospital, and restaurants.)

❷ A: 這個餐館兒的上海菜很地道，我很喜歡。
这个餐馆儿的上海菜很地道，我很喜欢。
(The Shanghai cuisine at this restaurant is quite authentic. I like it very much.)

B: 他們的上海菜是很地道，可是太貴了。
他们的上海菜是很地道，可是太贵了。
(Their Shanghai dishes are quite authentic, but too expensive.)

❸ A: 聽說你的同屋搬走了，不回來了。
听说你的同屋搬走了，不回来了。
(I hear that your roommate moved out, and isn't coming back.)

B: 沒錯，他是搬走了，他去了一個更有名的大學。
没错，他是搬走了，他去了一个更有名的大学。
(That's right. He did move out, and went to another university with an even better reputation.)

5. 不如

不如 means more or less the same thing as 没有 in comparative sentences.

A + 不如 + B (+ adjective, etc.)

❶　我跑得不如小李快。
(I don't run as fast as Little Li.)

❷　這台烘乾機不如那台烘乾機新。
这台烘干机不如那台烘干机新。
(This dryer is not as new as that one.)

Unlike 没有, however, 不如 does not always need to be followed by an adjective.

❸　他的中文不如我。
(His Chinese isn't as good as mine.)

❹　我唱歌不如他，但是跳舞他不如我。
(I don't sing as well as he does, but when it comes to dancing, he isn't as good as
I am.)

Furthermore, 不如 is generally used with adjectives that are positive in meaning such as
好, 漂亮, 好吃, 方便, 近, 暖和, etc.

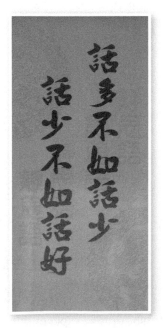

你同意嗎?
你同意吗?

Words & Phrases

A. 正好 (coincidentally)

正好 is an adverb.

❶ 我今天正好有時間，我跟你去買衣服吧。 [adverb]
我今天正好有时间，我跟你去买衣服吧。

(I happen to have some free time today. Let me go with you to buy some clothes.)

❷ 我去找他的時候，他正好要出門。 [adverb]
我去找他的时候，他正好要出门。

(When I went to look for him, he happened to be about to go out.)

正好 is also an adjective meaning "just right." It can be used as a predicate:

❸ 這雙鞋我穿著不大不小，正好。 [adjective as predicate]
这双鞋我穿着不大不小，正好。

(This pair of shoes is not too big and not too small for me. It's just right.)

❹ 你來得正好，我們都在找你呢。 [adjective as complement]
你来得正好，我们都在找你呢。

(You came at just the right time. We were all looking for you.)

B. 特別是 (especially)

特別 is often used together with 是.

❶ 這兒魚做得很好，特別是清蒸魚，味道好極了。
这儿鱼做得很好，特别是清蒸鱼，味道好极了。

(The fish here is really good, especially the steamed fish. It tastes fantastic.)

❷ 王小姐喜歡買東西，特別是碗盤。
王小姐喜欢买东西，特别是碗盘。

(Miss Wang likes to go shopping, especially for bowls and plates.)

❸   小柯不喜歡運動，特別是游泳。

小柯不喜欢运动，特别是游泳。

(Little Ke dislikes sports, especially swimming.)

❹   李先生覺得中國菜很難做，特別是糖醋魚。

李先生觉得中国菜很难做，特别是糖醋鱼。

(Mr. Li thinks Chinese food is difficult to prepare, especially sweet and sour fish.)

C. 麻煩/麻烦 ([may I] trouble [you]; troublesome)

When asking for a favor, it is polite to begin by saying 麻煩(你)/麻烦(你)…Here
麻煩/麻烦 is a verb, meaning "[May I] trouble [you to]…"

❶   小張，如果有人來電話，麻煩你告訴他我去飛機場了。

[verb]

小张，如果有人来电话，麻烦你告诉他我去飞机场了。

(Little Zhang, if someone calls, could you please tell him that I went to the airport?)

❷   服務員，麻煩給我一些餐巾紙。 [verb]

服务员，麻烦给我一些餐巾纸。

(Waiter, please give me some napkins.)

❸   麻煩你告訴老師我病了，不能去上課了。 [verb]

麻烦你告诉老师我病了，不能去上课了。

(Could you please tell the teacher that I'm sick and can't go to class?)

❹ A: 先生，這件行李我幫你拿進房間吧。

先生，这件行李我帮你拿进房间吧。

(Sir, let me help you carry this luggage to your room.)

   B: 不用，不麻煩你了。 [verb]

不用，不麻烦你了。

(That won't be necessary. I won't trouble you.)

麻煩/麻烦 can also be an adjective used as a predicate, meaning "troublesome."

❺   做中國菜很麻煩。 [adjective]
做中国菜很麻烦。
(Making Chinese food is a lot of trouble.)

❻   出國得辦護照、辦簽證，很麻煩。 [adjective]
出国得办护照、办签证，很麻烦。
(To go abroad you have to get your passport and visa ready; it's quite a hassle.)

❼   他這個人很麻煩，常常問一些很難的問題。 [adjective]
他这个人很麻烦，常常问一些很难的问题。
(He can be quite a pain. He often asks questions that are very difficult.)

D. 這(就)要看⋯(了)/这(就)要看⋯(了)(it depends on...)

This is a way to give flexible or indirect responses to a question.

❶   什麼菜好吃？這就要看你的口味了。
什么菜好吃？这就要看你的口味了。
(What dishes are delicious? That depends on your tastes.)

❷   學生：明天的考試難不難？
学生：明天的考试难不难？
(Student: Is tomorrow's test hard?)

老師：這就要看你準備得怎麼樣了。
老师：这就要看你准备得怎么样了。
(Teacher: That depends on whether you prepare well.)

❸ A: 快放假了，寒假你打算去中國玩嗎？
快放假了，寒假你打算去中国玩吗？
(It's almost vacation time. Do you plan on going to China this winter break?)

    B: 這就要看我媽媽讓不讓我去了。
这就要看我妈妈让不让我去了。
(It all depends on whether my mom will let me.)

> **E. 比如(説)/比如(说) (for example)**

比如(説)/比如(说) is used before citing examples. It is slightly more formal than 比方説/比方说.

❶　他去過很多國家，比如英國、日本、中國…
　　他去过很多国家，比如英国、日本、中国…
　　(He's been to many countries, for instance, England, Japan, China…)

❷　我們班的同學很多人唱歌唱得很好，比如說王朋，唱得
　　棒極了。
　　我们班的同学很多人唱歌唱得很好，比如说王朋，唱得
　　棒极了。
　　(Many of our classmates sing really well. Take Wang Peng, for example. He's a great singer.)

❸　這裏的飯館兒很多，比如東邊的"好吃飯館"，西邊的
　　"請再來"，南邊的"最便宜"，北邊的"大家喜歡來
　　餐廳"。
　　这里的饭馆儿很多，比如东边的"好吃饭馆"，西边的
　　"请再来"，南边的"最便宜"，北边的"大家喜欢来
　　餐厅"。
　　(There are many restaurants here, for example "Delicious" on the east side, "Come Again" on the west side, "Good Bargains" on the south side, and "Everybody's Favorite" on the north side.)

Language Practice

A. Name that Flavor

Look at the foods and drinks listed and take turns with your partner to tell what flavors they usually have.

EXAMPLE:　　飲料　　　　　　　　饮料

→　　　飲料一般很甜。　　　饮料一般很甜。

1. 可樂　　　　可乐
2. 西瓜　　　　西瓜
3. 蘋果　　　　苹果
4. 蛋糕　　　　蛋糕
5. 酸辣湯　　　酸辣汤
6. 糖醋魚　　　糖醋鱼
7. 清蒸魚　　　清蒸鱼
8. 四川菜　　　四川菜

B. Can You Take the Heat?

Ke Lin likes his food spicy, and Lin Xuemei likes hers sweet. How about you and your classmates? Ask your classmates if they like their food spicy, sweet, salty, and/or sour.

A: 你愛吃辣的、甜的、鹹的、　　　A: 你爱吃辣的、甜的、咸的、
　　還是酸的？　　　　　　　　　　　　还是酸的？

B: 我愛吃＿＿＿的。　　　　　　　　B: 我爱吃＿＿＿的。

Then report back to the class:

Kevin, Janet, ⋯跟我一樣，　　　　Kevin, Janet, ⋯跟我一样，
都愛吃＿＿的。　　　　　　　　　　都爱吃＿＿的。

or

Jose 跟我不一樣，　　　　　　　　Jose 跟我不一样，
他愛吃＿＿的。　　　　　　　　　　他爱吃＿＿的。

C. Food Critic for a Day

Imagine you are a food critic. Use the following information to practice commenting on Chinese dishes.

EXAMPLE:　　酸辣湯　　　　　　　　　酸辣汤

＋醋　　－鹽　　×糖　　　＋醋　　－盐　　×糖

→　這碗酸辣湯不怎麼樣。　这碗酸辣汤不怎么样。

應該多放點兒醋，少放　应该多放点儿醋，少放

點兒鹽，別放糖。　　　点儿盐，别放糖。

1. 糖醋魚
　　＋醋　　　＋糖　　×味精

2. 芥蘭牛肉
　　＋油　　　－鹽　　×味精

3. 菠菜豆腐湯
　　－油　　　－鹽　　×醋

4. 素餃子
　　＋青菜　　－鹽　　×醋

5. 冰茶
　　＋冰　　　－糖

1. 糖醋鱼
　　＋醋　　　＋糖　　×味精

2. 芥兰牛肉
　　＋油　　　－盐　　×味精

3. 菠菜豆腐汤
　　－油　　　－盐　　×醋

4. 素饺子
　　＋青菜　　－盐　　×醋

5. 冰茶
　　＋冰　　　－糖

D. Sales Pitch

Help the following businesses promote their goods.

EXAMPLE: bookstore   numerous   new   Chinese books

→   我們的書又多又新，   我们的书又多又新，
特別是中文書。   特别是中文书。

1. clothing store   pretty   inexpensive   shirts
2. furniture store   new   inexpensive   wardrobes
3. grocery store   fresh   inexpensive   spinach
4. fruit stand   big   fresh   apples
5. Chinese restaurant   pleasant-smelling   delicious   steamed fish
6. tea house   healthy   delicious   green tea

E. A Model Chinese Language Student

A model Chinese language student uses many strategies and takes every opportunity to improve his or her Chinese. Things that he or she does include listening to audio recording, practicing speaking with friends, studying new vocabulary, reviewing grammar, reading texts, writing characters, etc.

EXAMPLE: 上課   上课
→   他一上課就說中文。   他一上课就说中文。

Here are some opportunities that a model Chinese language student may seize to practice Chinese:

1. 起床   起床
2. 下課   下课
3. 回家   回家
4. 吃完晚飯   吃完晚饭
5. 放假   放假

F. A Caterer's Challenge

Mr. Li has hired a caterer to help him throw a dinner party. Here's a list of his guests' likes (✓), dislikes
(X), and dietary restrictions (▽).

牛肉	✓	✓	✓	▽
雞/鸡	✓	✓	✓	X
魚/鱼	✓	✓	✓	✓
豆腐	✓	X	✓	✓
菠菜/菠菜	▽	✓	X	✓
中國芥蘭/中国芥兰	✓	✓	X	✓
辣的菜/辣的菜	✓	X	✓	✓
味精	X	X	▽	X

Here are the caterer's specialties:

紅燒牛肉	红烧牛肉
芥蘭牛肉	芥兰牛肉
清蒸魚	清蒸鱼
家常豆腐	家常豆腐
涼拌黃瓜	凉拌黄瓜
小白菜	小白菜
素餃子	素饺子
菠菜湯	菠菜汤
酸辣湯	酸辣汤
雞湯	鸡汤

Work with a partner and help Mr. Li put together the menu.

a. Choose the dishes that will definitely work for all guests and give the reasons.

_____   _____

_____   _____

_____   _____

b. Using 恐怕, list the dishes that probably shouldn't be served and explain the reasons:

_____   _____

_____   _____

你想喝什麼飲料？
你想喝什么饮料？

c. Recommend a dish or two outside the menu that you and your partner think would be welcomed by all guests. Give the reasons using 又…又…

_____   _____

G. I Love My Parents' Cooking Because …

a. Using the adjectives you learned in this lesson, list the reasons why you love your mom's or dad's cooking. Is it because it's not oily but flavorful, free of charge, etc.?

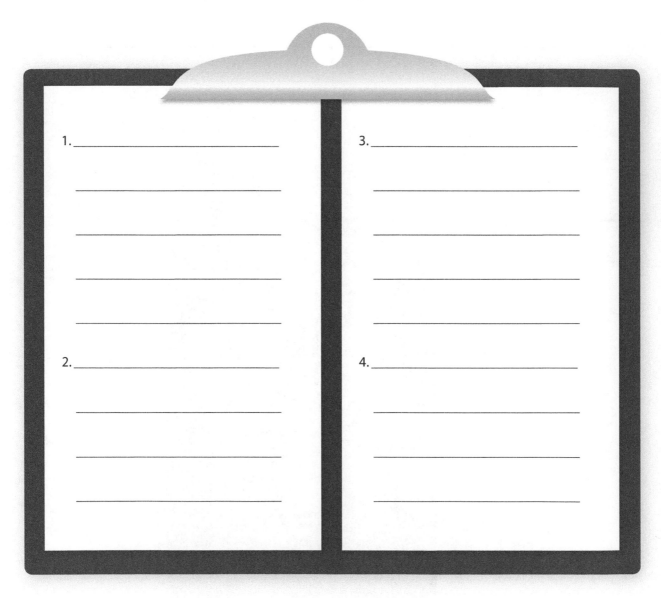

1._____   3._____

_____   _____

_____   _____

_____   _____

2._____   4._____

_____   _____

_____   _____

b. Then report to your class why you love your mom's or dad's cooking. Include 第一…, 第二…,… 除了……以外, 還/还…, or other connectors to explain your reasons.

Pinyin Text

Jīntiān shì zhōumò, gōngkè yě zuò wán le①, Zhāng Tiānmíng jiù gěi Kē Lín dǎ diànhuà, shuō tā hé tā de nǚpéngyou Lìshā xiǎng chī Zhōngguó fàn, wèn tā xiǎng bù xiǎng qù. Kē Lín shuō zhènghǎo tā yě xiǎng chī Zhōngguó fàn, jiù ràng Zhāng Tiānmíng zài sùshè ménkǒu děng zhe, tā kāi chē lái jiē tā.

Bàn ge zhōngtóu yǐhòu, Kē Lín de qìchē dào le. Zhāng Tiānmíng hé Lìshā shàng chē yí kàn②, chē li hái yǒu yí ge nǚháir, Kē Lín jièshào shuō, tā shì cóng Zhōngguó lái de liúxuéshēng, jiào Lín Xuěméi. Jǐ fēnzhōng yǐhòu, tāmen sì ge rén dào le nà jiā Zhōngguó fànguǎnr.

(The four of them follow the waitress to their table.)

Fúwùyuán:	Zhè shì càidān.
Kē Lín:	Xièxie. Lìshā, Tiānmíng, nǐmen xiǎng chī diǎnr shénme?
Zhāng Tiānmíng:	Zhèr shénme cài hǎochī?
Kē Lín:	Zhèr jī zuò de búcuò, yú yě hěn hǎo, tèbié shì qīngzhēng yú, wèidao hǎo jí le.
Lín Xuěméi:	Jièlán niúròu yě tǐng hǎo, yòu nèn yòu xiāng③.
Lìshā:	Kěyǐ diǎn❶ yí ge tāng ma?
Kē Lín:	Dāngrán kěyǐ, zhèr de bōcài dòufu tāng zuò de hěn hǎo, jiào yí ge ba.
Lín Xuěméi:	Zài lái yí ge qīngcài ba.
Lìshā:	Hǎo, hǎo.
Fúwùyuán:	Xiànzài kěyǐ diǎn cài le ma?
Kē Lín:	Kěyǐ. Yí ge qīngzhēng yú, yí ge jièlán niúròu, yí ge bōcài dòufu tāng. Jīntiān nǐmen yǒu shénme xīnxian de qīngcài?
Fúwùyuán:	Xiǎo báicài zěnmeyàng?
Kē Lín:	Xíng. Fúwùyuán, cài yào qīngdàn yì diǎnr, bié tài xián, shǎo fàng yóu, bié fàng wèijīng.
Zhāng Tiānmíng:	Máfan xiān lái sì bēi bīngshuǐ, zài duō gěi wǒmen yì xiē cānjīn zhǐ.
Fúwùyuán:	Hǎo, méi wèntí. Duì le, nín yào fàn ma?
Lín Xuěméi:	Wǒmen bú "yào fàn,"❷ wǒmen yào sì wǎn mǐfàn.
Fúwùyuán:	Duì, duì, duì, yào sì wǎn mǐfàn.

…

Zhāng Tiānmíng: Lín Xuěméi, Kē Lín shuō zhèr Zhōngguó cài hěn dìdào, shì zhēn de ma?

Lín Xuěméi: Zhè ge fànguǎnr de cài shì④ búcuò, dànshì bùrú⑤ wǒmen Hángzhōu de fànguǎnr.

Zhāng Tiānmíng: Wǒ tīng wǒ fùmǔ❸ shuō Zhōngguó gè ge dìfang de cài bù yíyàng, nǎr de cài zuì hǎochī?

Lín Xuěméi: Zhè jiù yào kàn nǐ de kǒuwèi le. Bǐrú wǒ ài chī tián de, jiù xǐhuan Shànghǎi cài; Kē Lín ài chī là de, jiù xǐhuan Sìchuān cài, Húnán cài. Yàoshi xǐhuan bǐjiào qīngdàn de, jiù chī Guǎngdōng cài.

Kē Lín: Xuěméi, nǐ bié shuō le, wǒ de kǒushuǐ dōu kuài liú chu lai le... Wǒmen hánjià qù Zhōngguó ba.

Lín Xuěméi: Qù Zhōngguó lǚxíng, chī Zhōngguó cài? Kěyǐ kǎolǜ.

Lìshā: Zhè ge zhúyì❹ búcuò, wǒ yě kěyǐ kǎolǜ.

Zhāng Tiānmíng: Yǒu chī yǒu wánr? Wǒ dāngrán kěyǐ kǎolǜ.

Lín Xuěméi: Zhēn de? Nà tài hǎo le! Dàjiā dōu qù!

Lìshā: Yàoshi néng qù Zhōngguó xué Zhōngwén jiù gèng hǎo le.

Kē Lín: Āi, wǒmen de cài lái le.

English Text

Today is a weekend, and he has already finished his homework, so Zhang Tianming calls Ke Lin and says that he and his girlfriend Lisa would like to eat Chinese food. He asks Ke Lin if he would like to go. Ke Lin says it so happens that he also wants to have Chinese food, so he asks Zhang Tianming to wait for him outside the dorm. He'll come pick him up.

Half an hour later Ke Lin's car arrives. Zhang Tianming and Lisa get into the car and see a girl. Ke Lin introduces her, saying that she is an international student from China named Lin Xuemei. In a few minutes they are at the Chinese restaurant.

(The four of them follow the waitress to their table.)

Waitress:	Here's the menu.
Ke Lin:	Thanks. Lisa, Tianming, what would you like to eat?
Zhang Tianming:	What's delicious here?
Ke Lin:	Their chicken is done very well. So is their fish, especially steamed fish. It tastes great.
Lin Xuemei:	Their beef with Chinese broccoli is also quite good, both tender and fragrant.
Lisa:	Can we order a soup?
Ke Lin:	Of course. Their spinach and tofu soup is very good. Let's order one.
Lin Xuemei:	Let's order another vegetable dish.
Lisa:	Yes, yes.
Waitress:	Are you ready to order?
Ke Lin:	Yes. A steamed fish, a beef with Chinese broccoli, a spinach and tofu soup. What fresh vegetables do you have today?
Waitress:	How about baby bok choy?
Ke Lin:	Fine. Waitress, we'd like our food light. Please don't make it too salty. Not too much oil, no MSG.
Zhang Tianming:	Please bring us four glasses of ice water first and give us some more napkins.
Waitress:	No problem. Oh, that's right. Do you want rice?
Lin Xuemei:	We don't "want rice" [like beggars]. We'd like four bowls of rice.
Waitress:	You're right. You'd like four bowls of rice.
...	
Zhang Tianming:	Lin Xuemei, Ke Lin says that the Chinese dishes here are very authentic. Is it true?
Lin Xuemei:	Their dishes are very good, but not as good as the ones in our restaurants in Hangzhou.
Zhang Tianming:	My parents say that the food is very different all over China. Which place has the best food?
Lin Xuemei:	That depends on your personal preferences. Take me for example. I like it sweet. That's why I like Shanghai cuisine. Ke Lin loves spicy food, so he likes Sichuan and Hunan food. If you like your food light, you can have Cantonese dishes...
Ke Lin:	Xuemei, say no more. My mouth is watering. ... Let's go to China over the winter break.

Lin Xuemei:	Go to China to have Chinese food? I'd consider it.
Lisa:	That's not a bad idea. I'll also consider it.
Zhang Tianming:	Food and fun? Of course I'll consider it, too.
Lin Xuemei:	Really? Fantastic! Let's all go.
Lisa:	If I could go to China to study Chinese, that would be even better.
Ke Lin:	Oh, here comes our food.

SELF-ASSESSMENT

How well can you do these things? Check (✔) the boxes to evaluate your progress and see which areas you may need to practice more.

I can	Very Well	OK	A Little
Name the four major types of Chinese cuisine	☐	☐	☐
Name several popular Chinese dishes I have learned	☐	☐	☐
Order my favorite Chinese dish(es)	☐	☐	☐
Specify which seasonings I want or don't want in my food	☐	☐	☐
Talk about what flavor(s) I prefer	☐	☐	☐

第四课　　第四课

買東西　买东西

4

 LEARNING OBJECTIVES

In this lesson, you will learn to use Chinese to

1. Name basic clothing, bedding, and bath items;
2. Describe your shopping preferences and criteria;
3. Disagree with others tactfully;
4. Present your arguments with rhetorical questions.

 RELATE AND GET READY

In your own culture/community—

- Can you purchase clothing and other necessities all in one shopping area?
- Do people usually pay for their purchases in cash, with checks, or with credit cards?
- Is there a sales tax?

Before You Study

Check the statements that apply to you.

☐ 1. I go shopping when stores offer discounts.

☐ 2. I prefer natural fibers.

When You Study

Listen to the audio recording and scan the text. Ask yourself the following questions before you begin a close reading of the text.

1. Where does the conversation take place?

張天明從家裏來的時候，媽媽給他買了一些衣服，像T恤衫❶、毛衣、牛仔褲❷什麼的，可是他覺得無論是樣子還是顏色都不太好①。今天是星期日，正好林雪梅和麗莎

LANGUAGE NOTES

❶ T恤衫 is a portmanteau word formed by combining the sounds and meanings of the Cantonese transliteration of the English "T-shirt" T恤 (pronounced *tiseot* in Cantonese) and the Mandarin morpheme 衫 "shirt." Modern Standard Chinese is based on the speech of Beijing and the vocabulary

☐ 3. I consider myself fashionable.
☐ 4. I stand by and care about brand names.
☐ 5. I have a credit card.

2. Do the characters share similar views?
3. Do they manage to obtain the items they require?

张天明从家里来的时候，妈妈给他买了一些衣服，像T恤衫❶、毛衣、牛仔裤❷什么的，可是他觉得无论是样子还是颜色都不太好①。今天是星期日，正好林雪梅和丽莎

and syntax of the modern Chinese literary canon. Contributions from various dialects have also enriched the vocabulary of standard spoken Chinese.

❷ 牛仔裤/牛仔裤 literally means "cowboy pants." 仔 is used in dialects for "boy." 牛仔 is a dialectal translation of the English word "cowboy."

也需要買衛生紙❸、牙膏、毛巾、洗衣粉這些日用品，於是②柯林就帶他們來到附近一家最大的購物中心。

柯林：　你要買什麼衣服？

張天明：　我想買一套運動服。

柯林：　這邊兒就是。你看看這一套，樣子、大小、長短都合適，而且打八折。

張天明：　顏色也不錯。多少錢？什麼牌子的？

林雪梅：　價錢不貴。這個牌子沒聽說過。

麗莎：　不過是純棉❹的。

張天明：　牌子不好不行，我想買名牌的。

柯林：　你真時髦！穿名牌！那件好像是名牌的⋯哎呀，太貴了！

張天明：　買東西，我只買名牌的，要不然就不買，因為名牌的衣服質量❺好。

麗莎：　不錯。有的衣服便宜是便宜，可是牌子不好❸，穿一、兩次就不想穿了，只好再買一件。這樣買兩件衣服的錢比買一件名牌的還多。

林雪梅：　你說的有道理❻。

柯林：　買衣服只考慮便宜當然不好，但是也不必❼非買名牌的不可。我買衣服的標準，第一是穿著舒服，第二是物美價廉，是什麼牌子的，時髦不時髦，

LANGUAGE NOTES

❸ 衛生紙／卫生纸 is also called 手紙 in northern spoken Chinese.

❹ 純棉／纯棉: This word is used as an adjective before a noun, e.g., 我買了一件純棉襯衫／我买了一件纯棉衬衫 (I bought a pure cotton shirt.). To use it as a predicate, put 的 after it: 這條褲子是純棉的／这条裤子是纯棉的 (These pants are 100 percent cotton).

也需要买卫生纸❸、牙膏、毛巾、洗衣粉这些日用品，
于是②柯林就带他们来到附近一家最大的购物中心。

柯林：　你要买什么衣服？

张天明：我想买一套运动服。

柯林：　这边儿就是。你看看这一套，样子、大小、长短
都合适，而且打八折。

张天明：颜色也不错。多少钱？什么牌子的？

林雪梅：价钱不贵。这个牌子没听说过。

丽莎：　不过是纯棉❹的。

张天明：牌子不好不行，我想买名牌的。

柯林：　你真时髦！穿名牌！那件好像是名牌的…哎呀，
太贵了！

张天明：买东西，我只买名牌的，要不然就不买，因为名牌
的衣服质量❺好。

丽莎：　不错。有的衣服便宜是便宜，可是牌子不好③，
穿一、两次就不想穿了，只好再买一件。这样买
两件衣服的钱比买一件名牌的还多。

林雪梅：你说的有道理❻。

柯林：　买衣服只考虑便宜当然不好，但是也不必❼非买
名牌的不可。我买衣服的标准，第一是穿着舒服，
第二是物美价廉，是什么牌子的，时髦不时髦，

---

❺ 質量/质量 is a mainland Chinese usage. In Taiwan, the word for quality is 品質/品质 (pǐnzhí). This has a slightly different meaning on the mainland, referring to someone or something's essential qualities, including someone's "moral fiber," 道德品質/道德品质 (dàodé pǐnzhì).

❻ 有道理 means "to make sense." It is often used to convey one's agreement with an opinion that someone else has just expressed.

我都不在乎。因為穿衣服是為了自己，不是為了給別人看。

張天明：　我不同意。難道④你喜歡看雪梅穿不好看的衣服嗎？

柯林：　　雪梅穿什麼衣服都好看，對不對？

林雪梅：　你別貧⑧了！

張天明：　哎，柯林，你身上這件衣服怎麼是名牌的，你不是不穿名牌嗎？

柯林：　　我是說不必非買名牌不可，可是沒說不穿名牌呀。這件是打折的時候買的。

林雪梅：　哎，麗莎，我們去日用品那邊看看。

張天明：　你們去吧，我先去付錢，咱們⑨一會兒見。

(Zhang Tianming is at the check-out counter...)

售貨員：　先生，付現金，還是用信用卡？

張天明：　我刷卡。

售貨員：　先生，加上稅一共是一百八十六塊四。

張天明：　好…謝謝！再見。

After You Study

Challenge yourself to complete the following tasks in Chinese.

1. List the items that Lin Xuemei and Lisa would like to buy.

LANGUAGE NOTES

❼ 不必 is synonymous with 不用. Its positive form is 得 or 必須/必须 (bìxū), not 必. Its interrogative form is 用不用… or 必須…嗎/必须…吗.

❽ The literal meaning of 貧/贫 is "poor." In northern Chinese dialect usage, it also means "to talk too much" or "to make too many jokes." It's mildly derogatory.

我都不在乎。因为穿衣服是为了自己，不是为了给别人看。

张天明： 我不同意。难道④你喜欢看雪梅穿不好看的衣服吗？

柯林： 雪梅穿什么衣服都好看，对不对？

林雪梅： 你别贫⑧了！

张天明： 哎，柯林，你身上这件衣服怎么是名牌的，你不是不穿名牌吗？

柯林： 我是说不必非买名牌不可，可是没说不穿名牌呀。这件是打折的时候买的。

林雪梅： 哎，丽莎，我们去日用品那边看看。

张天明： 你们去吧，我先去付钱，咱们⑨一会儿见。

(Zhang Tianming is at the checkout counter...)

售货员： 先生，付现金，还是用信用卡？

张天明： 我刷卡。

售货员： 先生，加上税一共是一百八十六块四。

张天明： 好…谢谢！再见。

---

2. List the four characters' shopping philosophies.
3. List your shopping criteria to determine which of the characters best represents your shopping views.

---

❾ 咱們/咱们 is a colloquial usage. It includes both the speaker and the listener, whereas 我們/我们 doesn't necessarily include the listener. Therefore, 咱們/咱们 sounds more intimate in tone.

VOCABULARY

1.	像		xiàng	v	such as
2.	T恤衫		tīxùshān	n	t-shirt
3.	毛衣		máoyī	n	woolen sweater
4.	牛仔褲	牛仔裤	niúzǎikù	n	jeans
5.	無論	无论	wúlùn	conj	regardless of...; whether it be... [See Grammar 1.]
6.	需要		xūyào	v/n	to need; needs
7.	衛生紙	卫生纸	wèishēngzhǐ	n	toilet paper
8.	牙膏		yágāo	n	toothpaste
9.	毛巾		máojīn	n	towel
10.	洗衣粉		xǐyīfěn	n	laundry powder
11.	於是	于是	yúshì	conj	so; therefore; thereupon [See Grammar 2.]
12.	購物	购物	gòuwù	v	to shop
13.	牌子		páizi	n	brand
14.	價錢	价钱	jiàqian	n	price
15.	純棉	纯棉	chúnmián	adj	pure cotton; 100 percent cotton
16.	名牌(兒)	名牌(儿)	míngpái(r)	n	famous brand; name brand
17.	時髦	时髦	shímáo	adj	fashionable, stylish
18.	哎呀	哎呀	āiyā	interj	(an exclamation to express surprise) gosh; ah
19.	質量	质量	zhìliàng	n	quality
20.	只好		zhǐhǎo	adv	to be forced to; to have no choice but

21.	道理		dàoli	n	reason; sense
22.	不必		búbì	adv	need not; not have to
23.	非…不可		fēi...bù kě		have to; nothing but... would do
24.	標準	标准	biāozhǔn	n/adj	criterion; standard
25.	物美價廉	物美价廉	wù měi jià lián		attractive goods at inexpensive prices
26.	在乎		zàihu	v	to mind; to care
27.	同意		tóngyi	v	to agree
28.	難道	难道	nándào	adv	Do you mean to say... [See Grammar 4.]
29.	好看		hǎokàn	adj	nice-looking; attractive
30.	貧	贫	pín	adj	gabby; glib
31.	咱們	咱们	zánmen	pr	we; us
32.	一會兒	一会儿	yíhuìr	nm	in a moment; a little while
33.	現金	现金	xiànjīn	n	cash
34.	加		jiā	v	to add
35.	稅		shuì	n	tax

Enlarged Characters

| 褲 | 無 | 衛 | 膏 | 購 | 價 | 髦 | 質 |
| 裤 | 无 | 卫 | 膏 | 购 | 价 | 髦 | 质 |

What do you think 起 means here?

Culture Highlights

1 Bargaining is expected almost everywhere in mainland China. Even in mid-priced department stores, it doesn't hurt to ask if you could get a discount. That is because department stores sometimes rent counter space to private vendors and manufacturers. How much you end up paying depends on your bargaining skills. Often, you can start bargaining by cutting the offering price as much as fifty percent, particularly when buying clothes and shoes. However, there's no bargaining in supermarkets, large chain stores like Wal-Mart, or upscale department stores, and there is no sales tax in China.

2 If you open a personal bank account in China, you will receive a deposit book along with an ATM card. However, you won't receive a checkbook since personal checking accounts are not common in China. Typically people pay for their purchases with either cash or credit cards.

11:00 —23:00
请勿食用非本餐厅食物、酒水、饮料
贵重物品请随身携带
本餐厅不能刷卡，消费请用现金
请保管好您的随身物品
请勿携带宠物入内

在這個飯館兒吃飯得怎麼付錢?
在这个饭馆儿吃饭得怎么付钱?

Grammar

1. 無論···, 都···/无论···, 都···

無論/无论 signifies that the result will remain the same under any condition or circumstance. It must be used together with a question pronoun or an alternative construction.

❶   明天無論誰請客我都不去。

明天无论谁请客我都不去。

(No matter who's paying tomorrow, I'm not going.)

[誰/谁 is a question pronoun. Together with 無論/无论, it means *doesn't matter who*, or *anybody*.]

❷ **A:** 你想去城裏的哪個購物中心？

你想去城里的哪个购物中心？

(Which shopping center in town do you want to go to?)

  B: 城裏的購物中心我都沒去過，所以無論去哪個都可以。

城里的购物中心我都没去过，所以无论去哪个都可以。

(I haven't been to any shopping center in town, so going to any of them will be fine.)

[哪個/哪个 is a question pronoun.]

❸   我們已經說好明天去買東西，你無論願意不願意都得跟我們去。

我们已经说好明天去买东西，你无论愿意不愿意都得跟我们去。

(We've already decided to go shopping tomorrow. Whether you're willing or not, you have to go with us.)

[願意不願意/愿意不愿意 is an alternative construction meaning *willing or not willing*.]

❹   他無論在家裏還是在學校，總是做功課，很少看見他
玩兒。

他无论在家里还是在学校，总是做功课，很少看见他
玩儿。

(Whether he's at home or at school, he's always studying. You seldom see him relax.)
[在家裏還是在學校 / 在家里还是在学校 is an alternative
construction meaning *doesn't matter (whether it's) at home or at school*.]

2. Conjunction 於是/于是

The conjunction 於是/于是 connects two clauses. The second clause is a new situation
or action caused by the first clause.

❶   我給他打了很多次電話都沒有人接，於是就給他發了
一封電子郵件。

我给他打了很多次电话都没有人接，于是就给他发了
一封电子邮件。

(I called him many times, but nobody answered, so I sent him an e-mail.)

❷   晚飯後，他去一家購物中心買運動鞋，那裏沒有他喜歡
的，於是又開車去了另一個購物中心。

晚饭后，他去一家购物中心买运动鞋，那里没有他喜欢
的，于是又开车去了另一个购物中心。

(After dinner he went to a shopping center to get a pair of sneakers. The shopping
center didn't have the ones he liked, so he drove to another shopping center.)

❸   週末孩子們要去山上，沒想到星期六早上下雨了，於是
他們就不去了。

周末孩子们要去山上，没想到星期六早上下雨了，于是
他们就不去了。

(The kids were going to go to the mountains over the weekend, but it rained
unexpectedly Saturday morning, so they didn't go.)

❹ 小明在商店看見一件毛衣，樣子、顏色他都很喜歡，
於是就買下來了。

小明在商店看见一件毛衣，样子、颜色他都很喜欢，
于是就买下来了。

(Little Ming saw a sweater at the store. He liked the style and the color, so he
bought it.)

In Examples ❶–❹, where there is a discernible causal relationship, 於是/于是 can be
replaced by 所以. However, with 於是/于是, the sequential relationship of the two
actions is also emphasized.

If, however, the emphasis is clearly on cause and effect, and the two actions do not have a
sequential relationship, only 所以 can be used.

❺ 這次考試，因為我沒有準備，所以考得很不好。

这次考试，因为我没有准备，所以考得很不好。

(I didn't prepare for the exam, so I did really badly.)

[Lack of preparation is the direct cause of poor performance on the exam.]

❻ 上海人多車多，所以開車很容易緊張。

上海人多车多，所以开车很容易紧张。

(There are so many people and cars in Shanghai that it is easy to get nervous while
you drive.)

[Crowds and cars lead to nervousness.]

❼ 這兩天他不太舒服，所以不想吃東西。

这两天他不太舒服，所以不想吃东西。

(He's been under the weather the past two days. That's why he's lost his appetite
for food.)

[Poor health results in a loss of appetite.]

3. Adj/V+是+Adj/V, 可是/但是…

This structure is equivalent to "although…(yet)…"

❶ A: 我打算學音樂。
　　我打算学音乐。
　　(I plan to study music.)

B: 學音樂好是好，可是以後找工作不太容易。
　　学音乐好是好，可是以后找工作不太容易。
　　(It *is* good to study music, but it may not be easy to find a job later.)

❷ A: 這件衣服太貴了，別買！
　　这件衣服太贵了，别买！
　　(This piece of clothing is too expensive. Don't buy it.)

B: 這件衣服貴是貴，可是牌子好。
　　这件衣服贵是贵，可是牌子好。
　　(It *is* expensive, but it's a good brand.)

❸ A: 明天晚上是林雪梅的生日晚會，你去嗎？
　　明天晚上是林雪梅的生日晚会，你去吗？
　　(Lin Xuemei's birthday party is tomorrow evening. Will you be going?)

B: 我去是去，可是會晚一點兒。
　　我去是去，可是会晚一点儿。
　　(I will be going, but I will be a bit late.)

4. Adverb 難道/难道

難道/难道 (Do you mean to say...) is used in rhetorical questions.

❶   你做菜放那麼多鹽和味精，難道你不在乎自己的
健康嗎？

你做菜放那么多盐和味精，难道你不在乎自己的
健康吗？

(You use so much salt and MSG when you cook. Don't you care about your own health?)

❷   他來美國十年了，難道他連一個英文詞都不認識嗎？
他来美国十年了，难道他连一个英文词都不认识吗？

(Do you mean that he has been in America for ten years and can't recognize even one English word?)

❸   你說這件事不是他做的，難道是你做的嗎？
你说这件事不是他做的，难道是你做的吗？

(You said he didn't do it. Are you telling me that you did it?)

❹   你已經有八張信用卡了，難道你還想再辦一張？
你已经有八张信用卡了，难道你还想再办一张？

(You already have eight credit cards. Do you really want to get another one?)

難道/难道 can be used before or after the subject, but the question always takes the
嗎/吗 form, as shown in ❶, ❷, and ❸. Sometimes the 嗎/吗 can be omitted, as in
❹. Note also that rhetorical questions require some kind of context. Therefore, 難道/
难道 cannot be used out of the blue.

Words & Phrases

A. ···什麼的/···什么的 (...etc.)

This expression is used to cap a series of items.

❶　他要買毛衣、牛仔褲什麼的。
　　他要买毛衣、牛仔裤什么的。
(He wants to buy sweaters, jeans, etc.)

❷　媽媽昨天晚上請客，做了很多菜，像紅燒牛肉、
　　清蒸鱼、家常豆腐什麼的，都很好吃。
　　妈妈昨天晚上请客，做了很多菜，像红烧牛肉、
　　清蒸鱼、家常豆腐什么的，都很好吃。
(Mom invited some guests over last night. She made many dishes—beef in soy sauce, steamed fish, family-style tofu, and so on. They were all delicious.)

❸　我們這棟宿舍的傢具不錯，像床、桌子、書架什麼的，
　　都又好又新。
　　我们这栋宿舍的家具不错，像床、桌子、书架什么的，
　　都又好又新。
(The furniture in our dorm is not bad. The beds, desks, bookshelves, and so on are all good and new.)

❹　他床上放了很多東西，有被子、毯子、衣服什麼的。
　　他床上放了很多东西，有被子、毯子、衣服什么的。
(There's lots of stuff on his bed: a quilt, a blanket, clothes, etc.)

B. 大小, 長短/长短, 寬窄/宽窄 (kuānzhǎi)··· (size, length, width...)

Opposites such as 大, 小, 長/长, 短, 寬/宽 (kuān), 窄 (zhǎi)··· can be combined to form abstract nouns meaning size, length, width, and so on.

❶   你看看這一套，樣子、大小、長短都合適···
你看看这一套，样子、大小、长短都合适···
(Take a look at this suit. The style, size, and length are all suitable.)

❷   你穿中號的，這套運動服也是中號的，大小正好合適。
你穿中号的，这套运动服也是中号的，大小正好合适。
(You wear size medium. This sweatsuit is also a medium. The size is just right.)

❸   這條褲子長短正好。
这条裤子长短正好。
(The length of these pants is just right.)

C. 打折 (to discount; to sell at a discount)

打折 can either be used generally to mean "on sale" or more specifically with numbers to mean "a certain percentage off." 20 percent off is (打) 八折, 25 percent off is (打) 七五折, and 50 percent off is (打)五折 or (打)對折/对折.

❶   這個週末很多東西都打折，我們去買吧。
这个周末很多东西都打折，我们去买吧。
(Many things are on sale this weekend. Let's go shopping.)

❷   這個書架上個月八十塊，現在打七折，是五十六塊錢。
这个书架上个月八十块，现在打七折，是五十六块钱。
(This bookshelf was eighty dollars last month. Now it is 30 percent off. It's fifty-six dollars.)

❸　　我買了一張飛機票，打五折，一百二十五塊錢。
　　　我买了一张飞机票，打五折，一百二十五块钱。
　　　(I bought a plane ticket at half price for $125.)

中文怎麼說？英文什麼意思？
中文怎么说？英文什么意思？

D. (要)不然 (otherwise)

❶　　這兒的冬天冷得很，你得再買一條毯子，要不然容易
　　　感冒。
　　　这儿的冬天冷得很，你得再买一条毯子，要不然容易
　　　感冒。
　　　(The winter here is really cold. You've got to buy another blanket, otherwise it's easy
　　　to catch a cold.)

❷　　找房子不要找離馬路太近的，要不然會很吵。
　　　找房子不要找离马路太近的，要不然会很吵。
　　　(When you are looking for a house, find a place that's not too close to the street.
　　　Otherwise it'll be too noisy.)

❸ 別吃那麼多肉，多吃點青菜，要不然你會越來越胖。

別吃那么多肉，多吃点青菜，要不然你会越来越胖。

(Don't eat so much meat. Have more green leafy vegetables or you'll put on more and more weight.)

E. 非…不可 (have to; must)

This construction sometimes means that if one doesn't do something, there will be negative consequences.

❶ 你再不起床，上課非晚了不可。

你再不起床，上课非晚了不可。

(If you stay in bed any longer, you'll definitely be late for class.)

❷ 你得的這個病非打針不可，要不然會越來越重。

你得的这个病非打针不可，要不然会越来越重。

(You have no choice but to get an injection for this illness. Otherwise, it will get more and more serious.)

The construction can also show strong resolution and will.

❸ 張天明買衣服非買名牌不可。

张天明买衣服非买名牌不可。

(Zhang Tianming insists on buying only designer clothes.)

❹ 我明年畢業以後非找一個錢多的工作不可，要不然就再上學。

我明年毕业以后非找一个钱多的工作不可，要不然就再上学。

(I'm determined to find a lucrative job after I graduate next year. Otherwise, I'll go back to school.)

❺ 小林吃魚非吃清蒸魚不可，別的做法他不喜歡。

小林吃鱼非吃清蒸鱼不可，别的做法他不喜欢。

(When Little Lin eats fish, he insists on steamed fish. He doesn't care for fish cooked in any other way.)

F. 標準/标准 (criterion; standard)

標準/标准 is both a noun and an adjective.

❶   你認為一個好老師的標準是什麼？ [noun]

你认为一个好老师的标准是什么？

(What do you think are the criteria for a good teacher?)

❷   這個大學收研究生有什麼標準？ [noun]

这个大学收研究生有什么标准？

(What are the criteria for accepting graduate students at this university?)

As an adjective, 標準/标准 can be an attributive or a predicate.

❸   他説的是標準的北京話。 [attributive]

他说的是标准的北京话。

(What he speaks is standard Beijing dialect.)

❹   我説的上海話不太標準。 [predicate]

我说的上海话不太标准。

(My Shanghainese is not very standard.)

G. 在乎 (to mind; to care)

在乎 is a verb and its negative form, 不在乎, is used more often than the affirmative form, 在乎.

❶   別人説什麼，我不在乎。

别人说什么，我不在乎。

(I don't care what other people say.)

❷   你的車不見了，你怎麼一點都不在乎？

你的车不见了，你怎么一点都不在乎？

(Your car has disappeared. How can you not care in the least?)

❸   他很在乎別人怎麼看他。
           他很在乎别人怎么看他。

(He cares a lot about how other people see him.)

Language Practice

A. Stock Up on Necessities

If you were in China, you would want to know how to name some of the basic household necessities before heading to the store. Practice with a partner and see how many you can pronounce correctly.

1.

2.

3.

4.

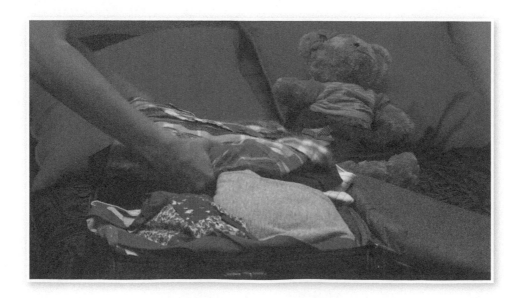

B. Complete Your Wardrobe

You've received a gift card from your favorite apparel store, and you want to update your wardrobe. With the help of a partner, get your shopping list ready. Then report back to the class what you wish to purchase, and estimate the price of each item. Make sure to note your size and color preferences so your shopping trip will go smoothly.

_____

_____

_____

_____

_____

_____

_____

_____

_____

C. Name Your Price!

You are very budget-conscious and like a good bargain. Role play with a classmate. With one person as a potential buyer and the other a seller, bargain and figure out how deep the discount has to be before you will purchase the item.

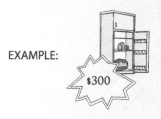

EXAMPLE:

→ **A:** 這個冰箱多少錢你才買？　　**A:** 这个冰箱多少钱你才买？

B: 這個冰箱打＿＿折我才買。　**B:** 这个冰箱打＿＿折我才买。

A: 打了＿＿折，是＿＿錢。　　**A:** 打了＿＿折，是＿＿钱。
　　好，賣了。　　　　　　　　　　好，卖了。

1.

$ 500

4.

$1000

2.

$300

5.

$50

3.

$100

6.

$ 40

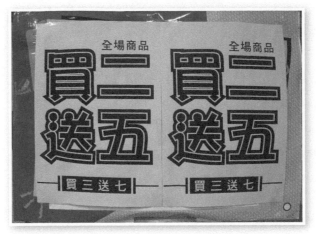

Read these sale signs in Chinese. What do they mean?

D. What's on Your Shopping List?

Here are some criteria that most people have when shopping. List your own top five criteria when you shop for clothes, with 1 as the most important. Then compare your list with your partner's, and explain your rankings to each other. Please include 第一，第二，第三… when you report your rankings.

標準	标准	價錢	价钱
樣子	样子	質量	质量
顏色	颜色	牌子	牌子
大小、長短	大小、长短		

1. _____

2. _____

3. _____

4. _____

5. _____

E. Regardless...

a. Your friend Mr. Studious is an avid reader. He reads all the time:

whether he's in class or out of class;

whether he's in the library or in the dorm;

no matter what day of the week it is;

no matter whom he is with.

Describe Mr. Studious' reading habits with sentences in the 無論···都···/无论···都··· pattern.

b. You have an exam early tomorrow morning, but your friend has just invited you to dinner at 7:00 pm today. Tell your friend that you cannot go, regardless of:

who has issued the invitation;

which restaurant it is;

whether it is a Chinese meal or a Japanese one;

whether the food is authentic or not.

Again, say these sentences in the 無論···都···/无论···都··· pattern.

F. The Polite Critic

a. Your friend enjoys cooking Chinese food and wants you to critique the meal he has just prepared. You want to give your honest opinions, but don't want to hurt your friend's feelings.

EXAMPLE:	糖醋魚　香　鹹	糖醋鱼　香　咸
→	**A:** 我做的糖醋魚香不香？	**A:** 我做的糖醋鱼香不香？
	B: 香是香，可是有點兒鹹。	**B:** 香是香，可是有点儿咸。

1.	菠菜豆腐湯	好喝	鹹	1.	菠菜豆腐汤	好喝	咸
2.	清蒸魚	嫩	油	2.	清蒸鱼	嫩	油
3.	芥蘭牛肉	好吃	甜	3.	芥兰牛肉	好吃	甜
4.	家常豆腐	香	酸	4.	家常豆腐	香	酸

b. You are a fashion consultant. In a mini-consultation with your client, tactfully call his or her attention to something that he or she may have neglected.

EXAMPLE: good quality   length is not right

→ Client: 我覺得這條牛仔褲   Client: 我觉得这条牛仔裤
                  質量很好。   质量很好。
   Consultant: 質量好是好，   Consultant: 质量好是好，
                  可是長短不合適。   可是长短不合适。

1.   pretty color   size is not right

2.   cheap price   not pure cotton

3.   perfect fit   not fashionable enough

4.   nice style   too expensive

這件T恤衫是不是純棉的？
这件T恤衫是不是纯棉的？

G. He'd Have It No Other Way

Mr. Zhang is particular about everything and always wants things done his way. Let's see if you can tell the class some of Mr. Zhang's fastidious habits.

EXAMPLE: 住房子　大房子
→ 張先生住(房子)，非住大
房子不可。

住房子　大房子
张先生住(房子)，非住大
房子不可。

1. 吃飯　　　日本菜
2. 喝茶　　　英國茶
3. 穿衣服　　名牌的
4. 開車　　　跑車
5. 打球　　　網球

1. 吃饭　　　日本菜
2. 喝茶　　　英国茶
3. 穿衣服　　名牌的
4. 开车　　　跑车
5. 打球　　　网球

Do you know anyone who always wants things done in a certain way? Give an example or two.

H. You Mean to Tell Me You Don't Know?!

a. Your classmate is clueless about the things happening around him. Luckily for him, you've been paying attention in class. Answer his questions and explain what's going on with the exam tomorrow.

EXAMPLE: need to prepare for the exam   exam cancelled

→ A: 我得準備考試。
B: 難道你不知道明天不
考試了嗎?

A: 我得准备考试。
B: 难道你不知道明天不
考试了吗?

1. why there isn't an exam tomorrow   the teacher is sick
2. what the teacher's illness is   the teacher caught a cold and had a fever
3. want to send flowers to the teacher   the teacher is allergic to flowers

b. Your mother has come to visit you at school and is shocked at your unhealthy eating habits. Listen and respond as she warns you about the consequences of a poor diet.

EXAMPLE: 鹽　　盐

→ 少吃鹽，難道你不知道吃 太多鹽對身體健康沒有 好處嗎?　　少吃盐，难道你不知道吃 太多盐对身体健康没有 好处吗?

1. 糖　　　糖
2. 油　　　油
3. 辣的　　辣的
4. 味精　　味精
5. 可樂　　可乐

I. Become a Modeling Agent

A good agent working for a modeling agency has to be able to scout potential fashion models. Suppose you think that a classmate has style and is a good candidate to become a model. Describe what he/she is wearing and what he/she looks like. Make sure that your description follows a certain logic. Describe his or her clothes from top to bottom and then his or her appearance—figure, hair, eyes, etc.

_____

_____

_____

_____

_____

Pinyin Text

Zhāng Tiānmíng cóng jiā li lái de shíhou, māma gěi tā mǎi le yì xiē yīfu, xiàng tīxùshān①, máoyī, niúzǎikù②shénme de, kěshì tā juéde wúlùn shì yàngzi háishi yánsè dōu bú tài hǎo①. Jīntiān shì xīngqīrì, zhènghǎo Lín Xuěméi hé Lìshā yě xūyào mǎi wèishēngzhǐ③, yágāo, máojīn, xǐyīfěn zhè xiē rìyòngpǐn, yúshì② Kē Lín jiù dài tāmen lái dào fùjìn yì jiā zuì dà de gòuwù zhōngxīn.

Kē Lín:	Nǐ yào mǎi shénme yīfu?
Zhāng Tiānmíng:	Wǒ xiǎng mǎi yí tào yùndòngfú.
Kē Lín:	Zhèbianr jiù shì. Nǐ kàn kan zhè yí tào, yàngzi, dàxiǎo, chángduǎn dōu héshì, érqiě dǎ bā zhé.
Zhāng Tiānmíng:	Yánsè yě búcuò. Duōshao qián? Shénme páizi de?
Lín Xuěméi:	Jiàqian bú guì. Zhè ge páizi méi tīngshuō guo.
Lìshā:	Búguò shì chúnmián④ de.
Zhāng Tiānmíng:	Páizi bù hǎo bù xíng, wǒ xiǎng mǎi míngpái de.
Kē Lín:	Nǐ zhēn shímáo! Chuān míngpái! Nà jiàn hǎoxiàng shì míngpái de... Āiyā, tài guì le!
Zhāng Tiānmíng:	Mǎi dōngxi, wǒ zhǐ mǎi míngpái de, yàobùrán jiù bù mǎi, yīnwèi míngpái de yīfu zhìliàng⑤ hǎo.
Lìshā:	Búcuò. Yǒude yīfu piányi shì piányi, kěshì páizi bù hǎo③, chuān yī, liǎng cì jiù bù xiǎng chuān le, zhǐhǎo zài mǎi yí jiàn. Zhèyàng mǎi liǎng jiàn yīfu de qián bǐ mǎi yí jiàn míngpái de hái duō.
Lín Xuěméi:	Nǐ shuō de yǒu dàoli⑥.
Kē Lín:	Mǎi yīfu zhǐ kǎolǜ piányi dāngrán bù hǎo, dànshì yě búbì⑦fēi mǎi míngpái de bù kě. Wǒ mǎi yīfu de biāozhǔn, dì yī shì chuān zhe shūfu, dì èr shì wù měi jià lián, shì shénme páizi de, shímáo bù shímáo, wǒ dōu bú zàihu. Yīnwèi chuān yīfu shì wèile zìjǐ, bú shì wèile gěi biéren kàn.
Zhāng Tiānmíng:	Wǒ bù tóngyì. Nándào④ nǐ xǐhuan kàn Xuěméi chuān bù hǎokàn de yīfu ma?
Kē Lín:	Xuěméi chuān shénme yīfu dōu hǎokàn, duì bu duì?
Lín Xuěméi:	Nǐ bié pín⑧le!
Zhāng Tiānmíng:	Āi, Kē Lín, nǐ shēn shang zhè jiàn yīfu zěnme shì míngpái de, nǐ bú shì bù chuān míngpái ma?

Kē Lín:	Wǒ shì shuō búbì fēi mǎi míngpái bù kě, kěshì méi shuō bù chuān míngpái ya. Zhè jiàn shì dǎ zhé de shíhou mǎi de.
Lín Xuěméi:	Āi, Lìshā, wǒmen qù rìyòngpǐn nàbian kàn kan.
Zhāng Tiānmíng:	Nǐmen qù ba, wǒ xiān qù fù qián, zánmen⁹ yíhuìr jiàn.

(Zhang Tianming is at the check-out counter...)

Shòuhuòyuán:	Xiānsheng, fù xiànjīn, háishi yòng xìnyòngkǎ?
Zhāng Tiānmíng:	Wǒ shuā kǎ.
Shòuhuòyuán:	Xiānsheng, jiā shang shuì yígòng shì yì bǎi bāshí liù kuài sì.
Zhāng Tiānmíng:	Hǎo...Xièxie! Zàijiàn.

English Text

Before Zhang Tianming came to school, his mom bought him some clothes such as T-shirts, sweaters, jeans, and so on, but he doesn't think they are very good either in terms of style or color. Today is Sunday, and it just so happens that Lin Xuemei and Lisa need to buy some daily necessities such as toilet paper, toothpaste, towels, and laundry detergent, so Ke Lin takes them to the biggest shopping center nearby.

Ke Lin:	What clothes do you want to buy?
Zhang Tianming:	I'd like to buy a sweatsuit set.
Ke Lin:	Here they are. Look at this one. The style, size, and length are all very suitable. Plus, it's 20 percent off.
Zhang Tianming:	The color isn't bad, either. How much money? What's the brand?
Lin Xuemei:	The price is not expensive. I've never heard of the brand.
Lisa:	But it's pure cotton.
Zhang Tianming:	It won't do if it's not a good brand. I want name brand.
Ke Lin:	You're really fashionable, wearing name brands! That one looks like it's name brand. Oh my, way too expensive.
Zhang Tianming:	When it comes to shopping, I only buy name brand or I won't buy, because name-brand clothes are better quality.
Lisa:	That's right. Some clothes are inexpensive, but they are not good brands. After you've worn them once or twice, you don't want to wear them anymore and you have to buy another set. That way the

cost of buying two sets of clothes is higher than buying just the one name brand.

Lin Xuemei: What you say makes sense.

Ke Lin: Of course it's not good if you only consider price when shopping for clothes, but you don't have to insist on name brands. My criteria for buying clothes is comfort first, and good quality at a reasonable price second. What brand they are and whether they are fashionable or not, I don't care. You wear your clothes for yourself, not for others to look at.

Zhang Tianming: I don't agree. Are you telling me you like to see Lin Xuemei wear ugly clothes?

Ke Lin: Xuemei looks good in whatever clothes she's wearing. Isn't that right?

Lin Xuemei: Don't be so glib.

Zhang Tianming: Ke Lin, how come the clothes you are wearing are name brand? I thought you didn't wear name brand.

Ke Lin: I said you don't have to buy name brand, but I didn't say I don't wear name brand. I bought this when it was on sale.

Lin Xuemei: Lisa, let's go over to the daily necessities to have a look.

Zhang Tianming: You go ahead. I'll go pay first. We'll see each other in a little bit.

(Zhang Tianming is at the check-out counter...)

Sales clerk: Sir, cash or credit card?

Zhang Tianming: I'll swipe my credit card.

Sales clerk: Sir, with tax it's $186.40.

Zhang Tianming: All right. ... Thank you! Goodbye.

SELF-ASSESSMENT

How well can you do these things? Check (✔) the boxes to evaluate your progress and see which areas you may need to practice more.

I can	Very Well	OK	A Little
Name basic clothing items and household necessities	☐	☐	☐
State my criteria when shopping for clothes	☐	☐	☐
Disagree tactfully and express my perspective politely	☐	☐	☐
Make rhetorical statements to emphasize my opinions	☐	☐	☐

第五课　第五课
选课　选课

 LEARNING OBJECTIVES

In this lesson, you will learn to use Chinese to

1. State your major area of study/academic department and some required general courses you have taken;
2. Talk about what you plan to do after graduating;
3. Explore what will enhance your future job opportunities;
4. Explain whether your family members have an influence on your choice of major and career path;
5. Share tips on how to save money for your education.

 RELATE AND GET READY

In your own culture/community—

• When do college students declare a major?
• What are the most common schools/colleges found in a typical university?
• Approximately how many credits are needed to graduate from college?

Before You Study

Check the statements that apply to you.

☐ 1. I have already declared my major.

☐ 2. I plan to double major.

☐ 3. I have an academic advisor.

When You Study

Listen to the audio recording and scan the text. Ask yourself the following questions before you begin a close reading of the text.

1. Where does the conversation take place?

2. Do the two characters know what courses they are going to take next semester?

 張天明這個學期選了四門課：世界歷史、電腦、政治學❶
和中文。這幾門課都很有意思，他也學到了不少東西。
因為張天明在家的時候常常跟父母說中文，所以一年級

LANGUAGE NOTES

❶ 學/学 can be used as a suffix meaning "academic subject," e.g., 政治學/政治学 (political science), 經濟學/经济学 (economics), 醫學/医学 (medical science), 化學/化学 (chemistry), etc.

4. I have been able to take whatever classes I wanted to take.
5. I believe the classes I've been taking are good preparation for the job market.
6. I would like to apply to graduate school.

3. Do the two characters' interests match their career choices?
4. Do the two characters know what they want to do after graduating?
5. Do the two characters get the advice they need?

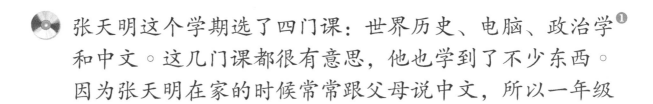

张天明这个学期选了四门课：世界历史、电脑、政治学 [1]
和中文。这几门课都很有意思，他也学到了不少东西。
因为张天明在家的时候常常跟父母说中文，所以一年级的中文課，對他來說^①，聽和說很容易，只是寫漢字有點兒難。除了中文課以外，其他幾門課都得花很多時間準備，還經常要寫文章，所以他覺得有點兒受不了。這個學期已經過了一半，馬上又得選下學期的課了，張天明希望下個學期能輕鬆點兒。後天要去見指導教授❷，討論選課的事，他想先找別的同學聊聊。這一天下午，他在籃球場上正好碰見大四的李哲，就一邊和李哲打球，一邊聊了起來。

張天明：　怎麼樣，下學期的課你選好^②了嗎？

李哲：　　還沒有呢。你呢？

張天明：　我肯定要選中文，至於^③另外^④兩門課選什麼，還沒想好。對了，你還得再上幾門課才能畢業？

李哲：　　我想拿雙學位❸，還得上四門課。我想再^⑤選一門化學、一門經濟，另外^④再選兩門電腦系的課，這樣學分就夠了。

張天明：　對，我決定了，也選經濟和電腦！我的問題解決了，太好了！我後天就告訴我的指導教授。

李哲：　　是嗎？我後天也去見指導教授。

張天明：　李哲，你畢業以後打算做什麼？

李哲：　　我想念研究生，要麼上工學院，要麼上管理學院^⑥，我還沒跟指導教授談。你想選什麼專業？

LANGUAGE NOTES

❷ 指導教授/指导教授 is "academic advisor." In mainland China, professors advising graduate students are called 導師/导师 (mentors).

的中文课，对他来说[1]，听和说很容易，只是写汉字有点儿难。除了中文课以外，其它几门课都得花很多时间准备，还经常要写文章，所以他觉得有点儿受不了。这个学期已经过了一半，马上又得选下学期的课了，张天明希望下个学期能轻松点儿。后天要去见指导教授[2]，讨论选课的事，他想先找别的同学聊聊。这一天下午，他在篮球场上正好碰见大四的李哲，就一边和李哲打球，一边聊了起来。

张天明：　怎么样，下学期的课你选好[2]了吗？

李哲：　　还没有呢。你呢？

张天明：　我肯定要选中文，至于[3]另外[4]两门课选什么，还没想好。对了，你还得再上几门课才能毕业？

李哲：　　我想拿双学位[3]，还得上四门课。我想再[5]选一门化学、一门经济，另外[4]再选两门电脑系的课，这样学分就够了。

张天明：　对，我决定了，也选经济和电脑！我的问题解决了，太好了！我后天就告诉我的指导教授。

李哲：　　是吗？我后天也去见指导教授。

张天明：　李哲，你毕业以后打算做什么？

李哲：　　我想念研究生，要么上工学院，要么上管理学院[6]，我还没跟指导教授谈。你想选什么专业？

---

❸ 雙學位/双学位 means "dual degree." 雙/双 means "double." It can only be used before nouns as an attributive, e.g., 雙手/双手 (both hands), 雙人床/双人床 (double bed). It can't be used as a predicate.

張天明: 我想學文學。可是我媽媽說，學文科❹將來找工作不
容易，而且賺錢也少，她希望我念金融。但是我對
金融沒有興趣，整天跟數字打交道，多沒意思。

李哲: 我的父母跟你的父母差不多。其實，我最喜歡的是
哲學，因為我喜歡想問題。我們班很多同學的父母
都不太管孩子選什麼專業，比我們自由。

張天明: 你要申請哪些學校？

李哲: 我想申請離我姐姐家比較近的學校，這樣我就可以
搬到她家去住，把房租跟飯錢省下來。

張天明: 不過在姐姐家裏住可能不太自由。

LANGUAGE NOTES

❹ 科 means divisions or branches of learning at a college or university, e.g., 文科 (humanities), 理科
(sciences), 工科 (engineering), etc.

张天明：　我想学文学。可是我妈妈说，学文科❹将来找工作不
　　　　　容易，而且赚钱也少，她希望我念金融。但是我对
　　　　　金融没有兴趣，整天跟数字打交道，多没意思。

李哲：　　我的父母跟你的父母差不多。其实，我最喜欢的是
　　　　　哲学，因为我喜欢想问题。我们班很多同学的父母
　　　　　都不太管孩子选什么专业，比我们自由。

张天明：　你要申请哪些学校？

李哲：　　我想申请离我姐姐家比较近的学校，这样我就可以
　　　　　搬到她家去住，把房租跟饭钱省下来。

张天明：　不过在姐姐家里住可能不太自由。

李哲：　　你的話沒錯，但是住在姐姐家的好處也不少。我再考慮考慮。

張天明：　哎，我給你一個建議吧。你沒有什麼工作經驗，先找個地方實習一下，對將來找工作肯定有好處。

李哲：　　你這個建議真不錯，我看我也不必去找指導教授了，就聽你的"指導"吧！

張天明：　別、別、別，還是聽聽教授的意見吧。

After You Study

Challenge yourself to complete the following tasks in Chinese.

1. List the courses that Zhang Tianming is currently taking.
2. List the courses that Zhang Tianming is going to take next semester.
3. List the courses that Li Zhe needs to graduate.

Sichuan University

李哲：　　你的话没错，但是住在姐姐家的好处也不少。我再
　　　　　考虑考虑。

张天明：　哎，我给你一个建议吧。你没有什么工作经验，先
　　　　　找个地方实习一下，对将来找工作肯定有好处。

李哲：　　你这个建议真不错，我看我也不必去找指导教授
　　　　　了，就听你的"指导"吧！

张天明：　别、别、别，还是听听教授的意见吧。

4. List Zhang Tianming's and Li Zhe's favorite subjects.
5. Give your advice to Zhang Tianming.
6. Give your advice to Li Zhe.

National Sun Yat-sen University

VOCABULARY

1.	選	选	xuǎn	v	to choose
2.	門	门	mén	m	(measure word for academic courses)
3.	世界		shìjiè	n	world
4.	歷史	历史	lìshǐ	n	history
5.	其他		qítā	pr	other; else
6.	經常	经常	jīngcháng	adv	often; frequently
7.	文章		wénzhāng	n	essay; article
8.	受不了		shòu bu liǎo	vc	cannot take it; unable to bear
9.	輕鬆	轻松	qīngsōng	adj	light; relaxed
10.	指導	指导	zhǐdǎo	v/n	to guide; guidance
11.	教授		jiàoshòu	n	professor
12.	討論	讨论	tǎolùn	v	to discuss
13.	碰見	碰见	pèng jiàn	vc	to bump into; to run into
14.	肯定		kěndìng	adv	definitely
15.	至於	至于	zhìyú	prep	as for; as to [See Grammar 3.]
16.	畢業	毕业	bì yè	vo	to graduate
17.	學位	学位	xuéwèi	n	(academic) degree
18.	化學	化学	huàxué	n	chemistry
19.	經濟	经济	jīngjì	n	economics; economy
20.	系		xì	n	department (of a college or university)
21.	學分	学分	xuéfēn	n	academic credit
22.	決定	决定	juédìng	v/n	to decide; decision

23.	解決	解决	jiějué	v	to solve; to resolve
24.	要麼…	要么…	yàome...	conj	if it's not..., it's...; either...or...
	要麼…	要么…	yàome...		[See Grammar 6.]
25.	工學院	工学院	gōng xuéyuàn	n	school of engineering
26.	管理學院	管理学院	guǎnlǐ xuéyuàn	n	school of management
27.	談	谈	tán	v	to talk; to discuss
28.	文學	文学	wénxué	n	literature
29.	科		kē	n	a branch of academic or vocational study
30.	將来	将来	jiānglái	n	future
31.	賺錢	赚钱	zhuàn qián	vo	make money
32.	金融		jīnróng	n	finance; banking
33.	整天		zhěng tiān		all day long
34.	數字	数字	shùzì	n	numeral; figure; digit
35.	打交道		dǎ jiāodào	vo	to deal with
36.	其實	其实	qíshí	adv	actually
37.	哲學	哲学	zhéxué	n	philosophy
38.	管		guǎn	v	to control, manage; to mind, to care about
39.	申請	申请	shēnqǐng	v	to apply (to a school or job)
40.	省下來	省下来	shěng xia lai	vc	to save (money, time)
41.	建議	建议	jiànyì	n/v	suggestion; to suggest
42.	經驗	经验	jīngyàn	n/v	experience; to experience

| 43. | 意見 | 意见 | yìjiàn | n | opinion |

Proper Noun

| 44. | 李哲 | | Lǐ Zhé | | Li Zhe (a personal name) |

Enlarged Characters

選　腦　鬆　導　畢　濟
选　脑　松　导　毕　济

T恤衫上寫著什麼？
T恤衫上写着什么？

Culture Highlights

1 The educational system in China is much more compartmentalized than in some other countries. Typically, high-school students are streamed into two separate tracks, sciences and humanities. College applicants have to declare their majors on their college application forms. Thus when high school graduates are admitted to colleges or universities, they are admitted directly into specialized departments. Because a student's college application can have a crucial impact on his or her future career, parents usually play a large role in the application process. Once students are in college, it is generally difficult to switch majors. However, in recent years some universities have attempted to be more flexible by allowing students the opportunity to explore their options before declaring a major. There is also a move to put more emphasis on general education, 通識教育/通识教育 (tōngshí jiàoyù) so that students will become well-rounded in both the humanities and sciences.

中国语言文学系
外国语言文学学院
新闻学院
哲学系
历史学系
文物与博物馆学系
经济学院
法学院
国际关系与公共事务学院
社会发展与公共政策学院
数学科学学院
物理系
环境科学与工程系
信息科学与工程学院
软件学院
化学系
生命科学学院
管理学院
力学与工程科学系
光源与照明工程系
高分子科学系
材料科学系
上海医学院

你認識哪些系、哪些學院？
你认识哪些系、哪些学院？

② The word for "graduate school" on the mainland is 研究生院, whereas in Taiwan, it is 研究所. However, 研究所 can mean either "graduate school" or "research institute." In mainland China, the word 研究所 refers only to research institutes, which may or may not be affiliated with universities. "To go to graduate school" is 念研究生 on the mainland and 念研究所 in Taiwan. In many countries, people apply to graduate school by submitting an application to one or more schools. But in both mainland China and Taiwan, admission is given based on people's scores on the graduate school entrance exams.

To whom does this reference room belong?

This is a sign on the door of a reading room. Who can have access to the room?

Grammar

1. 對⋯來説 / 对⋯来说

對他來説/对他来说 means "as far as he's concerned."

❶   對她來説，今年最需要做的事情是選一個好大學。
對她来说，今年最需要做的事情是选一个好大学。
(As far as she's concerned, the thing most needed to be done this year is to pick a good college.)

❷   對小王來説，今年找到工作最重要，要不然吃飯、住房子都會有問題。
对小王来说，今年找到工作最重要，要不然吃饭、住房子都会有问题。
(As far as Xiao Wang is concerned, the most important thing this year is to find a job. Otherwise, both food and housing would become problematic.)

對⋯來説/对⋯来说 can only convey the speaker's opinion. See in **❸** how it can be used together with 覺得/觉得.

❸   (我覺得)對他來説，有工作比沒工作好，可是他覺得工作不好比沒有工作更糟。
(我觉得)对他来说，有工作比没工作好，可是他觉得工作不好比没有工作更糟。
([I think that] for him, it's better to have a job than to have no job. However, in his view, having a lousy job is worse than having no job.)

2. Resultative Complements

The structure of a sentence containing a resultative complement is:

subject + verb + resultative complement (+ object)

Resultative complements are an important part of Chinese grammar. Generally speaking, as long as an action produces a certain result, a resultative complement must be used. For example, "extending one's hand" 伸手 (shēn shǒu) results in one's arm being stretched out, hence 伸出手. Opening the door 開門/开门 means having the door open, therefore, we say 開開門/开开门.

Whether a verb can be combined with an adjective or a verb to form a "verb + resultative complement" is not random, but rather follows certain patterns. Therefore, it is best to memorize each verb together with its resultative complement as if they were one unit.

Depending on their meanings, resultative complements fall into the following categories:

A. Resultative complements elucidating the verb:

❶ 我搬完家就去購物中心買日用品。
我搬完家就去购物中心买日用品。
(我—搬家，搬—完)
(I'll go get some household necessities at the shopping center as soon as I finish moving.)
[I will have moved; the act of moving will be completed.]

❷ 下學期的課你選好了嗎？(你—選課，選—好)
下学期的课你选好了吗？(你—选课，选—好)
(Have you finished selecting classes for next semester?)
[好 = "properly, readily" done selecting. You select, and are done selecting.]

B. Resultative complements indicating a new state or a change on the part of the agent of the action or the subject. In other words, by performing a certain action, the person brings upon himself or herself the result indicated by the complement:

❸ 老師説的話我聽懂了。(我—聽，我—懂)
老师说的话我听懂了。(我—听，我—懂)
(I understood what the teacher said.)
[My listening resulted in my understanding.]

❹ 張教授寫文章寫累了。(張教授—寫，張教授—累)
张教授写文章写累了。(张教授—写，张教授—累)
(Professor Zhang was tired from writing articles.)
[Professor Zhang wrote, and he became tired.]

C. Resultative complements indicating a new state or change on the part of the recipient of the action or the object; in other words, the complement indicates the action's result on the object.

❺ 你怎麽把妹妹打哭了？(你—打妹妹，妹妹—哭)
你怎么把妹妹打哭了？
(Why did you hit your sister and make her cry?)
[You hit; your younger sister started to cry.]

❻ 他搬走了一把椅子。(他—搬椅子，椅子—走)
(He took away a chair.)
[He moved the chair; the chair is now gone.]

❼ 你要把衣服洗乾淨才能去看電影。
(你—洗衣服，衣服—乾淨)
你要把衣服洗干净才能去看电影。
(你—洗衣服，衣服—干净)
(You have to wash the clothes clean [finish the laundry] before you can go see the movie.)
[You wash the clothes; the clothes will be clean as a result.]

3. Preposition 至於/至于

至於/至于 is used to introduce new subject matter which is related in some way to the subject of the preceding discussion, or a different aspect of the issue in question.

❶ A: 我們明年去旅行，好嗎？
我们明年去旅行，好吗？
(Let's take a trip next year. How about it?)

B: 我們先討論去不去，至於什麼時候去，以後再說。
我们先讨论去不去，至于什么时候去，以后再说。
(Let's first discuss whether we'll go or not. As for when to go, we'll talk about that later.)

❷ A: 你跟你太太喜歡吃四川菜還是廣東菜？
你跟你太太喜欢吃四川菜还是广东菜？
(Do you and your wife like Sichuanese or Cantonese cuisine?)

B: 我喜歡吃廣東菜，至於我太太，她喜歡吃四川菜。
我喜欢吃广东菜，至于我太太，她喜欢吃四川菜。
(I like Cantonese. As for my wife, she likes Sichuanese.)

❸ A: 你看這條牛仔褲的大小、樣子、顏色怎麼樣？
你看这条牛仔裤的大小、样子、颜色怎么样？
(What do you think of the size, style, and color of this pair of jeans?)

B: 這條牛仔褲，對你來說大小、樣子都合適。至於顏色，我覺得太難看了。
这条牛仔裤，对你来说大小、样子都合适。至于颜色，我觉得太难看了。
(Both the size and style are perfect for you. As for the color, I think it's ugly.)

4 A: 我想買衣服，這個商店怎麼樣？

我想买衣服，这个商店怎么样？

(I would like to buy some clothes. How is this store?)

B: 買日用品，這個商店不錯，比較便宜。至於買衣服，還是去大一點的購物中心吧。

买日用品，这个商店不错，比较便宜。至于买衣服，还是去大一点的购物中心吧。

(This store is good for daily necessities. It's quite cheap. As for clothes, you'd better go to a bigger shopping center.)

4. 另外

There are three ways to use 另外. One of them is before a noun or a demonstrative pronoun as seen in **1**, **2**, and **3**.

1   下個學期我打算選三門課。一門電腦，另外兩門課選什麼，還沒決定。

下个学期我打算选三门课。一门电脑，另外两门课选什么，还没决定。

(I plan to take three courses next semester. One of them will be computer science. As for the other two, I haven't decided yet.)

2   這裏有兩個大學，一個男校，另外一個是女校，都很不錯。

这里有两个大学，一个男校，另外一个是女校，都很不错。

(There are two colleges here. One is a men's college and the other one is a women's college. Both are quite good.)

❸ 他三個妹妹都有工作，一個是律師，另外兩個是大學
教授。

他三个妹妹都有工作，一个是律师，另外两个是大学
教授。

(All three of his younger sisters have jobs. One is a lawyer and the other two are
college professors.)

另外 can also be used as an adverb before a verb phrase, as seen in **❹**, **❺**, and **❻** or as a
conjunction at the beginning of a sentence as in **❼**.

❹ 下個學期我要選一門化學課，另外再選兩門電腦系的
課，學分就夠了。

下个学期我要选一门化学课，另外再选两门电脑系的
课，学分就够了。

(Next semester I'll take a chemistry course, plus two more computer science courses.
Then I'll have enough credits.)

❺ 在這個州買吃的東西，除了東西的價錢以外，另外還得
付百分之八的稅。

在这个州买吃的东西，除了东西的价钱以外，另外还得
付百分之八的税。

(When you buy food in this state, you have to pay eight percent in tax on top of the
price.)

❻ 上個週末我買了一些日用品，另外還買了一件T恤衫。
上个周末我买了一些日用品，另外还买了一件T恤衫。

(Last weekend I bought some household necessities. I also bought a T-shirt.)

❼ 請你給我訂兩張飛機票，另外，麻煩你再幫我買一個大
一點兒的包。

请你给我订两张飞机票，另外，麻烦你再帮我买一个大
一点儿的包。

(Please book two plane tickets for me. And also, may I trouble you to get a slightly
bigger bag for me?)

5. 再, 又, and 還/还 Compared

Both 又 and 再 indicate repetition of an action. 又 is usually used with actions that have already taken place as seen in ❶. 再, on the other hand, indicates recurrences in the future as seen in ❷. However, before 是 or certain modal verbs such as 想, 能, 要, 可以, or 會/会, one can use 又 for a future recurrence of an action as seen in ❸ and ❹.

❶ 我上星期申請了一個實習工作，昨天又申請了一個。
我上星期申请了一个实习工作，昨天又申请了一个。
(I applied for an internship last week. I applied for another one yesterday.)

❷ 先生，您剛才點的菜我沒聽清楚，麻煩您再說一次。
先生，您刚才点的菜我没听清楚，麻烦您再说一次。
(Sir, I didn't hear clearly what dishes you just ordered. Could I trouble you to say them again?)

❸ 明天又是星期天了。
明天又是星期天了。
(Tomorrow will be Sunday again.)

❹ 她今天下午又要去見指導教授了。
她今天下午又要去见指导教授了。
(She's going to see her advisor again this afternoon.)

還/还 indicates an increase in quantity or amount:

❺ 歷史課我選了一門了，還得選一門。
历史课我选了一门了，还得选一门。
(I've already taken one history class. I have to take one more.)

❻ 我點了一個清蒸魚，一個豆腐，還點了一盤餃子。
我点了一个清蒸鱼，一个豆腐，还点了一盘饺子。
(I ordered steamed fish, tofu, and also a plate of dumplings.)

---

6. 要麼···, 要麼··· / 要么···, 要么···

要麼···, 要麼··· / 要么···, 要么··· is a selective conjunction. It means "choosing between two or more possibilities or desires."

❶ 你要麼學醫, 要麼學經濟, 就是不能學文學。

你要么学医, 要么学经济, 就是不能学文学。

(You have to study either medicine or economics. It just can't be literature.)

❷ **A:** 你這個寒假打算做什麼?

你这个寒假打算做什么?

(What do you plan to do this winter break?)

B: 要麼打工, 要麼實習。

要么打工, 要么实习。

(Either work part-time or get an internship.)

❸ **A:** 今天晚飯想吃點什麼素菜?

今天晚饭想吃点什么素菜?

(What kind of vegetable would you like for dinner tonight?)

B: 要麼吃菠菜, 要麼吃芥蘭。

要么吃菠菜, 要么吃芥兰。

(Either spinach or Chinese broccoli.)

企業管理研究生班

大专免试入学 / 在 职 学 习 / 可申请硕士学位
人力资源方向 / 战略管理方向 / 市场营销方向

金融硕士班

免试入学、符合条件可申请硕士学位

金融学理论与实践的系统结合、高度应用性
和前瞻性的课程设置, 特设以下研究方向:

誰會對這兩個廣告有興趣?

谁会对这两个广告有兴趣?

Words & Phrases

A. 只是 or 就是 (it's just that)

只是 or 就是 signifies a turn in thought; it is similar to 不過/不过 in usage and tone (see Words & Phrases point F). It is, however, milder in tone than 但是 and 可是. Note that 只是 or 就是 usually appears in the second clause of a sentence. The first clause is often positive in meaning, whereas the second clause modifies the first clause, pointing out a flaw in something that might otherwise be perfect. In this respect 只是 is different from 但是, 可是, and 不過/不过.

❶ 你要搬到校外去住，我不是不同意，只是我覺得太早了一點。

你要搬到校外去住，我不是不同意，只是我觉得太早了一点。

(It's not that I object to your moving off campus. It's just that it's too soon.)

❷ 那件毛衣樣子好是好，只是價錢太貴。

那件毛衣样子好是好，只是价钱太贵。

(It's true that the style of that sweater is good. It's just that the price is too expensive.)

❸ 這個飯館很好，也不貴，就是常常沒有位子。

这个饭馆很好，也不贵，就是常常没有位子。

(This restaurant is very good, and it's not expensive either. It's just that often there aren't any tables.)

B. 受不了 (unable to bear)

❶ 今天太熱，我真的受不了。

今天太热，我真的受不了。

(It's so hot today. I truly can't take it.)

❷ 很久沒吃中國飯了，小張快受不了了。

很久没吃中国饭了，小张快受不了了。

(It's been awhile since Xiao Zhang last had a Chinese meal. It's getting so that he's almost unable to stand it anymore.)

❸ 我的同屋每天夜裏兩三點鐘才睡覺，我真受不了。

我的同屋每天夜里两三点钟才睡觉，我真受不了。

(My roommate doesn't go to bed until two or three in the morning. I can't stand it.)

C. 肯定 (definitely)

肯定 is an adverb that indicates there is no doubt whatsoever.

❶ **A:** 小林會說中文嗎？

小林会说中文吗？

(Can Little Lin speak Chinese?)

B: 他是在中國出生，在中國長大的，肯定會說中文。

他是在中国出生，在中国长大的，肯定会说中文。

(He was born and raised in China. He most certainly can speak Chinese.)

❷ **A:** 老柯身上穿的那套運動服是名牌嗎？

老柯身上穿的那套运动服是名牌吗？

(Is the sweatsuit that Old Ke is wearing name-brand?)

B: 肯定不是。聽說他是花十塊錢買的。名牌的衣服怎麼會那麼便宜？

肯定不是。听说他是花十块钱买的。名牌的衣服怎么会那么便宜？

(Most certainly not. I hear he spent ten dollars (or yuan) on it. How could designer clothes be so cheap?)

❸ **A:** 你姐姐做菜，油放得少，鹽也放得少，肯定不好吃。
你姐姐做菜，油放得少，盐也放得少，肯定不好吃。
(Your older sister adds very little oil and very little salt when she cooks. There's no way the food will taste good.)

B: 那也不見得。油少、鹽少的菜不一定不好吃。
那也不见得。油少、盐少的菜不一定不好吃。
(That's not necessarily true. Food with only a little oil and a little salt doesn't necessarily taste bad.)

D. 跟…打交道 (to deal with...)

This phrase usually means to come in contact with certain people or objects because of necessity or the nature of one's work or study.

❶ 購物中心的售貨員整天跟買東西的人打交道。
购物中心的售货员整天跟买东西的人打交道。
(The salespeople at the shopping center deal with shoppers all day long.)

❷ 我媽媽在銀行(yínháng)工作，天天跟錢和數字打交道。
我妈妈在银行(yínháng)工作，天天跟钱和数字打交道。
(My mom works at a bank. She deals with money and numbers every day.)

❸ 我現在在小學教英文，每天跟小孩兒打交道，很高興。
我现在在小学教英文，每天跟小孩儿打交道，很高兴。
(I now teach English at an elementary school. I deal with children every day. I'm very happy.)

E. 這樣/这样 (in this way)

這樣/这样 refers to what has just been mentioned. It connects a clause with the previous clause.

❶   我想申請離家比較近的學校，這樣我就可以搬回家去住。

我想申请离家比较近的学校，这样我就可以搬回家去住。

(I'd like to apply to a school that's closer to home. That way I can move back home.)

❷   學外語得經常聽錄音、念課文，這樣才能提高聽和說的水平。

学外语得经常听录音、念课文，这样才能提高听和说的水平。

(To learn a foreign language you have to listen to the audio recordings and read the lessons aloud frequently. This is the only way to improve your listening and speaking abilities.)

❸   選課以前你應該聽聽指導教授的意見，這樣你的課才能選得合適。

选课以前你应该听听指导教授的意见，这样你的课才能选得合适。

(Before you decide on your courses you should consult with your advisor. This is the only way to choose the appropriate courses.)

❹   買東西應該等商店打折的時候去買，這樣才能買到便宜的東西。

买东西应该等商店打折的时候去买，这样才能买到便宜的东西。

(You should shop when the stores are having sales. This is the only way to find bargains.)

> ### F. 不過/不过 (but)

不過/不过 introduces a turn in thought, but is less emphatic than 但是 or 可是.

❶ 醫生一般賺錢都不少，不過太忙、太累。
醫生一般赚钱都不少，不过太忙、太累。
(Doctors generally make a lot of money, but they are too busy and too tired.)

❷ 學電腦又忙又累，不過將來找工作比較容易。
学电脑又忙又累，不过将来找工作比较容易。
(Studying computer science keeps you very busy and very tired, but it's relatively easy to find a job later.)

❸ 打折以後的衣服便宜是便宜，不過有的時候大小、
樣子、顏色不一定合適。
打折以后的衣服便宜是便宜，不过有的时候大小、
样子、颜色不一定合适。
(Discounted clothes may be inexpensive, but sometimes they are not the right size, style, or color.)

Language Practice

> ### A. It's All about Classes!

Work with a partner and take turns to ask each other, among the courses listed:

a. which courses you have taken and which course you were most/least interested in.

A: 你選過什麼課?   A: 你选过什么课?

B: _____   B: _____

A: 你對哪一門課最有興趣?   A: 你对哪一门课最有兴趣?

B: _____   B: _____

A: 你對哪一門課最沒有興趣？   A: 你对哪一门课最没有兴趣？

B: _____   B: _____

b. which courses you want to take next semester and which course(s) will be good for finding a job later.

A: 下個學期你想選什麼課？   A: 下个学期你想选什么课？

B: _____   B: _____

A: 什麼課對將來找工作很有   A: 什么课对将来找工作很有
   好處？   好处？

B: _____   B: _____

_____   _____

A: 還有什麼對將來找工作也   A: 还有什么对将来找工作也
   很有好處？   很有好处？

B: _____   B: _____

_____   _____

B. Graduation in Sight

Pair up with a partner. Tell each other what your major is, whether you wish to double major, how many credits you still need to graduate, and whether you plan to find a job or apply to graduate school after graduating.

EXAMPLE:

major	double major	credits	job	graduate school
√	X	30	√	X
(finance)				

我的專業是金融，   我的专业是金融，
我不打算拿雙學位。   我不打算拿双学位。

我還需要三十個學分才能
畢業。

畢業以後，我打算找工作，
不打算念研究生。

我还需要三十个学分才能
毕业。

毕业以后，我打算找工作，
不打算念研究生。

Yours:

major	double major	credits	job	graduate school

Your Partner's:

major	double major	credits	job	graduate school

Note: If you haven't chosen a major yet, you can say:

我還沒決定選什麼專業。　　　我还没决定选什么专业。

C. Can You Deal with a Heavy Course Load?

Go around the class. Ask your classmates what kind of course load in a semester is manageable for them.

a. 一個學期上幾門課會讓你
受不了？

b. 一個學期上幾門課你會覺得
比較輕鬆？

a. 一个学期上几门课会让你
受不了？

b. 一个学期上几门课你会觉得
比较轻松？

Tally your classmates' answers, and report back to the class.

_____個同學覺得上_____門課
會讓他們受不了。

　　_____個同學覺得上_____門課
會比較輕鬆。

…

_____个同学觉得上_____门课
会让他们受不了。

　　_____个同学觉得上_____门课
会比较轻松。

…

D. All Things Considered

With the help of the chart, practice with a partner how to give your opinions on various aspects of the topic in question.

topic	aspect 1	aspect 2	aspect 3	aspect 4
university	professors	libraries	classrooms	dorms
jeans	style	color	size	price
apartment	size	furniture	security deposit	rent
restaurant	steamed fish	Chinese broccoli	beef in soy sauce	hot and sour soup

EXAMPLE: university

A: 這個大學怎麼樣？

B: 我覺得這個大學教授很
　 有名，圖書館書很多，
　 教室很新，至於宿舍，
　 我覺得有點兒舊。

A: 这个大学怎么样？

B: 我觉得这个大学教授很
　 有名，图书馆书很多，
　 教室很新，至于宿舍，
　 我觉得有点儿旧。

1. jeans
2. apartment
3. restaurant

E. It Comes with the Job

Based on the pictures, describe what these people have to deal with because of the nature of their jobs.

EXAMPLE:

→ 經濟學教授整天跟數字打
交道。

經濟學教授整天跟數字打
交道。

经济学教授整天跟数字打
交道。

 1. 　　2. 　　3.

F. Is There a Control Freak in Your Life?

Are your parents/siblings/teachers/friends concerned about every detail of your life/study/work? Do they try to micromanage you all the time? Mark their tendencies on the chart, and report the information to the class.

	parent(s)	sibling(s)	friend(s)	teacher(s)
Example: wardrobe	√	X	X	X
1. wardrobe				
2. food				
3. classes				
4. major				
5. work				

EXAMPLE: wardrobe

→ 我父母常常管我穿什麼
衣服。

我父母常常管我穿什么
衣服。

1. wardrobe
2. food
3. classes
4. major
5. work

G. Creative Money-Saving Tips

Brainstorm with your partner and come up with ways to save money to pay for your education.

EXAMPLE:

A: 怎麼樣可以把錢省下來
付學費？

B: 住在家裏可以把錢省下來
付學費。

A: 怎么样可以把钱省下来
付学费？

B: 住在家里可以把钱省下来
付学费。

1.

2.

3.

...

H. Do You Know Your Schools and Colleges?

Draw a line connecting the Chinese words with their English equivalents.

人文學院	school of engineering	人文学院
醫學院	school of management	医学院
工學院	business school	工学院
理學院	medical school	理学院
藥學院	college of humanities	药学院
法學院	college of sciences	法学院
商學院	law school	商学院
管理學院	school of pharmacology	管理学院

Can you figure out what kind of college this is?

Pinyin Text

Zhāng Tiānmíng zhè ge xuéqī xuǎn le sì mén kè: shìjiè lìshǐ, diànnǎo, zhèngzhìxué❶ hé Zhōngwén. Zhè jǐ mén kè dōu hěn yǒu yìsi, tā yě xué dào le bù shǎo dōngxi.Yīnwèi Zhāng Tiānmíng zài jiā de shíhou chángcháng gēn fùmǔ shuō Zhōngwén, suǒyǐ yī niánjí de Zhōngwén kè, duì tā lái shuō①, tīng hé shuō hěn róngyì, zhǐshì xiě Hànzì yǒu diǎnr nán. Chúle Zhōngwén kè yǐwài, qítā jǐ mén kè dōu děi huā hěn duō shíjiān zhǔnbèi, hái jīngcháng yào xiě wénzhāng, suǒyǐ tā juéde yǒu diǎnr shòu bu liǎo. Zhè ge xuéqī yǐjīng guò le yí bàn, mǎshàng yòu děi xuǎn xià xuéqī de kè le, Zhāng Tiānmíng xīwàng xià ge xuéqī néng qīngsōng diǎnr. Hòutiān yào qù jiàn zhǐdǎo jiàoshòu❷, tǎolùn xuǎn kè de shì, tā xiǎng xiān zhǎo bié de tóngxué liáo liao. Zhè yì tiān xiàwǔ, tā zài lánqiú chǎng shang zhènghǎo pèng jiàn dà sì de Lǐ Zhé, jiù yì biān hé Lǐ Zhé dǎ qiú, yì biān liáo le qi lai.

Zhāng Tiānmíng:	Zěnmeyàng, xià xuéqī de kè nǐ xuǎn hǎo② le ma?
Lǐ Zhé:	Hái méiyǒu ne. Nǐ ne?
Zhāng Tiānmíng:	Wǒ kěndìng yào xuǎn Zhōngwén, zhìyú③ lìngwài④ liǎng mén kè xuǎn shénme, hái méi xiǎng hǎo. Duì le, nǐ hái děi zài shàng jǐ mén kè cái néng bì yè?
Lǐ Zhé:	Wǒ xiǎng ná shuāng xuéwèi❸, hái děi shàng sì mén kè. Wǒ xiǎng zài⑤ xuǎn yì mén huàxué, yì mén jīngjì, lìngwài④ zài xuǎn liǎng mén diànnǎo xì de kè, zhèyàng xuéfēn jiù gòu le.
Zhāng Tiānmíng:	Duì, wǒ juédìng le, yě xuǎn jīngjì hé diànnǎo! Wǒ de wèntí jiějué le, tài hǎo le! Wǒ hòutiān jiù gàosu wǒ de zhǐdǎo jiàoshòu.
Lǐ Zhé:	Shì ma? Wǒ hòutiān yě qù jiàn zhǐdǎo jiàoshòu.
Zhāng Tiānmíng:	Lǐ Zhé, nǐ bì yè yǐhòu dǎsuàn zuò shénme?
Lǐ Zhé:	Wǒ xiǎng niàn yánjiūshēng, yàome shàng gōng xuéyuàn, yàome shàng guǎnlǐ xuéyuàn⑥, wǒ hái méi gēn zhǐdǎo jiàoshòu tán. Nǐ xiǎng xuǎn shénme zhuānyè?
Zhāng Tiānmíng:	Wǒ xiǎng xué wénxué. Kěshì wǒ māma shuō, xué wénkē❹ jiānglái zhǎo gōngzuò bù róngyì, érqiě zhuàn qián yě shǎo, tā xīwàng wǒ niàn jīnróng. Dànshì wǒ duì jīnróng méi yǒu xìngqù, zhěngtiān gēn shùzì dǎ jiāodao, duō méi yìsi.
Lǐ Zhé:	Wǒ de fùmǔ gēn nǐ de fùmǔ chàbuduō. Qíshí, wǒ zuì xǐhuan de shì zhéxué, yīnwèi wǒ xǐhuan xiǎng wèntí. Wǒmen bān hěn duō tóngxué

de fùmǔ dōu bú tài guǎn háizi xuǎn shénme zhuānyè, bǐ wǒmen zìyóu.

Zhāng Tiānmíng: Nǐ yào shēnqǐng nǎ xiē xuéxiào?

Lǐ Zhé: Wǒ xiǎng shēnqǐng lí wǒ jiějie jiā bǐjiào jìn de xuéxiào, zhèyàng wǒ jiù kěyǐ bān dào tā jiā qù zhù, bǎ fángzū gēn fànqian shěng xia lai.

Zhāng Tiānmíng: Búguò zài jiějie jiā li zhù kěnéng bú tài zìyóu.

Lǐ Zhé: Nǐ de huà méi cuò, dànshì zhù zài jiějie jiā de hǎochù yě bù shǎo. Wǒ zài kǎolǜ kǎolǜ.

Zhāng Tiānmíng: Āi, wǒ gěi nǐ yí ge jiànyì ba. Nǐ méiyǒu shénme gōngzuò jīngyàn, xiān zhǎo ge dìfang shíxí yí xià, duì jiānglái zhǎo gōngzuò kěndìng yǒu hǎochù.

Lǐ Zhé: Nǐ zhè ge jiànyì zhēn búcuò. Wǒ kàn wǒ yě búbì qù zhǎo zhǐdǎo jiàoshòu le, jiù tīng nǐ de "zhǐdǎo" ba!

Zhāng Tiānmíng: Bié, bié, bié, hái shì tīng ting jiàoshòu de yìjiàn ba.

English Text

Zhang Tianming is taking four courses this semester: World History, Computer Science, Political Science, and Chinese. These classes are all very interesting, and he has learned a lot of things. Because Zhang Tianming often speaks Chinese with his parents at home, first-year Chinese for him is very easy in terms of listening and speaking; only writing Chinese characters is a little difficult. Apart from Chinese, preparing for his other classes takes up a lot of his time, and he also has to write many essays, so he finds his course load a bit too much. This semester is half over. Soon he'll have to choose next semester's classes. Zhang Tianming hopes that he can relax a bit more next semester. The day after tomorrow he will see his advisor to discuss course selection, and he wants to talk with other schoolmates first. This afternoon he happens to run into Li Zhe on the basketball court, so he begins to chat with Li Zhe while they play basketball.

Zhang Tianming: So have you finished picking your classes for next semester?

Li Zhe: Not yet. How about you?

Zhang Tianming: I definitely want to take Chinese. As for the other two classes, I'm still thinking. Oh yeah, how many classes do you still have to take before you can graduate?

Li Zhe:	I'd like to do a double major, so I still need four more classes. I want to take another chemistry class, an econ class, plus two classes with the Computer Science Department. Then I'll have enough credits.
Zhang Tianming:	That's it. I've decided. I'll also take Economics and Computer Science. My problem is solved. This is great. I'll tell my advisor the day after tomorrow.
Li Zhe:	Yeah? The day after tomorrow is the day I'll meet with my advisor, too.
Zhang Tianming:	Li Zhe, what do you want to do after you graduate?
Li Zhe:	I'd like to go to graduate school, either engineering or business school. I haven't discussed it yet with my advisor. What do you want to major in?
Zhang Tianming:	I'd like to study literature, but my mom says it's difficult to find a job if I study the humanities. Besides, I won't make much money. She hopes that I will study finance, but I'm not interested in finance. How boring—dealing with numbers all day long.
Li Zhe:	My parents are not too different from yours. As a matter of fact, what interests me the most is philosophy because I like to think about [philosophical] problems. Many of our classmates' parents don't care what majors their children pick. They have more freedom than we do.
Zhang Tianming:	Which schools do you want to apply to?
Li Zhe:	I'd like to apply to a school near my sister's place. This way I can move into her house and save room and board.
Zhang Tianming:	But staying at your sister's place may be a bit constricting.
Li Zhe:	What you say is true, but staying at my sister's place has many advantages. I need to think about it some more.
Zhang Tianming:	Hey, I have a suggestion. You don't have a lot of working experience; you could find a place to intern first. It'll be good when you look for a job.
Li Zhe:	That's a good suggestion. It seems like I don't need to see my advisor. I can listen to your advice!
Zhang Tianming:	Oh no, no. You'd better listen to your advisor's opinion.

SELF-ASSESSMENT

How well can you do these things? Check (✔) the boxes to evaluate your progress and see which areas you may need to practice more.

I can	Very Well	OK	A Little
Name my major and other required courses	☐	☐	☐
Talk about my plans for after graduation	☐	☐	☐
Talk about ways to enhance my future job prospects	☐	☐	☐
Discuss whether my parents have a say in choosing my major and career path	☐	☐	☐
List ways to save money for school	☐	☐	☐

Let's Review! (Lessons 1-5)

I. Chinese Character Crossword Puzzles

You have learned many vocabulary items from Lessons 1–5. You may have noticed that some words/phrases share the same characters. Let's see whether you can recall these characters. The common character is positioned in the center of the cluster of rings. The block arrows indicate which way you should read the words. Work with a partner and see how many association rings you can complete. Of course, you may add more rings if you can think of additional words/phrases sharing the same characters or you may create your own clusters of rings.

EXAMPLE:

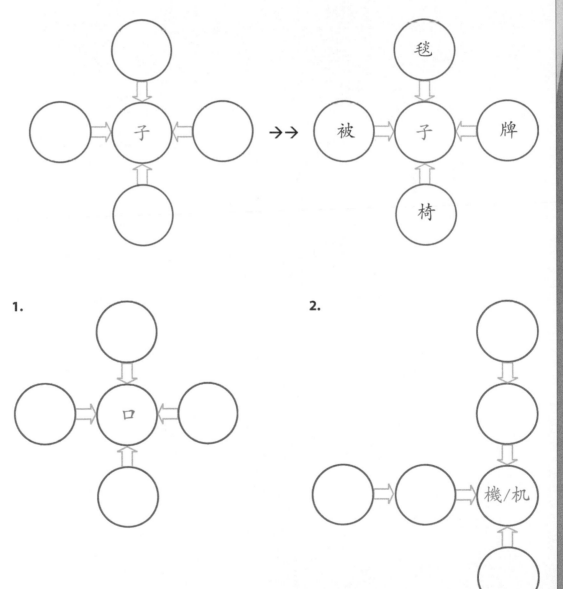

3.

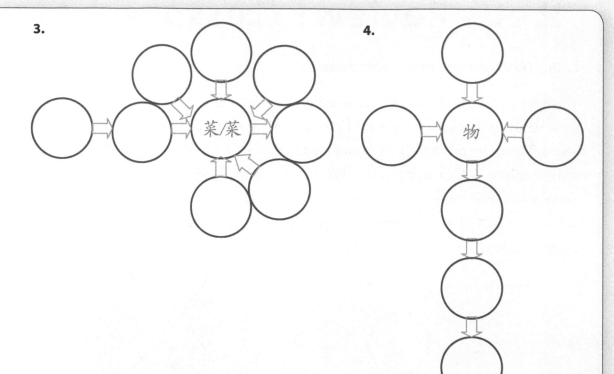

菜/菜

4.

物

5.

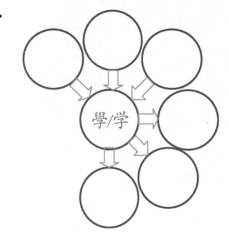

學/学

6.   Create Your Own

II. Make a Word List

A. Brainstorm with a partner and ask each other what words will come to mind when you want to

1. describe your dorm room/apartment: **2.** prioritize your shopping criteria:

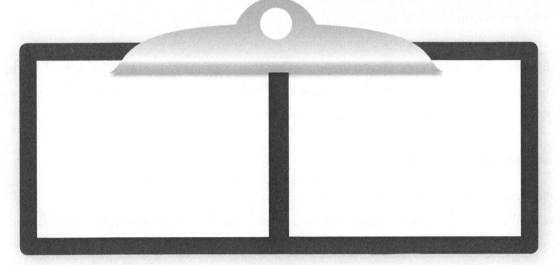

3. specify your preferences when ordering food: **4.** talk about your academic studies:

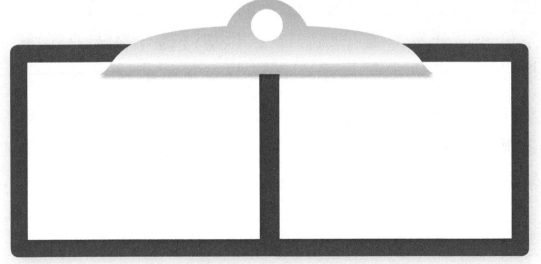

B. Brainstorm with a partner and ask each other what words or phrases will help when you want to:

1. agree with someone: _____

2. politely disagree with someone: _____

3. discuss the pros and cons of something: _____

4. make a polite request: _____

5. voice your disagreement rhetorically: _____

III. Organize Your Thoughts

Select a topic from the four listed in II A. Discuss with your partner

a. what you want to say;

b. what words or phrases from II B will help you express your opinion;

c. what should be said first, next, and last;

d. what transitions may be needed; and

e. what cohesive devices should be used to connect your sentences.

It may be a good idea to jot down sentences that you wish to say, then number them in the order you think they should be presented, and finally consider how to make your sentences a coherent discourse. Then present your work to the class.

IV. Let Me Explain Myself

Explain yourself in paragraphs.

How would you help make Speaker B sound more logical while justifying his/her choice of major? Use the following conjunctions when necessary to complete the following paragraph.

另外	雖然/虽然	可是	所以	再說/再说

A: 你想好選什麼專業了嗎？

B: 想好了。我決定學化學。

A: 為什麼選化學？你昨天不是說要跟我一樣，上管理學院嗎？

B: _____管理學院的課不難，_____很沒有意思。_____我對數字、金融也沒什麼興趣。_____上管理學院的人太多了，畢業以後找工作不見得容易。我聽說學藥學找工作比較容易，_____我打算先學化學專業，將來念藥學研究生。

A: 你想好选什么专业了吗？

B: 想好了。我决定学化学。

A: 为什么选化学？你昨天不是说要跟我一样，上管理学院吗？

B: _____管理学院的课不难，_____很没有意思。_____我对数字、金融也没什么兴趣。_____上管理学院的人太多了，毕业以后找工作不见得容易。我听说学药学找工作比较容易，_____我打算先学化学专业，将来念药学研究生。

第六课
男朋友
女朋友

第六课
男朋友
女朋友

6

 LEARNING OBJECTIVES

In this lesson, you will learn to use Chinese to

1. Say if you have an upbeat personality;
2. State if you share the same interests or hobbies with others;
3. Inquire if everything is OK and find out what has happened;
4. Describe typical behaviors of a forgetful person;
5. Give a simple description of what you look for in a boyfriend/ girlfriend.
6. Tell what makes you anxious or angry.

 RELATE AND GET READY

In your own culture/community—

• What do people look for in a date?

• Do people introduce their dates to their parents?

• Is dating always intended for people to find their future life partner?

Before You Study

Check the statements that apply to you.

☐ 1. I have an extroverted personality.

☐ 2. I get along well with my friends.

When You Study

Listen to the audio recording and scan the text. Ask yourself the following questions before you begin a close reading of the text.

1. Why is Lisa in a bad mood?

 麗莎這幾天好像有什麼❶心事。昨天林雪梅問了她好幾❷次，她才說她跟張天明鬧彆扭了。

　　雪梅剛認識麗莎的時候，聽麗莎說，她和張天明在高中就是同學。天明人很好，性格十分開朗，學習也不

LANGUAGE NOTES

❶ In colloquial Chinese, 什麼／什么 is sometimes used not as a question pronoun, but rather as an indefinite reference. It can be omitted without affecting the meaning of the sentence.

☐ 3. I am a forgetful person.

☐ 4. I have gone through a break-up before.

2. Does Xuemei understand Lisa's frustration? Why or why not?

3. What is Xuemei's worry, if any?

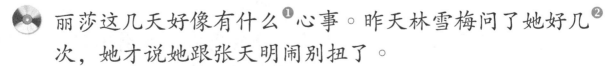 丽莎这几天好像有什么^❶心事。昨天林雪梅问了她好几^❷次，她才说她跟张天明闹别扭了。

　　雪梅刚认识丽莎的时候，听丽莎说，她和张天明在高中就是同学。天明人很好，性格十分开朗，学习也不

---

❷ 好 can be used as a mild intensifier, e.g., 好幾個人/好几个人, quite a few people. 幾/几 here is not a question pronoun, but suggests a small, indefinite number, "a few."

錯。在興趣上①她跟天明不太一樣，天明是個球迷，電視裏一有球賽，他就非看不可，麗莎是個歌迷，一有演唱會就去聽。麗莎說，他們的興趣愛好雖然不同③，但是一直相處得很好。

林雪梅想來想去②，想不出他們之間到底發生了什麼事兒。是因為文化背景不同嗎？還是天明有了新的女朋友？正好今天晚上有空，雪梅就去找麗莎。

雪梅：你跟天明怎麼了？

麗莎：哎，別提④了，他心裏根本沒有我。

雪梅：到底是怎麼回⑤事兒？

麗莎：兩個星期前我跟他約好去看一個演唱會，沒想到他那天晚上一直玩兒電腦，把演唱會的事兒忘得一乾二淨。你說我能不生氣嗎？

雪梅：別生氣了，柯林也常常這樣，一看球賽就什麼事兒都忘了。

麗莎：還有更叫⑥人生氣的呢。上個星期六我要他陪我去看電影，他很高興地③④答應了，可是八點的電影，我等到八點一刻他還沒到。打他手機，才知道他跑⑦到另一家電影院去了。這些雖然都是小事兒，但是叫我非常生氣，覺得他根本不在乎我。真想跟他吹了。

雪梅：噢，原來⑤是這樣。哎，這個天明，怎麼這麼⑧馬虎！難怪你心情不好。後來呢？

麗莎：後來他見到我，不停地給我道歉，說對不起，態度特別好。這讓我覺得他對我還是真心的。

LANGUAGE NOTES

❸ 同 is an adjective meaning "same; alike." It usually doesn't appear by itself.

❹ 提 here means "to mention." When someone is in a bad mood and says, "別提了", the speaker is not so much asking the other person to drop the topic as indicating his emotional response to the subject.

错。在兴趣上①她跟天明不太一样，天明是个球迷，电视里一有球赛，他就非看不可，丽莎是个歌迷，一有演唱会就去听。丽莎说，他们的兴趣爱好虽然不同③，但是一直相处得很好。

林雪梅想来想去②，想不出他们之间到底发生了什么事儿。是因为文化背景不同吗？还是天明有了新的女朋友？正好今天晚上有空，雪梅就去找丽莎。

雪梅： 你跟天明怎么了？

丽莎： 哎，别提④了，他心里根本没有我。

雪梅： 到底是怎么回⑤事儿？

丽莎： 两个星期前我跟他约好去看一个演唱会，没想到他那天晚上一直玩儿电脑，把演唱会的事儿忘得一干二净。你说我能不生气吗？

雪梅： 别生气了，柯林也常常这样，一看球赛就什么事儿都忘了。

丽莎： 还有更叫⑥人生气的呢。上个星期六我要他陪我去看电影，他很高兴地③④答应了，可是八点的电影，我等到八点一刻他还没到。打他手机，才知道他跑⑦到另一家电影院去了。这些虽然都是小事儿，但是叫我非常生气，觉得他根本不在乎我。真想跟他吹了。

雪梅： 噢，原来⑤是这样。哎，这个天明，怎么这么⑧马虎！难怪你心情不好。后来呢？

丽莎： 后来他见到我，不停地给我道歉，说对不起，态度特别好。这让我觉得他对我还是真心的。

---

⑤ 回 is a measure word. It can indicate frequency of an action or be used before the noun 事.
⑥ 讓/让 and 叫 are interchangeable when they are used in the sense of "making someone do something."
⑦ 跑 here is a colloquial usage meaning "to go."
⑧ 這麼/这么 is usually pronounced zème rather than zhème in northern China.

雪梅：　是啊，別生氣了！馬虎跟心裏沒有你是兩回事兒。
　　　　你聽說過嗎？中國有一句話："小兩口吵架不記
　　　　仇。"⑨哈哈！如果有一天不吵了，說不定你們就真的
　　　　會分手。

麗莎：　我看你跟柯林兩個人挺好的，也不怎麼吵架。

雪梅：　實際上，柯林跟天明差不多，常常忘這忘那⑩、丟三拉
　　　　四⑥的。他一會兒忘了我的生日，一會兒找不到鑰匙，
　　　　一會兒又…有的時候真讓人着急。

麗莎：　是嗎？原來柯林也有馬虎的時候。對了，你交男朋友
　　　　的事兒，家裏知道嗎？

雪梅：　這個嗎…我還沒把我跟柯林的事兒告訴家裏呢。

After You Study

Challenge yourself to complete the following tasks in Chinese.

1. List what Lisa finds attractive about Zhang Tianming.
2. Tell the differences between Zhang Tianming and Lisa.

LANGUAGE NOTES

❾ 小兩口吵架不記仇/小两口吵架不记仇 This is a colloquial saying about "lovers' quarrels," literally, "when a young couple fights they don't hold grudges." Xuemei is teasing here since Lisa and Tianming are not married.

雪梅：   是啊，别生气了！马虎跟心里没有你是两回事儿。
你听说过吗？中国有一句话："小两口吵架不记
仇。"❾哈哈！如果有一天不吵了，说不定你们就真的
会分手。

丽莎：   我看你跟柯林两个人挺好的，也不怎么吵架。

雪梅：   实际上，柯林跟天明差不多，常常忘这忘那❿、丢三拉
四❻的。他一会儿忘了我的生日，一会儿找不到钥匙，
一会儿又…有的时候真让人着急。

丽莎：   是吗？原来柯林也有马虎的时候。对了，你交男朋友
的事儿，家里知道吗？

雪梅：   这个吗…我还没把我跟柯林的事儿告诉家里呢。

---

3. List the incidents that upset Lisa.
4. List the incidents that Xuemei shares with Lisa.
5. Describe how you would react if you were in Lisa and Xuemei's positions, respectively.

---

❿ In 忘這忘那/忘这忘那 (forget this and forget that), both 這/这 (this) and 那 (that) are indefinite references, just like their English equivalents.

VOCABULARY

1.	心事		xīnshì	n	something weighing on one's mind
2.	鬧彆扭	闹别扭	nào bièniu	vo	to have a small conflict; to be at odds (with someone)
3.	高中		gāozhōng	n	senior high school
4.	性格		xìnggé	n	personality; character
5.	十分		shífēn	adv	very
6.	開朗	开朗	kāilǎng	adj	extroverted; open and sunny in disposition
7.	迷		mí	n/v	fan; to be infatuated with
8.	演唱會	演唱会	yǎnchànghuì	n	vocal concert
9.	愛好	爱好	àihào	n/v	hobby; interest; to love (something)
10.	不同		bù tóng		different; not the same
11.	相處	相处	xiāngchǔ	v	to get along
12.	之間	之间	zhī jiān		between; among
13.	到底		dàodǐ	adv	what on earth; what in the world; in the end
14.	發生	发生	fāshēng	v	to happen; to occur; to take place
15.	背景		bèijǐng	n	background
16.	提		tí	v	to mention; to bring up
17.	心		xīn	n	heart; mind
18.	根本		gēnběn	adv	at all; simply
19.	回		huí	m	(measure word for frequency of an action)
20.	一乾二淨	一干二净	yì gān èr jìng		completely; thoroughly [See Grammar 6.]

21. 生氣	生气	shēng qì	vo	to get angry
22. 叫		jiào	v	to make (someone do something)
23. 陪		péi	v	to accompany
24. 答應	答应	dāying	v	to agree (to do something); to promise; to answer
25. 電影院	电影院	diànyǐngyuàn	n	movie theater
26. 吹		chuī	v	to end a relationship; (lit.) to blow
27. 噢	噢	ō	interj	oh!
28. 原來	原来	yuánlái	adv/adj	as a matter of fact; original; former [See Grammar 5.]
29. 馬虎	马虎	mǎhu	adj	careless; perfunctory; mediocre
30. 難怪	难怪	nánguài	adv	no wonder
31. 心情		xīnqíng	n	mood
32. 不停		bùtíng	adv	continuously; incessantly
33. 道歉		dào qiàn	vo	to apologize
34. 態度	态度	tàidu	n	attitude
35. 真心		zhēnxīn	n	sincere; wholehearted
36. 句		jù	m	(measure word for sentences)
37. 吵架		chǎo jià	vo	to quarrel
38. 記仇	记仇	jì chóu	vo	to bear a grudge; to harbor resentment
39. 哈		hā	ono	(imitating laughter)
40. 說不定	说不定	shuōbudìng	adv	perhaps; maybe
41. 分手		fēn shǒu	vo	to break up; to part company
42. 實際上	实际上	shíjìshang	adv	in fact; in reality; actually

43.	丢三拉四		diū sān là sì		scatterbrained; forgetful [See Grammar 6.]
44.	鑰匙	钥匙	yàoshi	n	key
45.	交朋友		jiāo péngyou	vo	to make friends

●北京电视台—6

6:10 奥运故事 365
6:25 国际足球杂志 7:00 天天体育
8:08 快乐健身一箩筐精彩回放
8:38 奥运会项目介绍
9:05 足球 100 分
10:59 福娃奥运漫游记
11:15 国际足球杂志 11:50 体坛资讯
12:20 快乐健身一箩筐精彩回放
12:50 奥运会项目介绍
13:15 奥运故事 365 13:30 奥运时段
14:10 中超(北京国安队—河南队)
16:00 NBA 精彩回放
17:50 快乐健身一箩筐精彩回放
18:25 足球世界波 19:00 篮球风云
19:35 桌上运动 20:30 各就各位
21:25 天天体育
22:35 篮球风云 23:05 京彩时刻
23:25 环法自行车赛精华
00:00 中超(北京国安队—河南队)
02:00 天天体育 03:00 足球 100 分

如果你是足球迷，你會看什麼？如果你是籃球迷，你會看什麼？
如果你是足球迷，你会看什么？如果你是篮球迷，你会看什么？

Enlarged Characters

鬧	彆	淨	態	鑰
闹	别	净	态	钥

這兩家電影院演的電影一樣，電影票都是新台幣210元一張。如果你跟你的朋友兩個人一起去看，你們會選哪一家？為什麼？

这两家电影院演的电影一样，电影票都是新台币210元一张。如果你跟你的朋友两个人一起去看，你们会选哪一家？为什么？

Culture Highlights

❶ Although customs and mores are changing, Western-style dating remains a rather foreign concept in China. Instead, people speak of 交朋友 or 談戀愛/谈恋爱 (tán liàn'ài) when a man and a woman start going out. The goal is invariably marriage. Teachers and parents usually discourage young people from forming romantic relationships at a young age. Parental opinion continues to play a large role in the choices of a marriage partner.

交友徵婚	徵婚	徵婚	代女徵婚	MS婚友會
	江西姑娘 張小姐 39歲	包小姐 44歲 容貌嬌美	小女34歲 現居廣州	為單身人士
	高1.66 外貌美麗 性格溫柔大方	廣州人 大專學歷 國企工作	大學本科 健康秀美文靜	介紹朋友或婚友
	在廣州生活及工作	覓有愛心善良有經濟基礎	待字閨中 覓30-45歲健康	有意英語電Maria
	尋真心有緣男士為伴侶	男士共普愛的新曲	素質好 美、加籍華裔為婿	604-
	電：86-1343	011-86-13	婚史不限 206-	女會員免費

這些是什麼廣告?
这些是什么广告?

❷ Valentine's Day has become quite popular with many young people in China in recent years. Some traditionalists have suggested 七夕 (qīxī), the seventh day of the seventh month of the lunar calendar, as a Chinese equivalent of Valentine's Day. The idea is based on an old legend about a cowherd (牛郎, Niúláng) and a heavenly weaving maiden (織女/织女, Zhīnǔ), who fall in love with each other and have two beautiful children. However, fate intervenes. According to one version of the story, the Queen Mother of the West recalls the Weaver Girl from the earth. The lovers are cruelly separated by the Milky Way, created by the Queen Mother with a flourish of her gold hairpin. A flock of magpies takes pity on the distraught Cowherd and Weaver Girl and forms a bridge, thus allowing them to be reunited. The Queen Mother is moved too, and agrees to let the lovers and their children come together as a family once a year on the bridge of magpies, on the seventh day of the seventh month of the lunar calendar. Interestingly enough, that day used to be called Girls' Day (女兒節/女儿节), when girls and young women prayed to the Weaver Girl to have some of her dexterity and cleverness.

Grammar

1. (在)⋯上

(在)⋯上 can be combined with an abstract noun to mean "in terms of," for instance, in terms of character, interest, studies, work, etc.

❶   在興趣上，麗莎跟天明不太一樣。
在兴趣上，丽莎跟天明不太一样。
(In terms of their interests, Lisa and Tianming are not quite the same.)

❷   小林最近在學習上有很多問題，所以心情不太好。
小林最近在学习上有很多问题，所以心情不太好。
(Little Lin has had a lot of problems with his studies lately, so he is not in a good mood.)

❸   在性格上，她以前的男朋友比現在的男朋友開朗多了。
在性格上，她以前的男朋友比现在的男朋友开朗多了。
(In terms of personality, her ex-boyfriend was much more extroverted than her current boyfriend.)

2. V來V去/V来V去

V來V去/V来V去 signifies a repetitive action, e.g., 走來走去/走来走去 (walk back and forth), 飛來飛去/飞来飞去 (fly here and there), 想來想去/想来想去 (think over and over), 說來說去/说来说去 (say again and again), 討論來討論去/讨论来讨论去 (discuss again and again), 研究來研究去/研究来研究去 (consider [research] again and again).

❶   你別在房間裏走來走去，大家都睡覺了。
你别在房间里走来走去，大家都睡觉了。
(Don't pace back and forth in the room. Everybody has gone to bed.)

❷ 這個問題我們討論來討論去，最後還是沒有辦法解決。

这个问题我们讨论来讨论去，最后还是没有办法解决。

(We discussed this problem again and again. In the end we still couldn't find a way to solve it.)

❸ 媽媽叫我學經濟，我想來想去還是選了電腦。

妈妈叫我学经济，我想来想去还是选了电脑。

(My mother wanted me to study economics. After thinking it over and over, I decided to study computer [science].)

3. Adverbials and 地 (de)

Some adverbials signify the manner of an action. The particle 地 (de) is usually required after these adverbials:

❶ 老教授慢慢地走進了教室。

老教授慢慢地走进了教室。

(The old professor slowly walked into the classroom.)

❷ 我用力地把桌子搬起來。

我用力地把桌子搬起来。

(I lifted the table with a great deal of effort.)

❸ 看見了我，妹妹很高興地問："姐姐，你陪我看碟，好嗎？"

看见了我，妹妹很高兴地问："姐姐，你陪我看碟，好吗？"

(When she saw me, my sister gladly asked, "Older sister, watch the DVD with me, OK?")

【舞蹈】

爱尔兰踢踏舞《大河之舞》访华演出
时间：07 月 24 日－ 27 日
场馆：国家大剧院歌剧院
票价：1280（VIP/980/780/580/380/180 元

芭蕾舞剧《大红灯笼高高挂》
时间：07 月 11 日－－ 13 日
场馆：天桥剧场
票价：500（VIP)/400/300/200/100/50 元

中央芭蕾舞团《天鹅湖》
时间：07 月 02 日
场馆：人民大会堂
票价：880/580/380/180/120/40 元

【舞台剧】

Disney　Live 迪士尼
舞台剧《三大经典童话》(白雪公主、灰姑娘、美女与野兽)
时间：7 月 15－20 日
场馆：北京展览馆剧场
票价：380/280/180/120 元

百老汇音乐剧《发胶星梦》
时间：07 月 25 日 －30 日
场馆：北京展览馆剧场
票价：880/680/480/380/280/180 元

" 相约北京"2008 文化活动——意大利卡达克罗体育舞蹈团访华演出
时间：07 月 11－12 日
场馆：北大讲堂
票价：280/180/80/50/30/20 元

This is a schedule of performances at an arts center. Can you find when "Snow White" and "Beauty and the Beast" will be performed?

4. 的, 得, and 地 Compared

These three structural particles are pronounced the same, but have different usages. 的 appears after attributives, 得 after verbs/adjectives, and 地 after adverbials. A rule of the thumb is as follows: 的 appears before nouns, 得 after verbs or adjectives, and 地 before verbs.

attributive	+	的	+	noun (phrase)
v/adj	+	得	+	complement
adverbial	+	地	+	verb (phrase)

a. 的 is used after attributives:

❶
請幫我買點新鮮的青菜水果。
请帮我买点新鲜的青菜水果。
(Please help me buy some fresh vegetables and fruits.)

❷
媽媽給我買的衣服是純棉的。
妈妈给我买的衣服是纯棉的。
(The clothes that my mom bought for me are 100 percent cotton.)

❸
你說的那位教授我不認識。
你说的那位教授我不认识。
(I don't know the professor you are talking about.)

b. 得 is used after verbs and adjectives to link descriptive complements:

❹
教授說我選課選得很好。
教授说我选课选得很好。
(My professor said I chose my classes well.)

❺
今天熱得連我都受不了了。
今天热得连我都受不了了。
(It's so hot today that not even I can stand it.)

❻
孩子們玩電腦玩得忘了吃飯。
孩子们玩电脑玩得忘了吃饭。
(The children had such a good time playing on the computer that they forgot to eat.)

c. 地 (de) is used to link adverbs with verbs:

❼
女兒的病還不好，王太太著急地給醫生打了一個電話。
女儿的病还不好，王太太着急地给医生打了一个电话。
(As her daughter's illness still hadn't gotten better, Mrs. Wang anxiously called the doctor.)

❽　看完電視，爺爺奶奶慢慢地走上樓去休息。
看完电视，爷爷奶奶慢慢地走上楼去休息。
(After watching TV, Grandma and Grandpa slowly walked upstairs to rest.)

---

5. 原來/原来 as Adverb and Adjective

原來/原来 has two meanings:

a. It is used upon the discovery of new information, implying a sudden realization. When used in this way, 原來/原来 is an adverb.

❶　我早就聽說有一個新同屋要來，原來就是你呀。
我早就听说有一个新同屋要来，原来就是你呀。
(I heard that a new roommate was coming. So it was you!)

❷　房間裏熱得很，原來窗戶沒開。
房间里热得很，原来窗户没开。
(The room was really hot. It turned out that the window was not open.)

❸　我覺得好像在哪兒見過你，原來你是我的同學的姐姐。
我觉得好像在哪儿见过你，原来你是我的同学的姐姐。
(I thought that I had seen you somewhere. [I didn't realize that] you're my classmate's older sister.)

b. It can be used as an adjective before a noun as in ❹ and ❺, or an adverb before a verb as in ❻, ❼, and ❽, meaning "in the past, before a change occurred." Note that in the adjectival use, 原來/原来 must be followed by 的.

❹　你還住在原來的宿舍嗎？
你还住在原来的宿舍吗？
(Are you still living in the same dorm where you used to live?)

❺   這棟樓還是原來的樣子，又小又舊。

這栋楼还是原来的样子，又小又旧。

(This building is still the same as it used to be—small and old.)

❻   他原來住在學校的宿舍裏，後來搬到校外去了。

他原来住在学校的宿舍里，后来搬到校外去了。

(He used to live in a dorm on campus, but later he moved off campus.)

❼   她原來吃肉，現在吃起素來了。

她原来吃肉，现在吃起素来了。

(She used to eat meat. Now she's a vegetarian.)

❽   我的同屋原來不喜歡吃菠菜，後來聽説菠菜對身體健康
有好處，就開始吃菠菜了。

我的同屋原来不喜欢吃菠菜，后来听说菠菜对身体健康
有好处，就开始吃菠菜了。

(My roommate didn't used to like spinach. Then he heard that spinach was good for
you. After that he started to eat spinach.)

6. Set Phrases

There are many set expressions in Chinese. Their form is often fixed and they are not meant
to be taken literally. In other words, their overall meaning is not the sum of the individual
words. For this reason, it's best to memorize the whole expression. These set expressions
are typically composed of four characters, and many of them are idioms, e.g., 一乾
二淨/一干二净 or 丢三拉四 from this lesson.

Set phrases function like words, but often in limited grammatical contexts. For instance,
一乾二淨/一干二净 is adjectival, but it's most often used as a complement. For
more examples, see C of Words & Phrases. 丢三拉四, which functions like a verb, can
be used as a predicate, but it can't have objects or complements. For more examples, see
F of the Words & Phrases section.

如果鑰匙丟了，就得找他們幫忙。
如果钥匙丢了，就得找他们帮忙。

Words & Phrases

> ### A. 到底 (what on earth; what in the world; in the end)

The word 到底 is often used in questions to press the other speaker for an answer.

❶ **A:** 你明天去看演唱會嗎？
你明天去看演唱会吗？
(Are you going to the concert tomorrow?)

B: 我想去，可是…
(I'd like to go, but...)

A: 你到底去不去？
(Are you going or not?)

❷   他們倆到底為什麼分手？沒有人知道。

他们俩到底为什么分手？没有人知道。

(What's the real reason those two broke up? No one knows.)

❸   畢業以後到底念研究生還是找工作，我還沒考慮好。

毕业以后到底念研究生还是找工作，我还没考虑好。

(Whether I really should go to graduate school or find a job after graduation, I still haven't thought it through.)

Note the embedded question in this example. The word 到底 implies that the speaker has been questioning himself in order to come to a conclusion.

B. 根本 (at all, simply)

Often used in negative sentences.

❶   老師今天介紹的語法，我根本不懂。

老师今天介绍的语法，我根本不懂。

(I simply don't get the grammar that the teacher introduced today.)

❷   他們倆鬧彆扭的事兒我根本沒聽說，你別問我。

他们俩闹别扭的事儿我根本没听说，你别问我。

(I've heard nothing at all about their falling out. Don't ask me.)

❸   你根本不認識他，怎麼知道他的性格怎麼樣？

你根本不认识他，怎么知道他的性格怎么样？

(You don't know him at all. How could you know what his personality is like?)

C. 一乾二淨/一干二净 (completely, thoroughly, spotless)

This idiom is mostly used after 得 as a complement. It means one of two things:

a) completely; thoroughly, "with nothing remaining," which is the meaning used in this lesson and in ❶ and ❷ below; or b) very clean, as in ❸.

❶ 上個學期學的漢字，他已經忘得一乾二淨了。

上个学期学的汉字，他已经忘得一干二净了。

(He has forgotten every single character that he learned last semester.)

❷ 他請我們去飯館吃飯，我去晚了一點，到那兒的時候，
他們已經把菜吃得一乾二淨了。

他请我们去饭馆吃饭，我去晚了一点，到那儿的时候，
他们已经把菜吃得一干二净了。

(He invited us to dinner. I was a little bit late. When I got there, they had already eaten everything.)

❸ 他把房間打掃得一乾二淨。

他把房间打扫得一干二净。

(He made the room spotless.)

D. 難怪/难怪 (no wonder)

An interjective adverb often used at the beginning of a sentence.

❶ 難怪他不知道這件事，他根本不看報紙！

难怪他不知道这件事，他根本不看报纸！

(No wonder he doesn't know this—he doesn't read newspapers at all.)

❷ 難怪他不申請念研究生，我剛知道他已經找到工作了。

难怪他不申请念研究生，我刚知道他已经找到工作了。

(No wonder he is not applying to graduate school. I just found out that he has already found a job.)

❸ 難怪這兩天他心情不好，原來他女朋友跟他吹了。

难怪这两天他心情不好，原来他女朋友跟他吹了。

(No wonder he's been in a bad mood the last couple of days. As it turns out, his girlfriend broke up with him.)

E. 實際上/实际上 (actually; in fact; in reality)

❶ 很多人以為我同屋比我大，實際上我比她大多了。

很多人以为我同屋比我大，实际上我比她大多了。

(A lot of people think my roommate is older than I am. Actually, I'm much older than she is.)

❷ 我一直以為整天跟數字打交道沒什麼意思，實際上挺好玩兒的。

我一直以为整天跟数字打交道没什么意思，实际上挺好玩儿的。

(I always had a misconception that it was boring to handle numbers and figures all day long. In fact, it's quite fun.)

❸ 小王實際上學分已經夠了，但他還想選兩門電腦課，明年春天再畢業。

小王实际上学分已经够了，但他还想选两门电脑课，明年春天再毕业。

(Little Wang actually has enough credits already, but he wants to take two more courses in computer science. He will graduate next spring.)

F. 丟三拉四 (scatterbrained; forgetful)

This means to be so scatterbrained as to leave things behind; to be careless and absentminded. 拉 can also be written as 落/落. See Language Note 2 in Lesson 1.

❶ 我哥哥經常丟三拉四的，我看有一天會把自己丟了。

我哥哥经常丢三拉四的，我看有一天会把自己丢了。

(My older brother is such a scatterbrain. I wouldn't be surprised if he forgot who he is one day.)

❷   你這麼丟三拉四的，難怪你女朋友老生氣。

你这么丢三拉四的，难怪你女朋友老生气。

(You're so forgetful and absentminded. No wonder your girlfriend is always angry with you.)

G. 一會兒…, 一會兒…, 一會兒又…／一会儿…, 一会儿…, 一会儿又… (one minute…, the next minute…)

Used in this way, 一會兒…, 一會兒…, 一會兒又…／一会儿…, 一会儿…, 一会儿又…suggests two or more alternative actions or states. If it is repeated three times, there needs to be a 又 after the third 一會兒／一会儿. The implication is that someone or something is constantly changing or unpredictable.

❶   小張覺得他哥哥很麻煩，一會兒叫他洗衣服，一會兒叫他出去買東西，一會兒又叫他做飯，小張根本不能做自己的事。

小张觉得他哥哥很麻烦，一会儿叫他洗衣服，一会儿叫他出去买东西，一会儿又叫他做饭，小张根本不能做自己的事。

(Little Zhang finds his older brother is a lot of trouble. One minute he's asking him to do laundry, the next he's asking him to go shopping or to cook. Little Zhang can't get any of his own things done at all.)

❷   你怎麼了？一會兒哭，一會兒笑。

你怎么了？一会儿哭，一会儿笑。

(What's wrong with you? One minute you're crying, the next you're laughing.)

❸   這幾天天氣很奇怪，一會兒很冷，一會兒很熱，不少人都感冒了。

这几天天气很奇怪，一会儿很冷，一会儿很熟，不少人都感冒了。

(The weather has been really strange the last few days. One minute it's very cold, the next it's very hot. Many people have caught cold.)

Language Practice

A. Personality Scale

Let's rate the following characters' personalities with 1 representing the least cheerful (一點也不開朗/一点也不开朗) and 5 the most cheerful (非常開朗/非常开朗).

	1	2	3	4	5
Homer Simpson	1	2	3	4	5
Fred Flintstone	1	2	3	4	5
Ron Weasley	1	2	3	4	5
Hermione Granger	1	2	3	4	5
Batman	1	2	3	4	5
Superman	1	2	3	4	5
You	1	2	3	4	5

Then, based on your ratings, make comparisons among the characters and yourself.

EXAMPLE: Homer Simpson vs. Fred Flintstone

→ Homer的性格沒有Fred那麼開朗。 Homer的性格没有Fred那么开朗。

or

→ Fred的性格比Homer開朗得多。   Fred的性格比Homer开朗得多。

1. Ron Weasley vs. Hermione Granger
2. Batman vs. Superman
3. You vs. Homer Simpson
4. You vs. Ron Weasley
5. You vs. Hermione Granger

Finally, ask your class to vote on who has the most upbeat personality.

_____性格最開朗。   _____性格最开朗。

B. Are They Alike or Not?

With the help of the pictures, discuss with a partner whether the characters share similar interests with each other and with you.

EXAMPLE 1:　

→ 在興趣上，張天明跟柯林　　　在兴趣上，张天明跟柯林
一樣，都喜歡看球賽。　　　一样，都喜欢看球赛。

EXAMPLE 2:

→ 在興趣上，柯林跟李哲不一樣，柯林喜歡看球賽，李哲喜歡看電影。

在兴趣上，柯林跟李哲不一样，柯林喜欢看球赛，李哲喜欢看电影。

1.

2.

3.

4. You

5. You

C. Who's a Space Cadet?

With the help of the pictures, identify who forgot what where.

EXAMPLE:

→ 張天明把電腦拉在出租車上了。　　张天明把电脑拉在出租车上了。

1.

2.

3.

4.

Among your friends and family members, who is often forgetful and/or absentminded?

EXAMPLE: My mother

→ 我媽媽常常忘這忘那、
　 丢三拉四的。要麽/
　 一會兒忘了買鹽，要麽/
　 一會兒把手機忘在車裏。

我妈妈常常忘这忘那、
丢三拉四的。要么/
一会儿忘了买盐，要么/
一会儿把手机忘在车里。

Friend/Family Member #1:
Friend/Family Member #2:
Friend/Family Member #3:

D. An EQ Evaluation

Work with a partner and confess to one another what may make you lose your cool and lower your EQ (emotional intelligence quotient).

a. List things that often put you in a lousy mood.

1. 下雨
2.
3.
4.

Then tell your partner what they are.

EXAMPLE:

→ 下雨會讓我心情不好。　　　　下雨会让我心情不好。

b. List the situations that may make you feel anxious.

1. _____

2. _____

3. _____

Then tell your partner what they are.

…會讓我着急。　　　　　　　…会让我着急。

c. List the situations that may cause you to lose your temper.

1. _____

2. _____

3. _____

Then tell your partner what they are.

…會讓我生氣。　　　　　　　…会让我生气。

E. What's the Matter?

When you sense there's something different or wrong, you can use 怎麼了/怎么了 to find out what's going on. Use the visuals to practice with a partner.

EXAMPLE:

→　**A:** 他怎麼了？　　　　　　**A:** 他怎么了？
　　B: 他發燒了。　　　　　　**B:** 他发烧了。

1.

2.

3.

 4.

 5.

F. Make Up Your Mind!

Little Lin is indecisive about everything. The people around him have gotten impatient and would like to get some answers. One of your classmates will be Little Lin. You and the rest of the class will pretend to be Little Lin's friends and family. Take turns with one another and use the cues to make Little Lin decide.

EXAMPLE: after graduation   find a job   go to graduate school

→ **A:** 小林，你畢業以後做
什麼?

B: 我還沒決定/不知道。
可能找工作，也可能
念研究生。

A: 你畢業以後到底找工作
還是念研究生?

B: _____

A: 小林，你毕业以后做
什么?

B: 我还没决定/不知道。
可能找工作，也可能
念研究生。

A: 你毕业以后到底找工作
还是念研究生?

B: _____

1. tomorrow	wear workout pants	wear jeans
2. next semester	take history	take philosophy
3. next year	live on campus	live off campus
4. after start dating	tell your mother	not tell your mother
5. when shopping	care about the quality	care about the price

G. The Ideal Boyfriend/Girlfriend

Here are some qualities that people look for in a prospective partner. Based on your own opinion, rearrange the list in descending order, with the most important quality on the top. Add other qualities if they are not listed here.

性格很開朗 *outgoing*　　　　性格很开朗
學習很好　　　　　　　　　学习很好
吵架不記仇 *grudge*　　　　吵架不记仇
興趣愛好跟我一樣 *same hobbies*　兴趣爱好跟我一样 —
文化背景跟我一樣 *same cultural background*　文化背景跟我一样
跟我相處得很好 *get along*　跟我相处得很好
很在乎我 *care about me*　　很在乎我 —
做事不馬虎 *not careless*　　做事不马虎

1: _____   6: _____

2: _____   7: _____

3: _____   8: _____

4: _____   9: _____

5: _____   10: _____

After finishing the list, work with a partner and see if your lists are similar. Then, explain to one another what's important to you when dating. Try to include conjunctions or other devices to build a discourse and present your opinions in a coherent and cohesive manner.

H. Deal Breaker

Here are some qualities that could lead to relationship trouble:

性格不開朗	性格不开朗
常常心情不好 *always in bad mood*	常常心情不好
吵架記仇 *hold grudge*	吵架记仇
跟我興趣愛好不同	跟我兴趣爱好不同
跟我文化背景不同	跟我文化背景不同
跟我相處得不好	跟我相处得不好
根本不在乎我 *does not care about me*	根本不在乎我
忘這忘那、丟三拉四 *forgetful*	忘这忘那、丢三拉四
做事非常馬虎 *careless*	做事非常马虎
做錯事不道歉 *does not apologize*	做错事不道歉

Which of them would make your relationship with your girlfriend/boyfriend unbearable and make you call it quits?

_____

You can then say:

如果我的男朋友/女朋友   如果我的男朋友/女朋友

_____   _____

我會跟他/她分手。   我会跟他/她分手。

Go around the class and listen to what your classmates have to say. Tally everyone's answers and see what the top deal breaker is for you and your classmates.

Pinyin Text

Lìshā zhè jǐ tiān hǎoxiàng yǒu shénme❶ xīnshì. Zuótiān Lín Xuěméi wèn le tā hǎo jǐ❷ cì, tā cái shuō tā gēn Zhāng Tiānmíng nào bièniu le.

Xuěméi gāng rènshi Lìshā de shíhou, tīng Lìshā shuō, tā hé Zhāng Tiānmíng zài gāozhōng jiù shì tóngxué. Tiānmíng rén hěn hǎo, xìnggé shífēn kāilǎng, xuéxí yě búcuò. Zài xìngqù shang① tā gēn Tiānmíng bú tài yíyàng, Tiānmíng shì ge qiúmí, diànshì li yì yǒu qiúsài, tā jiù fēi kàn bù kě, Lìshā shì ge gēmí, yì yǒu yǎnchànghuì jiù qù tīng. Lìshā shuō, tāmen de xìngqù àihào suīrán bù tóng❸, dànshì yìzhí xiāngchǔ de hěn hǎo.

Lín Xuěméi xiǎng lái xiǎng qù②, xiǎng bù chū tāmen zhījiān dàodǐ fāshēng le shénme shìr. Shì yīnwèi wénhuà bèijǐng bù tóng ma? Háishi Tiānmíng yǒu le xīn de nǚpéngyou? Zhènghǎo jīntiān wǎnshang yǒu kòng, Xuěméi jiù qù zhǎo Lìshā.

Xuěméi:	Nǐ gēn Tiānmíng zěnme le?
Lìshā:	Āi, bié tí❹ le, tā xīn li gēnběn méiyǒu wǒ.
Xuěméi:	Dàodǐ shì zěnme huí❺ shìr?
Lìshā:	Liǎng ge xīngqī qián wǒ gēn tā yuē hǎo qù kàn yí ge yǎnchànghuì, méi xiǎng dào tā nà tiān wǎnshang yìzhí wánr diànnǎo, bǎ yǎnchànghuì de shìr wàng de yì gān èr jìng. Nǐ shuō wǒ néng bù shēng qì ma?
Xuěméi:	Bié shēng qì le, Kē Lín yě chángcháng zhèyàng, yí kàn qiúsài jiù shénme shìr dōu wàng le.
Lìshā:	Hái yǒu gèng jiào❻ rén shēng qì de ne. Shàng ge xīngqīliù wǒ yào tā péi wǒ qù kàn diànyǐng, tā hěn gāoxìng de③④ dāying le, kěshì bā diǎn de diànyǐng, wǒ děng dào bā diǎn yí kè tā hái méi dào. Dǎ tā shǒujī, cái zhīdao tā pǎo❼ dào lìng yì jiā diànyǐngyuàn qù le. Zhè xiē suīrán dōu shì xiǎo shìr, dànshì jiào wǒ fēicháng shēng qì, juéde tā gēnběn bú zàihu wǒ. Zhēn xiǎng gēn tā chuī le.
Xuěméi:	Ō, yuánlái⑤ shì zhèyàng. Āi, zhè ge Tiānmíng, zěnme zème❽ mǎhu! Nánguài nǐ xīnqíng bù hǎo. Hòulái ne?
Lìshā:	Hòulái tā jiàn dào wǒ, bùtíng de gěi wǒ dào qiàn, shuō duìbuqǐ, tàidù tèbié hǎo. Zhè ràng wǒ juéde tā duì wǒ hái shì zhēnxīn de.
Xuěméi:	Shì a, bié shēng qì le! Mǎhu gēn xīn li méiyǒu nǐ shì liǎng huí shìr. Nǐ tīngshuō guo ma? Zhōngguó yǒu yí jù huà: "Xiǎoliǎngkǒu chǎo jià bú jì

chóu."⑨ Hā hā! Rúguǒ yǒu yì tiān bù chǎo le, shuōbudìng nǐmen jiù zhēn de huì fēn shǒu.

Lìshā: Wǒ kàn nǐ gēn Kē Lín liǎng ge rén tǐng hǎo de, yě bù zěnme chǎo jià.

Xuěméi: Shíjìshang, Kē Lín gēn Tiānmíng chàbuduō, chángcháng wàng zhè wàng nà⑩, diū sān là sì⑥ de. Tā yíhuìr wàng le wǒ de shēngrì, yíhuìr zhǎo bú dào yàoshi, yíhuìr yòu...Yǒude shíhou zhēn ràng rén zháojí.

Lìshā: Shì ma? Yuánlái Kē Lín yě yǒu mǎhu de shíhou. Duì le, nǐ jiāo nánpéngyou de shìr, jiā li zhīdao ma?

Xuěméi: Zhè ge ma...Wǒ hái méi bǎ wǒ gēn Kē Lín de shìr gàosu jiā li ne.

English Text

Something seems to be weighing on Lisa's mind these days. Lin Xuemei asked her about it several times yesterday. Only then did Lisa say that she had had a fight with Zhang Tianming.

When Xuemei first met Lisa, she heard Lisa say that she and Zhang Tianming were classmates in high school. Tianming is a good guy with a very outgoing personality, and he is a good student, too. In terms of interests, she and Tianming are not quite the same. Tianming is a sports fan. Whenever there is a ball game on TV, he has to watch it. Lisa is a fan of pop music. Whenever there is a concert, she will go and listen. Lisa says although they have different interests and hobbies they have always gotten along well.

Lin Xuemei racked her brains, but she still couldn't figure out what had really happened between the two of them. Is it because their cultural backgrounds are different? Or is it because Tianming has a new girlfriend? This evening Lin Xuemei happens to have some free time, so she goes looking for Lisa.

Xuemei: What's with you and Tianming?

Lisa: I don't want to talk about it. I simply don't matter to him.

Xuemei: What's really wrong?

Lisa: Two weeks ago he and I were supposed to go to a concert. Who knew? He spent the night playing on his computer. He completely forgot about the concert. How could I have not gotten upset?

Xuemei: Don't be upset anymore. Ke Lin is often like that, too. Whenever he starts watching a ball game, he forgets about everything else.

Lisa:　There was something even more maddening. Last Saturday I wanted him to go with me to the movies. He happily agreed. The film was at 8:00. I waited till 8:15. He still hadn't arrived. I called his cell phone. Only then did I find out that he had gone to another cinema. These were all small matters, but they made me really upset. I think I really don't matter to him. I wish I could just break up with him.

Xuemei:　Oh, so that's what happened. How could Tianming be such a scatterbrain? No wonder you're not happy. What happened afterwards?

Lisa:　When he saw me later, he kept apologizing to me. He seemed sincerely sorry and made me feel that he genuinely cared about me.

Xuemei:　That's right. Don't be upset any more. Being scatterbrained and not caring about you are two different things. Have you heard that there is a Chinese saying "couples don't hold grudges when they quarrel"? Haha, when you stop fighting, you may well go your separate ways.

Lisa:　You and Ke Lin seem very good together. You don't seem to fight a lot.

Xuemei:　Actually, Ke Lin is not much different from Tianming. He often forgets this or that and always leaves things behind. One minute he forgets my birthday, the next he can't find his keys, or something else… He sometimes really has me worried.

Lisa:　Really? Turns out Ke Lin has his moments of carelessness. Oh yes, does your family know you have a boyfriend?

Xuemei:　No…, I haven't told them yet.

SELF-ASSESSMENT

How well can you do these things? Check (✔) the boxes to evaluate your progress and see which areas you may need to practice more.

I can	Very Well	OK	A Little
Say if I have an upbeat personality	☐	☐	☐
State if I share similar interests with my friends	☐	☐	☐
Show my concern, ask if things are OK, and investigate further if necessary	☐	☐	☐
Describe a person who is absent-minded	☐	☐	☐
Give a simple description of the traits that I look for in a boyfriend/girlfriend	☐	☐	☐
Tell what makes I anxious or angry	☐	☐	☐

第七課
電腦和
網絡

第七课
电脑和
网络

 LEARNING OBJECTIVES

In this lesson, you will learn to use Chinese to

1. Find out if others are angry with you and apologize if so;
2. Reduce potential tension in a conversation by changing the subject;
3. Let people know about the trouble you had to go through because of their thoughtlessness or carelessness;
4. Name your activities on the internet and discuss how you make use of the internet;
5. Discuss the pros and the cons of using the internet.

 RELATE AND GET READY

In your own culture/community—

• Do people have easy access to the internet?
• What consumer habits have changed because of the internet?
• What impact has the internet had on society as a whole?

Before You Study

Check the statements that apply to you.

☐ 1. I cannot function well without my computer.
☐ 2. I spend a lot of time online every day.

When You Study

Listen to the audio recording and scan the text. Ask yourself the following questions before you begin a close reading of the text.

1. What do the four people plan to do on this day?

 張天明是個電腦迷，他的電腦從早到晚都開著。他在網
上看新聞，查資料，玩兒遊戲，有時候還在自己的網站
上寫博客。他說他可以沒有報紙，沒有電話，甚至①沒有
汽車，可是一會兒都❶離不開②電腦。他常常一上網，就

LANGUAGE NOTES

❶ 一會兒都/一会儿都 is similar to 一點兒都/一点儿都 and 一個都/一个都. They are all used in emphatic negative statements, "not for one moment," "not in the least," or "not a single one."

☐ 3. I have my own website or blog.

☐ 4. I get most of the information I use on a daily basis from the internet and not from books, newspapers, or libraries.

☐ 5. The internet makes my life more fun and convenient.

2. Why is Tianming late?

3. Does Tianming think he has a problem?

4. Does Lisa value the internet?

 张天明是个电脑迷，他的电脑从早到晚都开着。他在网上看新闻，查资料，玩儿游戏，有时候还在自己的网站上写博客。他说他可以没有报纸，没有电话，甚至①没有汽车，可是一会儿都❶离不开②电脑。他常常一上网，就忘了時間。昨天，麗莎、柯林、雪梅和他約好③今天一起去唱卡拉OK，時間到了也不見他來，他的手機也沒開，就給他發了一個電子郵件。十分鐘以後④，才看見天明急急忙忙地跑來。

天明：　對不起，對不起，我在網上下載了一個軟件，又查了一點兒東西，結果忘了時間了。

柯林：　查什麼？

天明：　我要寫一篇文章，查一些資料。

雪梅：　查資料？我們教授不讓我們用網上的东西，一定要用正式出版的書或者雜誌。他說網上的垃圾②太多了。

天明：　你的教授太落伍了，網上有很多資料很可靠很有用啊。網絡③世界又大又方便，你可以叫外賣、購物，你可以租房子、買車…，總之，衣食住行，什麼資料都查得到。

麗莎：　對，特別方便。要是想交女朋友，也可以上網找。

天明：　哎，麗莎，你還在生我的氣嗎？

麗莎：　你說我該④不該生氣？你每次都遲到，老是害得大家等你。

天明：　對不起、對不起，是我不好。下次不敢了。

柯林：　天明，你幾乎整天待在屋子⑤裏玩兒電腦，看起來真是玩兒上癮了。

天明：　上癮？沒那麼嚴重吧？現在是網絡時代，當然離不開電腦。

LANGUAGE NOTES

❷ 垃圾 (lājī) is pronounced lèsè in Taiwan.
❸ 網絡／网络 (wǎngluò) is known as 網路 (wǎnglù) in Taiwan.

忘了时间。昨天，丽莎、柯林、雪梅和他约好③今天一起去唱卡拉OK，时间到了也不见他来，他的手机也没开，就给他发了一个电子邮件。十分钟以后④，才看见天明急急忙忙地跑来。

天明：　对不起，对不起，我在网上下载了一个软件，又查了一点儿东西，结果忘了时间了。

柯林：　查什么？

天明：　我要写一篇文章，查一些资料。

雪梅：　查资料？我们教授不让我们用网上的东西，一定要用正式出版的书或者杂志。他说网上的垃圾②太多了。

天明：　你的教授太落伍了，网上有很多资料很可靠很有用啊。网络③世界又大又方便，你可以叫外卖、购物，你可以租房子、买车…，总之，衣食住行，什么资料都查得到。

丽莎：　对，特别方便。要是想交女朋友，也可以上网找。

天明：　哎，丽莎，你还在生我的气吗？

丽莎：　你说我该④不该生气？你每次都迟到，老是害得大家等你。

天明：　对不起、对不起，是我不好。下次不敢了。

柯林：　天明，你几乎整天待在屋子⑤里玩儿电脑，看起来真是玩儿上瘾了。

天明：　上瘾？没那么严重吧？现在是网络时代，当然离不开电脑。

---

❹ 該/该 is short for 應該/应该.
❺ 屋子 is more colloquial than 房間/房间.

麗莎： 我知道電腦和網絡在我們的生活中越來越重要，我也用電腦幫助❻我做翻譯練習，也上網比較價格❼，可是不像你，常常忘了時間，忘了朋友。

雪梅： 天明，聽麗莎說你不喜歡打電話，只喜歡發電郵。

柯林： 因為發電郵不花錢又省時間。

天明： 沒錯！免費，又快又方便。

雪梅： 可是有的時候，發電郵不如打電話感覺好。

柯林： 雪梅喜歡"電聊"❽。

麗莎： "電聊"？什麼是"電聊"？

柯林： 就是打"電"話"聊"天兒。懂了吧? 一直聊、不停地聊、從早到晚地聊…

你可以在這個地方做什麼?
你可以在这个地方做什么?

LANGUAGE NOTES

❻ Take care to distinguish among 幫/帮, 幫助/帮助, and 幫忙/帮忙. While they are synonymous with one another, they differ in usage. 幫忙/帮忙 is a VO compound. To help me out or give me a hand is 幫我的忙/帮我的忙. 幫忙/帮忙 cannot take another object: *幫忙我/帮忙我. 幫助/帮助 is a transitive verb, e.g., 幫助他學漢語/帮助他学汉语. The main difference between 幫/帮 and 幫助/帮助 is stylistic. 幫助/帮助 (lit. to aid and assist) is more formal than 幫/帮.

丽莎: 我知道电脑和网络在我们的生活中越来越重要，我也用电脑帮助❻我做翻译练习，也上网比较价格❼，可是不像你，常常忘了时间，忘了朋友。

雪梅: 天明，听丽莎说你不喜欢打电话，只喜欢发电邮。

柯林: 因为发电邮不花钱又省时间。

天明: 没错! 免费，又快又方便。

雪梅: 可是有的时候，发电邮不如打电话感觉好。

柯林: 雪梅喜欢"电聊"❽。

丽莎: "电聊"? 什么是"电聊"?

柯林: 就是打"电"话"聊"天儿。懂了吧? 一直聊、不停地聊、从早到晚地聊…

---

❼ 價格/价格 and 價錢/价钱 are similar in meaning. 價錢/价钱 is colloquial. In formal writing, 價格/价格 is used instead.

❽ 電聊/电聊 (to chat on the phone) is a facetious pun because it sounds the same as 電療/电疗 (diànliáo, electrotherapy).

雪梅： 怎麼？聽起來好像你不愛跟我聊天兒。

柯林： 不、不、不，我不是那個意思❾，我是開玩笑。我當然愛跟你聊天兒。好了，好了，不說這些了，咱們到底去哪家卡拉OK啊？

天明： 我上網查了，東邊兒那家不錯，那兒的歌都是麗莎喜歡的。你們看，我沒忘了朋友吧？

After You Study

Challenge yourself to complete the following tasks in Chinese.

1. List the things that Tianming can live without.
2. List what Tianming does or may do online.

LANGUAGE NOTES

❾ 我不是那個意思／我不是那个意思: "That's not what I mean" or "I don't mean what you think." This is something you say to dispel a misunderstanding.

雪梅：怎么？听起来好像你不爱跟我聊天儿。

柯林：不、不、不，我不是那个意思❾，我是开玩笑。我当然爱跟你聊天儿。好了，好了，不说这些了，咱们到底去哪家卡拉OK啊？

天明：我上网查了，东边儿那家不错，那儿的歌都是丽莎喜欢的。你们看，我没忘了朋友吧？

3. Describe how Lisa uses the internet.
4. List the reasons that Ke Lin prefers e-mail to phone calls.
5. List the reasons that Xuemei prefers phone calls to e-mail.

VOCABULARY

1.	網絡	网络	wǎngluò	n	network; internet
2.	新聞	新闻	xīnwén	n	news
3.	資料	资料	zīliào	n	material
4.	遊戲	游戏	yóuxì	n	game
5.	網站	网站	wǎngzhàn	n	website
6.	博客		bókè	n	blog
7.	甚至		shènzhì	adv	even [See Grammar 1.]
8.	卡拉OK		kǎlā-OK (ōukēi)	n	karaoke
9.	急忙		jímáng	adv	hastily; in a hurry
10.	下載	下载	xiàzài	v	to download
11.	軟件	软件	ruǎnjiàn	n	software
12.	結果	结果	jiéguǒ	conj/n	as a result; result
13.	正式		zhèngshì	adj	formal
14.	出版		chūbǎn	v	to publish
15.	雜誌	杂志	zázhì	n	magazine
16.	垃圾		lājī	n	garbage; trash
17.	落伍	落伍	luòwǔ	v	to lag behind; to be outdated
18.	可靠		kěkào	adj	dependable
19.	有用		yǒuyòng	adj	useful
20.	外賣	外卖	wàimài	n	takeout
21.	總之	总之	zǒngzhī	conj	in short; in brief

一般垃圾筒

請勿投入有回收標誌
之物品或容器

22.	衣食住行		yī shí zhù xíng		food, clothing, shelter and transportation; basic necessities of life
23.	遲到	迟到	chídào	v	to arrive late
24.	老是		lǎoshì	adv	always
25.	害		hài	v	to cause trouble; to do harm to
26.	敢		gǎn	mv	to dare
27.	幾乎	几乎	jīhū	adv	almost
28.	待		dāi	v	to stay
29.	屋子		wūzi	n	room
30.	上癮	上瘾	shàng yǐn	vo	to become addicted
31.	嚴重	严重	yánzhòng	adj	serious; grave
32.	時代	时代	shídài	n	era; age
33.	重要		zhòngyào	adj	important
34.	幫助	帮助	bāngzhù	v	to help
35.	翻譯	翻译	fānyì	v/n	to translate; interpreter; translation
36.	價格	价格	jiàgé	n	price
37.	免費	免费	miǎnfèi	v	to be free of charge
38.	感覺	感觉	gǎnjué	n/v	feeling; sense perception; to feel; to perceive
39.	開玩笑	开玩笑	kāi wánxiào	vo	to crack a joke; to joke around

免費上網
Free Internet Access
本設施
The
by

Enlarged Characters

戲	載	雜	遲	癮	嚴	譯
戏	载	杂	迟	瘾	严	译

Culture Highlights

1 New telecommunication technologies have given rise to many trendy new words. One example is 網聯/网联 (wǎnglián, internet link). If a banquet table is too big for the people sitting around it to clink glasses, the guests can propose to 網聯/网联 and tap their glasses lightly on the Lazy Susan in the middle of the table. One term that is sure to become part of the standard vocabulary is 博客 (bókè), a semi-transliteration of "blog." In Taiwan, blogs are called 部落格/部落格 (bùluògé), a semi-facetious transliteration of "blog." 部落/部落 means "tribe."

Another fad among young internet users is to appropriate and deliberately misuse very obscure characters. An example is 冏 (jiǒng), as in 今天考得很糟糕, 真冏 (I messed up today's exam. I'm really down.) The appeal of the character is not difficult to see. The combination of 八 on top of 口 seems a graphic depiction of a sad face with downcast eyebrows over the mouth—although the character is actually a variant of 炯 meaning "bright" or "brilliant." It sounds like 窘 meaning "embarrassing" or "awkward"; hence the usage.

2 Instant messaging is very popular in China. The dominant software is called QQ; it allows people to chat online in real time. What has turned it into a phenomenal success is the abundance of peripheral products such as QQ games, QQ music, and QQ (virtual) pets. Chinese people tend to prefer to text message rather than email one another.

Grammar

1. Conjunction 甚至

The conjunction 甚至 is used to single out an item for emphasis in order to stress the speaker's point of view:

❶   弟弟很聰明，才五歲，不但能看英文書，甚至能看
中文書。

弟弟很聪明，才五岁，不但能看英文书，甚至能看
中文书。

(My younger brother is really bright. He's only five, but he can read English books and even Chinese books.)

["Reading Chinese" shows how smart the speaker's younger brother is.]

❷   他很會做中國菜，甚至連清蒸魚都會做。

他很会做中国菜，甚至连清蒸鱼都会做。

(He's good at cooking Chinese food. He even knows how to cook steamed fish.)

["Making steamed fish" shows that he really knows how to make Chinese food.]

❸   他對中國的城市一点都不清楚，甚至連上海都沒聽
說過。

他对中国的城市一点都不清楚，甚至连上海都没听
说过。

(He doesn't know anything about Chinese cities. He hasn't even heard of Shanghai.)

[His ignorance of "Shanghai" shows how little he knows about Chinese cities.]

甚至 is often used together with 連/连···都··· or 連/连···也··· as seen in **❷** and **❸**.

2. Potential Complements

There are two kinds of potential complements.

A. verb + 得/不 + resultative complement/directional complement

❶   我一會兒都離不開電腦。

我一会儿都离不开电脑。

(I can't tear myself away from my computer even for a moment.)

❷   我的中文水平不高，看不懂中文雜誌。

我的中文水平不高，看不懂中文杂志。

(My Chinese is not good enough for reading Chinese magazines).

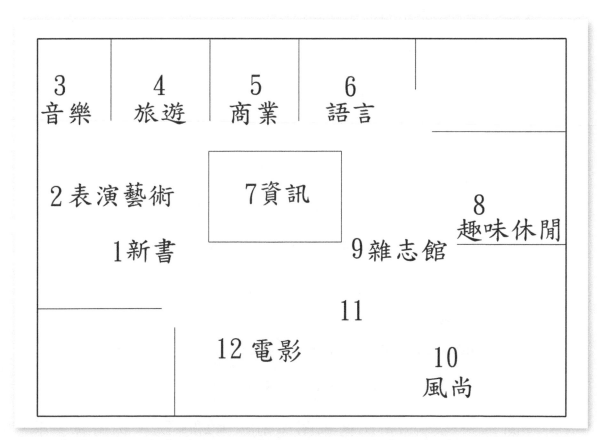

This is the floor plan of a bookstore. In which areas can you find new books, magazines, music, etc?

❸   房間的門太小，這張床搬不進去。

房间的门太小，这张床搬不进去。

(The door of this room is too small to fit the bed through it.)

❹   我的公寓很小，住不下兩個人。

我的公寓很小，住不下两个人。

(My apartment is too small for two people.)

This kind of potential complement expresses inability to realize a certain result due to subjective conditions, as in **❷**, "My Chinese is not good enough for reading Chinese magazines," or external circumstances, as in **❹**, "My apartment is too small for two people."

It should be noted that the negative form of potential complements cannot be replaced by 不能. Therefore, the following sentences are all incorrect:

(2a) *我的中文水平不高，不能看懂中文雜誌。

*我的中文水平不高，不能看懂中文杂志。

(3a) *房間的門太小，這張床不能搬進去。

*房间的门太小，这张床不能搬进去。

(4a) *我的公寓很小，不能住下兩個人。

*我的公寓很小，不能住下两个人。

Changing the potential complement to 不能 entails a change in meaning:

❺   我一會兒都離不開電腦。

我一会儿都离不开电脑。

(I can't tear myself away from my computer, not even for a moment.)

The inability has to do with the speaker. Compare:

(5a) 我一會兒都不能離開電腦，離開了，電腦會出問題。

我一会儿都不能离开电脑，离开了，电脑会出问题。

(I can't leave the computer even for a moment. If I do, something will go wrong with the computer.)

[Because of problems with the computer, I shouldn't be away from it.]

Note that the affirmative form of potential complements, however, can be replaced with "能 + verb + directional complement/resultative complement" as seen in (6a). One can even put 能 in front of the complement as seen in (6b).

❻ A: 你聽得懂老師說的話嗎？

你听得懂老师说的话吗？

(Can you understand what the teacher says?)

or

(6a) 你能聽懂老師說的話嗎？

你能听懂老师说的话吗？

(6b) 你能聽得懂老師說的話嗎？

你能听得懂老师说的话吗？

B: 我聽得懂。

我听得懂。

(Yes, I do.)

When both the affirmative and negative forms of potential complements are used to form a question, one can also use affirmative potential complements to reply; see (6c).

(6c) A: 你聽得懂聽不懂老師說的話？

你听得懂听不懂老师说的话？

B: 我聽得懂。

我听得懂。

In affirmative statements "能 + verb + complement" is much more common than "verb + 得 + complement." For instance, people say:

❼ 冬天你能看見很多爸爸媽媽帶著孩子去滑冰。

冬天你能看见很多爸爸妈妈带着孩子去滑冰。

(In winter, you can see many parents taking their children to go ice skating.)

Rather than:

(7a) 冬天你看得見很多爸爸媽媽帶著孩子去滑冰。

冬天你看得见很多爸爸妈妈带着孩子去滑冰。

B. verb + 得/不 + 了 (liǎo)

This kind of potential complement indicates whether subjective or objective conditions permit the realization of a certain action. It also often appears in negative form as seen in ❶ and ❷.

❶   我明天晚上有課，那個演唱會我去不了了。

我明天晚上有课，那个演唱会我去不了了。

(I have a class tomorrow evening. I won't be able to go to the concert.)

❷   那棟樓沒有水電，住不了人。

那栋楼没有水电，住不了人。

(That building doesn't have water or electricity. It's uninhabitable.)

This kind of potential complement is interchangeable with "(不) 能 + verb."

(1a) 我明天晚上有課，那個演唱會我不能去了。

我明天晚上有课，那个演唱会我不能去了。

(I have a class tomorrow evening. I won't be able to go to the concert.)

(2a) 那個樓沒有水電，不能住人。

那栋楼没有水电，不能住人。

(That building doesn't have water or electricity. It's not habitable.)

In questions, either the affirmative or the negative form can be used as seen in (3a), (3b), and (3c). However, when using the negative form in a question, as seen in (3b), the person who asks the question already assumes the negative outcome.

(3a) 那個演唱會你去得了嗎？

那个演唱会你去得了吗？

(Can you go to that concert?)

(3b) 那個演唱會你去不了嗎？

那个演唱会你去不了吗？

(You can't go to that concert anymore?)

(3c) 那個演唱會你去得了去不了？

那个演唱会你去得了去不了？

(Can you go to that concert or not?)

---

3. 好 as a Resultative Complement

好 as a resultative complement indicates bringing an action to completion and being ready for the next action:

❶ 飯做好了，快來吃吧！

饭做好了，快来吃吧！

(The food is ready. Hurry! Let's eat!)

❷ 明天的考試，我準備好了，可以睡覺了。

明天的考试，我准备好了，可以睡觉了。

(I am ready for tomorrow's test. I can go to bed [now].)

❸ 傢具買好了，明天就會送到新家去了。

家具买好了，明天就会送到新家去了。

(The furniture has been purchased. It'll be delivered to the new house tomorrow.)

❹ 你畢業以後是念研究生還是工作，考慮好了嗎？

你毕业以后是念研究生还是工作，考虑好了吗？

(Are you going to graduate school or looking for a job after you graduate? Have you thought it through?)

❺   昨天，麗莎、柯林和雪梅和他約好今天一起唱卡拉
OK，時間到了也不見他來。
昨天，丽莎、柯林和雪梅和他约好今天一起唱卡拉
OK，时间到了也不见他来。
(Yesterday Lisa, Ke Lin, and Xuemei made a date with him to go sing karaoke today,
but he didn't show up on time.)
[The fact that they had an agreement made his failure to show up all the more
unexpected.]

When 好 is used as a complement, it can also mean "well":

❻   (對客人): 你們在我家要吃好、玩兒好！
(对客人): 你们在我家要吃好、玩儿好！
([To guests]: You must eat well and have a good time in my house!)

❼   樓上太吵，我沒睡好。
楼上太吵，我没睡好。
(It was too noisy upstairs. I didn't sleep well.)

可以在這兒一邊吃飯，一邊唱卡拉OK。
可以在这儿一边吃饭，一边唱卡拉OK。

4. Connecting Sentences (II)

In narrative sentences time words can not only express the time of an action but can also serve as linking devices, as in this lesson:

❶ 昨天，麗莎、柯林、雪梅和他約好今天一起去唱卡拉OK，時間到了也不見他來，他的手機也沒開，就給他發了一個電子郵件。十分鐘以後，(他們)才看見天明急急忙忙地跑來。

昨天，丽莎、柯林、雪梅和他约好今天一起去唱卡拉OK，时间到了也不见他来，他的手机也没开，就给他发了一个电子邮件。十分钟以后，(他们)才看见天明急急忙忙地跑来。

(Yesterday Lisa, Ke Lin, Xuemei, and he agreed to sing karaoke today. At the appointed time he didn't show up. His cellphone wasn't turned on, so they sent him an email. Ten minutes later, [they] saw Tianming running towards them.)

Here is another example from Lesson Five:

❷ (張天明)後天要去見指導教授，討論選課的事，他想先找別的同學聊聊。這一天下午，他在籃球場上正好碰見大四的李哲，就一邊和李哲打球，一邊聊了起來。

(張天明)后天要去见指导教授，讨论选课的事，他想先找别的同学聊聊。这一天下午，他在篮球场上正好碰见大四的李哲，就一边和李哲打球，一边聊了起来。

([Zhang Tianming] has to see his advisor the day after tomorrow to discuss his course selections. He wants to talk with his schoolmates [about this]. One afternoon he happens to run into Li Zhe, a senior, on the basketball court, so he starts to play basketball and chat with him.)

In the above two sentences both 十分鐘以後/十分钟以后 and 這一天下午/这一天下午 have a linking function. Without these two time expressions the sentences would not be cohesive. Putting the time expressions after the subjects would make the sentences less cohesive as seen in (1a) and (2a):

(1a) 昨天，麗莎、柯林、雪梅和他約好今天一起去唱卡拉OK，時間到了也不見他來，他的手機也沒開，就給他發了一個電子郵件。他們十分鐘以後，才看見天明急急忙忙地跑來。

昨天，丽莎、柯林、雪梅和他约好今天一起去唱卡拉OK，时间到了也不见他来，他的手机也没开，就给他发了一个电子邮件。他们十分钟以后，才看见天明急急忙忙地跑来。

(2a) (張天明)後天要去見指導教授，討論選課的事，他想先找別的同學聊聊。他這一天下午，在籃球場上正好碰見大四的李哲，就一邊和李哲打球，一邊聊了起來。

(张天明)后天要去见指导教授，讨论选课的事，他想先找别的同学聊聊。他这一天下午，在篮球场上正好碰见大四的李哲，就一边和李哲打球，一边聊了起来。

Place expressions can also be cohesive devices:

❸ 我昨天去購物中心買東西，在那兒看見了我好久不見的兩個老同學。

我昨天去购物中心买东西，在那儿看见了我好久不见的两个老同学。

(I went to the shopping center yesterday to do some shopping. There I saw two old classmates whom I hadn't seen for a long time.)

❹ 開學前我坐飛機來學校，在飛機上我看了一個很有意思的電影。

开学前我坐飞机来学校，在飞机上我看了一个很有意思的电影。

(Before classes started, I flew to school. On the plane I saw a very interesting film.)

Without the two place expressions, the above two sentences would not be cohesive. Furthermore, to serve as linking devices the expressions must be placed at the beginning of a sentence. Otherwise they wouldn't serve the cohesive purpose, as seen in (3a) and (4a):

(3a) 我昨天去購物中心買東西。我在那兒看見了我好久不見的兩個老同學。

我昨天去购物中心买东西。我在那儿看见了我好久不见的两个老同学。

(4a) 開學前我坐飛機來學校。我在飛機上看了一個很有意思的電影。

开学前我坐飞机来学校。我在飞机上看了一个很有意思的电影。

If a noun or pronoun serves such a purpose, it must also be placed at the beginning of a sentence:

❺ 我一叫他，他馬上就來了。

我一叫他，他马上就来了。

(The minute I asked him, he came.)

❻ 他去年去了中國三個月，我今年要去中國半年。

他去年去了中国三个月，我今年要去中国半年。

(He went to China last year for three months. I'm going to China this year for half a year.)

Words & Phrases

A. 從⋯到⋯/从⋯到⋯ (from...to...)

For example: 從早到晚/从早到晚 (from morning till night), 從易到難/从易到难 (from easy to difficult), 從小到大/从小到大 (from childhood to adulthood), 從我家到你家/从我家到你家 (from my house to yours).

❶ 他明年暑假要到中國去實習，所以從早到晚都在學習
中文。

他明年暑假要到中国去实习，所以从早到晚都在学习
中文。

(He's going to intern in China next summer. That's why he's been studying Chinese from morning till night.)

❷ 學電腦要從易到難，慢慢兒來。

学电脑要从易到难，慢慢儿来。

(When it comes to learning how to use a computer, you have to go from easy to difficult, and take it slowly.)

❸ 他妹妹從小到大都不喜歡穿牛仔褲。

他妹妹从小到大都不喜欢穿牛仔裤。

(Since she was little, his younger sister has never liked wearing jeans.)

❹ 從你家到我家很遠，坐地鐵得四十分鐘。

从你家到我家很远，坐地铁得四十分钟。

(The distance from your house to mine is far. It takes forty minutes by subway.)

B. 結果/结果 (as a result)

結果/结果 is a conjunction. Used in the second clause of a compound sentence, 結果/结果 expresses a result of the condition indicated in the first clause:

❶ 上高中的時候，他一天到晚踢球，不學習，結果高中念
了五年才畢業。

上高中的时候，他一天到晚踢球，不学习，结果高中念
了五年才毕业。

(When he was in high school, he spent all his time playing soccer and didn't study. As a result, it took him five years to graduate from high school.)

❷ 他常常麻煩別人，可是一點也不願意幫助別人，結果一個朋友也没有。

他常常麻烦别人，可是一点也不愿意帮助别人，结果一个朋友也没有。

(He often asks people for favors, but won't help others at all. As a result, he doesn't have a single friend.)

❸ 他原來聽力不好，後來每天聽錄音，結果聽力比我們都好。

他原来听力不好，后来每天听录音，结果听力比我们都好。

(Originally, his listening comprehension wasn't very good, so he started listening to audio recordings every day. As a result, his listening comprehension is better than any of ours.)

C. 或者 (or)

或者 is used in non-interrogative sentences:

❶ A: 你平常週末做什麼？

你平常周末做什么？

(What do you usually do on weekends?)

B: 找朋友聊天兒或者寫博客。

找朋友聊天儿或者写博客。

(Shoot the breeze with my friends or blog.)

❷ 張老師叫你們去一個人，你或者你的同屋都可以。

张老师叫你们去一个人，你或者你的同屋都可以。

(Teacher Zhang asked one of you to go, either you or your roommate.)

❸ 你或者住學校，或者在校外租房子，都可以。

你或者住学校，或者在校外租房子，都可以。

(You can live on campus or rent housing off campus. Either is fine.)

In questions, use 還是/还是 instead.

4 **A:** 你畢業以後準備念研究生還是找工作？

你毕业以后准备念研究生还是找工作？

(After you graduate, are you going to graduate school or looking for a job?)

B: 我打算工作賺錢。

我打算工作赚钱。

(I plan to work and make some money.)

5 你上網還是去商店購物？

你上网还是去商店购物？

(Do you shop online or in stores?)

D. 害(得) (to cause trouble [so that]; to do harm [so that])

This verb means to make someone suffer or adversely affect someone.

1 你昨天晚上沒回來，害(得)我等了你一夜。

你昨天晚上没回来，害(得)我等了你一夜。

(You didn't come back last night. You made me wait for you all night.)

2 女朋友一個星期沒給他打電話，害(得)他吃不下飯，
睡不好覺。

女朋友一个星期没给他打电话，害(得)他吃不下饭，
睡不好觉。

(His girlfriend hasn't called him in a week. He hasn't been able to eat or sleep as a result.)

3 弟弟把我的手機拿走了，沒告訴我，害(得)我找了
半天。

弟弟把我的手机拿走了，没告诉我，害(得)我找了
半天。

(My younger brother took my cell phone and didn't tell me. As a result, I looked for it [in vain] for a long time.)

E. 幾乎/几乎 (almost)

幾乎/几乎 is an adverb. It can be interchanged with the adverbial 差不多, but is more formal than 差不多.

❶   他是個足球迷，幾乎每個週末都去看足球賽。

他是个足球迷，几乎每个周末都去看足球赛。

(He is a soccer fan. Almost every weekend he goes to watch a soccer game.)

❷   我這個學期很忙，幾乎一個月沒給媽媽發電郵了。

我这个学期很忙，几乎一个月没给妈妈发电邮了。

(I'm very busy this semester. I haven't e-mailed my mom in almost a month.)

❸   他玩兒電腦玩兒上癮了，幾乎從早到晚都在網上。

他玩儿电脑玩儿上瘾了，几乎从早到晚都在网上。

(He's addicted to the computer. Every day, he's online practically day and night.)

F. 看起來/看起来 (it seems)

This expression can be used before or after the subject.

❶   李阿姨這幾天常常哭，看起來心情很不好，她到底怎麼了？

李阿姨这几天常常哭，看起来心情很不好，她到底怎么了？

(Auntie Li has been crying a lot in the last few days. It seems she's in a bad mood. What's going on with her?)

❷   天氣不太好，很快就會下雨，(咱們)看起來(咱們)不能去公園打球了。

天气不太好，很快就会下雨，(咱们)看起来(咱们)不能去公园打球了。

(The weather isn't very good. It'll rain soon. It doesn't look like we'll be able to play ball in the park anymore.)

❸   老師： 你念課文念得很糟糕，看起來昨天沒有準備。
　　　　老师： 你念课文念得很糟糕，看起来昨天没有准备。
(Teacher: You didn't read the text aloud very well. It seems like you didn't prepare yesterday.)

　　　　學生： 對不起，老師，我下次一定好好兒準備。
　　　　学生： 对不起，老师，我下次一定好好儿准备。
(Student: I'm sorry, teacher. I'll definitely be well prepared next time.)

G. 聽起來/听起来 (it sounds)

聽起來/听起来 means "it sounds like." What follows is the speaker's interpretation or conclusion based on what he or she has heard.

❶   麗莎給天明打電話：天明，你怎麼還不來？音樂會快開
　　　　始了。
　　　　丽莎给天明打电话：天明，你怎么还不来？音乐会快开
　　　　始了。
(Lisa telephones Tianming: Tianming, how come you're still not here? The concert is about to start.)

　　　　天明： 哎，麗莎，我文章還沒寫完，網上的資料特別
　　　　　　　　　多，我還…
　　　　天明： 哎，丽莎，我文章还没写完，网上的资料特别
　　　　　　　　　多，我还…
(Tianming: Gosh, Lisa, I still haven't finished my paper. There is so much information on the internet. I still…)

　　　　麗莎： 聽起來你不想來了？
　　　　丽莎： 听起来你不想来了？
(Lisa: Sounds like you don't want to come anymore.)

　　　　天明： …
(Tianming: …)

麗莎：　算了吧！我自己去。

丽莎：　算了吧！我自己去。

(Lisa: Forget it. I'll go by myself.)

❷ **A:** 我找了一個公寓，離學校很近，房間很大，房租也
不貴。

我找了一个公寓，离学校很近，房间很大，房租也
不贵。

(I found an apartment that is close to campus. The rooms are very big, and the rent is
not expensive.)

B: 聽起來挺不錯的，你就租吧。

听起来挺不错的，你就租吧。

(Sounds great. Why don't you rent it?)

❸ 今天電視裏有一個賣電腦的廣告，聽起來又便宜又好，
我真想訂購一台。

今天电视里有一个卖电脑的广告，听起来又便宜又好，
我真想订购一台。

(There was a computer commercial on TV today. It sounded very inexpensive and very
good. I really wanted to order one.)

Language Practice

A. What Do You Do Online?

Make a list of that you do online, e.g. blogging, playing games, researching, downloading software,
chatting with friends, etc. Order them in the frequency that you do each activity, with #1 as the most
frequent. Then, list the things you never do online. Compare your two lists with a partner's lists, and see
how similar or different your lists are. Finally, report back to the class on the similarities and/or differences
between your lists.

我常常上網/上网⋯

1.＿＿＿＿＿＿＿＿＿＿＿＿

2.＿＿＿＿＿＿＿＿＿＿＿＿

3.＿＿＿＿＿＿＿＿＿＿＿＿

4.＿＿＿＿＿＿＿＿＿＿＿＿

5.＿＿＿＿＿＿＿＿＿＿＿＿

6.＿＿＿＿＿＿＿＿＿＿＿＿

7.＿＿＿＿＿＿＿＿＿＿＿＿

⋯

我不上網/上网⋯

1.＿＿＿＿＿＿＿＿＿＿＿＿

2.＿＿＿＿＿＿＿＿＿＿＿＿

3.＿＿＿＿＿＿＿＿＿＿＿＿

4.＿＿＿＿＿＿＿＿＿＿＿＿

5.＿＿＿＿＿＿＿＿＿＿＿＿

⋯

(Classmate's name) 跟我一樣，
都常常上網＿＿＿＿＿＿
or
(Classmate's name) 跟我一樣，
都不上網＿＿＿＿＿＿

(Classmate's name) 跟我一样，
都常常上网＿＿＿＿＿＿

(Classmate's name) 跟我一样，
都不上网＿＿＿＿＿＿

B. I Can't Live Without…

Ask yourself if there's any gadget, such as a computer, a cell phone, an MP3 player, a video game system, etc., that you cannot live without. Tell the class about your necessary gadgets using appropriate verbs and nouns.

EXAMPLE:

張天明每天都得上網，
他的生活離不開網絡。

张天明每天都得上网，
他的生活离不开网络。

You

我每天都得＿＿＿＿＿＿＿，
我的生活離不開＿＿＿＿＿。
…

我每天都得＿＿＿＿＿＿＿，
我的生活离不开＿＿＿＿＿。
…

After listening to everyone's confessions, see if there is a most prized possession shared by a majority of the people in your class: ＿＿＿＿＿＿＿＿＿＿.

C. Pros and Cons of the Internet

Tell a partner what positive and/or negative impact the internet has had on your daily life.

Pros	Cons
＿＿＿＿＿＿＿＿＿	＿＿＿＿＿＿＿＿＿
＿＿＿＿＿＿＿＿＿	＿＿＿＿＿＿＿＿＿
＿＿＿＿＿＿＿＿＿	＿＿＿＿＿＿＿＿＿
＿＿＿＿＿＿＿＿＿	＿＿＿＿＿＿＿＿＿

Poll your classmates and see what good and bad effects the internet has had on their lives; then see if everyone agrees.

D. Do You Have a High EQ?

Work with a partner and see if you can raise your EQ by expressing the following in Chinese:

1. It sounds like you're mad. What's the matter? _____

2. It seems that you're not pleased. What's going on? _____

3. Sorry! I've made you mad. _____

4. I am sorry. Are you angry with me? _____

5. Don't be angry. I was joking. _____

6. I didn't mean it. Please don't be mad at me. _____

7. Don't be mad. I apologize (to you). _____

8. How could I be so careless? I apologize (to you). _____

9. I am so sorry. It's all my fault. _____

10. It's my fault. I will not (dare to) do it again. _____

E. Let's Change the Subject

We've all had moments when we wish we could change the subject quickly or wrap up an awkward conversation. Depending on the situation, some of the most useful lines to use are:

1. 好了，好了，不說了⋯
2. 行、行、行，咱們不說這些了⋯
3. 行了，行了，我不跟你吵了⋯

1. 好了，好了，不说了⋯
2. 行、行、行，咱们不说这些了⋯
3. 行了，行了，我不跟你吵了⋯

Work with a partner to compose a conversation with

a. two people discussing/arguing about a matter for a while and then

b. with one person changing the subject or wrapping up the conversation using one of the three lines listed above.

_____

_____

_____

_____

_____

Act out the conversation you have composed, and ask your instructor and classmates to judge whether the lines are used appropriately.

F. Time to Vent!

Sometimes we just have to complain about the grief or trouble that we have endured. Here is one way to do it in Chinese. Let's practice with the help of the pictures.

EXAMPLE:

→ 空調開得太冷，害得我感冒了。　　空调开得太冷，害得我感冒了。

1.

2.

3.

4.

5.

G. What Happened? Please Tell.

Based on the following sentences, give a narration of what happened to Little Lin yesterday. Don't forget to include who, where, and when. Connect your sentences using time phrases, place expressions and pronouns.

1. 小林昨天早上八點起床。	1. 小林昨天早上八点起床。
2. 小林八點半去教室上課。	2. 小林八点半去教室上课。
3. 小林在教室裏看見同學們都在看電影，沒上課，不知道為什麼。	3. 小林在教室里看见同学们都在看电影，没上课，不知道为什么。
4. 小林過了一會兒，才想起來，老師叫大家今天八點來看電影。	4. 小林过了一会儿，才想起来，老师叫大家今天八点来看电影。
5. 馬上小林給老師道歉説："對不起，老師，我來晚了。"	5. 马上小林给老师道歉说："对不起，老师，我来晚了。"
→	→

小林昨天早上八點起
床，＿＿＿＿＿去教室
上課，＿＿＿＿＿看見
同學們都在看電影，沒
上課，不知道為什麼。
＿＿＿＿＿才想起來，
老師叫大家今天八點來
看電影。＿＿＿＿＿
給老師道歉說："對
不起，老師，我來晚
了。"

小林昨天早上八点起
床，＿＿＿＿＿去教室
上课，＿＿＿＿＿看见
同学们都在看电影，没
上课，不知道为什么。
＿＿＿＿＿才想起来，
老师叫大家今天八点来
看电影。＿＿＿＿＿
给老师道歉说："对
不起，老师，我来晚
了。"

Pinyin Text

Zhāng Tiānmíng shì ge diànnǎomí, tā de diànnǎo cóng zǎo dào wǎn dōu kāi zhe. Tā zài wǎng shang kàn xīnwén, chá zīliào, wánr yóuxì, yǒu shíhou hái zài zìjǐ de wǎngzhàn shang xiě bókè. Tā shuō tā kěyǐ méiyǒu bàozhǐ, méiyǒu diànhuà, shènzhì① méiyǒu qìchē, kěshì yíhuìr dōu❶ lí bù kāi② diànnǎo. Tā chángcháng yí shàng wǎng, jiù wàng le shíjiān. Zuótiān, Lìshā, Kē Lín, Xuěméi hé tā yuē hǎo③ jīntiān yìqǐ qù chàng kǎlā-ōukēi, shíjiān dào le yě bú jiàn tā lái, tā de shǒujī yě méi kāi, jiù gěi tā fā le yí ge diànzi yóujiàn. Shí fēnzhōng yǐhòu④, cái kàn jiàn Tiānmíng jí jí máng máng de pǎo lai.

Tiānmíng: Duìbuqǐ, duìbuqǐ, wǒ zài wǎng shang xiàzài le yí ge ruǎnjiàn, yòu chá le yì diǎnr dōngxi, jiéguǒ wàng le shíjiān le.

Kē Lín: Chá shénme?

Tiānmíng: Wǒ yào xiě yì piān wénzhāng, chá yì xiē zīliào.

Xuěméi: Chá zīliào? Wǒmen de jiàoshòu bú ràng wǒmen yòng wǎng shang de dōngxi, yídìng yào yòng zhèngshì chūbǎn de shū huòzhě zázhì. Tā shuō wǎng shang de lājī❷ tài duō le.

Tiānmíng: Nǐ de jiàoshòu tài luòwǔ le, wǎng shang yǒu hěn duō zīliào hěn kěkào hěn yǒuyòng a. Wǎngluò❸ shìjiè yòu dà yòu fāngbiàn, nǐ kěyǐ jiào wàimài, gòuwù, nǐ kěyǐ zū fángzi, mǎi chē … zǒngzhī, yī shí zhù xíng, shénme zīliào dōu chá de dào.

Lìshā: Duì, tèbié fāngbiàn. Yàoshi xiǎng jiāo nǚpéngyou, yě kěyǐ shàng wǎng zhǎo.

Tiānmíng: Āi, Lìshā, nǐ hái zài shēng wǒ de qì ma?

Lìshā: Nǐ shuō wǒ gāi④ bù gāi shēng qì? Nǐ měi cì dōu chídào, lǎoshì hài de dàjiā děng nǐ.

Tiānmíng: Duìbuqǐ, duìbuqǐ, shì wǒ bù hǎo. Xià cì bù gǎn le.

Kē Lín: Tiānmíng, nǐ jīhū zhěngtiān dāi zài wūzi⑤ li wánr diànnǎo, kàn qi lai zhēn shì wánr shàng yǐn le.

Tiānmíng: Shàng yǐn? Méi nàme yánzhòng ba? Xiànzài shì wǎngluò shídài, dāngrán lí bù kāi diànnǎo.

Lìshā: Wǒ zhīdao diànnǎo hé wǎngluò zài wǒmen de shēnghuó zhōng yuè lái yuè zhòngyào, wǒ yě yòng diànnǎo bāngzhù⑥ wǒ zuò fānyì liànxí, yě shàng wǎng bǐjiào jiàgé⑦, kěshì bú xiàng nǐ, chángcháng wàng le shíjiān, wàng le péngyou.

Xuěméi: Tiānmíng, tīng Lìshā shuō nǐ bù xǐhuan dǎ diànhuà, zhǐ xǐhuan fā diànyóu.

Kē Lín: Yīnwèi fā diànyóu bù huā qián yòu shěng shíjiān.

Tiānmíng: Méi cuò! Miǎnfèi, yòu kuài yòu fāngbiàn.

Xuěméi: Kěshì yǒude shíhou, fā diànyóu bùrú dǎ diànhuà gǎnjué hǎo.

Kē Lín: Xuěméi xǐhuan "diàn liáo."⑧

Lìshā: "Diàn liáo"? Shénme shì "diàn liáo"?

Kē Lín: Jiù shì dǎ "diàn" huà "liáo" tiānr. Dǒng le ba? Yìzhí liáo, bùtíng de liáo, cóng zǎo dào wǎn de liáo.

Xuěméi: Zěnme? Tīng qi lai hǎoxiàng nǐ bú ài gēn wǒ liáo tiānr.

Kē Lín: Bù, bù, bù, wǒ bú shì nà ge yìsi⑨, wǒ shì kāi wánxiào. Wǒ dāngrán ài gēn nǐ liáo tiānr. Hǎo le, hǎo le, bù shuō zhè xiē le, zánmen dàodǐ qù nǎ jiā kǎla-ōukèI a?

Tiānmíng: Wǒ shàng wǎng chá le, dōngbianr nà jiā búcuò, nàr de gē dōu shì Lìshā xǐhuan de. Nǐmen kàn, wǒ méi wàng le péngyou ba?

English Text

Zhang Tianming is a computer fanatic. His computer is on from morning till night. He reads news, does research, and plays games online. Sometimes he writes his blog on his website. He says he can do without newspapers, telephones, and even a car, but he can't leave his computer for a moment. When he goes online, very often he loses track of time. Yesterday Lisa, Xuemei, Ke Lin and he agreed to sing karaoke today, but at the appointed time he didn't show up. His cellphone wasn't turned on, so they sent him an email. Ten minutes later they saw him running towards them.

Tianming: Sorry, I'm sorry. I downloaded some software, searched for a few things and lost track of time.

Ke Lin: What were you searching for?

Tianming: I have to write an article. I needed to look up some information.

Xuemei: Looking for information? Our professor doesn't allow us to use anything from the internet. We have to use formally published books and journals. He says there is too much junk on the internet.

Tianming:	Your professor is too out of touch. Lots of information on the internet is very reliable and useful. The online world is huge and convenient. You can order takeout, shop, you can rent housing, buy a car….Anyway, from clothes to food, from housing to transportation, you can find all kinds of information.
Lisa:	That's right, it's really convenient. If you want to find a girlfriend, you can also go online.
Tianming:	Lisa, are you still mad at me?
Lisa:	You tell me if I should be mad or not. You're late every time. You always keep everyone waiting.
Tianming:	I'm sorry. I'm really sorry. It's my fault. There won't be a next time.
Ke Lin:	Tianming, you stay all day in your room playing on your computer. Seems you are getting addicted.
Tianming:	Addicted? Surely it's not as serious as that? Ours is the internet age. Of course, we can't do without computers.
Lisa:	I know that computers and the internet are becoming more and more important in our lives. I also use my computer to do my translation exercises and go online to compare prices, but I'm not like you, always forgetting the time and your friends.
Xuemei:	I hear Lisa say that you don't like to make phone calls. You only like to send emails.
Ke Lin:	Because email saves money and time.
Tianming:	That's right. It's free, quick and convenient.
Xuemei:	But sometimes emails don't feel as good as phone calls.
Ke Lin:	Xuemei likes "tele-chatting."
Lisa:	"Tele-chatting"? What's "tele-chatting"?
Ke Lin:	Chatting on the phone. Got it? Chatting continuously, chatting non-stop, from morning till night…
Xuemei:	What? Sounds like you don't like chatting with me.
Ke Lin:	No, no, no. That's not what I meant. I was joking. Of course, I love chatting with you. OK, that's enough. No more talk of that. Where are we going to sing karaoke?
Tianming:	I looked online. There's a place on the east side that's quite good. They have all the songs that Lisa likes. You see, I didn't forget my friends.

SELF-ASSESSMENT

How well can you do these things? Check (✔) the boxes to evaluate your progress and see which areas you may need to practice more.

I can	Very Well	OK	A Little
Apologize if I find out I have caused others distress	☐	☐	☐
Change the subject during a conversation	☐	☐	☐
Complain about the trouble that others have caused	☐	☐	☐
Talk about my online activities	☐	☐	☐
Discuss the positive and/or negative impact of the internet on my life	☐	☐	☐

第八课　　第八课

打工　　打工

 LEARNING OBJECTIVES

In this lesson, you will learn to use Chinese to

1. Review your monthly income and spending patterns;
2. Talk about how you balance your personal budget;
3. Name some possible reasons to work part-time while in school;
4. Discuss the pros and cons of working part-time while in school;
5. Describe what you dislike or what bothers you.

 RELATE AND GET READY

In your own culture/community—

- Are parents expected to provide their children with financial support for college?
- Do teenagers and college students often take on part-time jobs?
- Do people generally have savings in the bank?
- Is it easy to apply for student loans?

Before You Study

Check the statements that apply to you.

☐ 1. I have a part-time job.

☐ 2. I think work-study jobs are a good idea.

☐ 3. I think working while in school detracts from academics.

When You Study

Listen to the audio recording and scan the text. Ask yourself the following questions before you begin a close reading of the text.

1. Do Tianming's parents have the means to support their children's education?

2. Why is Tianming surfing the internet?

 張天明的父母收入雖然不少，但是供❶天明和姐姐上大學，經濟上還是有些壓力。他們希望孩子們能受到良好的教育，所以孩子一生下來①就開始給他們存❷教育費。

LANGUAGE NOTES

❶ 供 means to supply, e.g., 供水 (to supply water), but it can also mean to provide financial support, e.g., 供孩子上學/供孩子上学 (to support one's children's education), 供房子 (to pay one's mortgage).

4. I know how to find scholarship opportunities.
5. I think student loans are nothing to be nervous about.
6. I would like to save more money.

3. Is it common to find college students waiting tables in restaurants in China?
4. What kind of trouble is Lisa's roommate in?

张天明的父母收入虽然不少，但是供❶天明和姐姐上大学，经济上还是有些压力。他们希望孩子们能受到良好的教育，所以孩子一生下来①就开始给他们存❷教育费。

❷ 存 means to leave something somewhere for safe keeping, e.g., 在銀行存錢/在银行存钱 (to deposit money at a bank), 在機場存車/在机场存车 (to park one's car at an airport), 在超市 (chāoshì) 存包 (to check one's bag in a supermarket), 把東西存在朋友家/把东西存在朋友家 (to leave things at a friend's place).

可是因為學費和生活費不斷提高，家裏每年還得另外拿出很多錢來。張天明覺得自己已經是大人了，應該找工作掙錢來②減輕父母的負擔，所以就上網看看有沒有適合自己的工作③。這時候麗莎和雪梅走了進來。

雪梅：	天明，你在網上看什麼呢？
張天明：	我想打點兒工，少花一點兒家裏的錢。
雪梅：	你父母的工作都很好，需要你打工掙錢嗎？打工會不會影響學習？
張天明：	我想打工，除了為了減輕家庭經濟負擔以外，更重要的是想取得一些工作經驗。如果打工時間不太多，不會影響學習。
麗莎：	我也想打工掙點兒零用錢。
雪梅：	你不是有獎學金嗎？
麗莎：	獎學金不夠交學費，我還申請了政府的學生貸款。哎，雪梅，中國大學生也打工嗎？
雪梅：	以前不用，因為那時候上大學不用交學費。現在大學收費了，所以不少大學生也想辦法打工掙錢。
麗莎：	中國大學生一般在哪兒打工？在餐館兒當服務員嗎？
雪梅：	在餐館兒打工的大學生也有，但是很少。中國城市裏有很多從農村來找工作的人，飯館兒喜歡找他們，因為工資③比較低。

LANGUAGE NOTES

❸ Public employees' salaries have been called 工資/工资 in mainland China since 1949. The Taiwanese equivalent is 薪水/薪水 (xīnshuǐ).

可是因为学费和生活费不断提高，家里每年还得另外拿出很多钱来。张天明觉得自己已经是大人了，应该找工作挣钱来②减轻父母的负担，所以就上网看看有没有适合自己的工作③。这时候丽莎和雪梅走了进来。

雪梅：　天明，你在网上看什么呢？

张天明：　我想打点儿工，少花一点儿家里的钱。

雪梅：　你父母的工作都很好，需要你去打工挣钱吗？打工会不会影响学习？

张天明：　我想打工，除了为了减轻家庭经济负担以外，更重要的是想取得一些工作经验。如果打工时间不太多，不会影响学习。

丽莎：　我也想打工挣点儿零用钱。

雪梅：　你不是有奖学金吗？

丽莎：　奖学金不够交学费，我还申请了政府的学生贷款。哎，雪梅，中国大学生也打工吗？

雪梅：　以前不用，因为那时候上大学不用交学费。现在大学收费了，所以不少大学生也想办法打工挣钱。

丽莎：　中国大学生一般在哪儿打工？在餐馆儿当服务员吗？

雪梅：　在餐馆儿打工的大学生也有，但是很少。中国城市里有很多从农村来找工作的人，饭馆儿喜欢找他们，因为工资❸比较低。

麗莎：　你打過工嗎？

雪梅：　打過，我做過家教❹，教英語。我的同學有的做翻譯，有的管理電腦。

張天明：看起來不少學生都是一邊讀書一邊打工掙錢。

麗莎：　說到錢，我的同屋今天跟我借錢❺。她說她媽媽生氣了，不給她錢了。

雪梅：　為什麼？

麗莎：　她父母把她這個學期的飯錢都交了，可是她嫌學校餐廳的菜難吃，不是叫外賣，就是跟同學去飯館，還經常亂買東西，亂花錢，欠了銀行和信用卡公司很多錢。上個月父母給的零用錢，她不到❻十天就花完了，又跟媽媽要了一些，還是不夠。

雪梅：　難怪她媽媽生氣。她怎麼不想想❹，父母掙錢多不容易啊？

張天明：我可⑤做不出這樣的事情。

麗莎：　誰不知道❹你是父母的乖孩子！好吧，你慢慢兒找，我們走了。

LANGUAGE NOTES

❹ 家教 is short for 家庭教師/家庭教师.

❺ 借錢/借钱 can mean either to borrow or to lend money, depending on the context: A 跟B借錢/ A 跟B借钱 (A borrows money from B), A借錢給B/A借钱给B, A 把錢借給B/A 把钱借给B (A lends money to B).

丽莎：　　　你打过工吗？

雪梅：　　　打过，我做过家教❹，教英语。我的同学有的做翻译，有的管理电脑。

张天明：　　看起来不少学生都是一边读书一边打工挣钱。

丽莎：　　　说到钱，我的同屋今天跟我借钱❺。她说她妈妈生气了，不给她钱了。

雪梅：　　　为什么？

丽莎：　　　她父母把她这个学期的饭钱都交了，可是她嫌学校餐厅的菜难吃，不是叫外卖，就是跟同学去饭馆，还经常乱买东西，乱花钱，欠了银行和信用卡公司很多钱。上个月父母给的零用钱，她不到❻十天就花完了，又跟妈妈要了一些，还是不够。

雪梅：　　　难怪她妈妈生气。她怎么不想想❹，父母挣钱多不容易啊？

张天明：　　我可⑤做不出这样的事情。

丽莎：　　　谁不知道❹你是父母的乖孩子！好吧，你慢慢儿找，我们走了。

---

❻ 不到 means "has not reached a certain number," "less than," e.g., 認識不到一個月/认识不到一个月 (have known each other for less than a month), 現在不到六點/现在不到六点 (it's not yet six o'clock), 機票不到一千元/机票不到一千元 (the airline ticket costs less than a thousand dollars).

After You Study

Challenge yourself to complete the following tasks in Chinese.

1. List the expenses that Tianming's parents try to pay for.

2. List the reasons why Tianming wants to work.

存自行車的地方
存自行车的地方

3. List the financial arrangements that Lisa has made to support her college education.

4. List the part-time jobs that college students in China often take on.

5. List the behaviors that have landed Lisa's roommate in financial trouble.

存包的地方

1.	收入		shōurù	n	income
2.	供		gōng	v	to provide; to support financially
3.	壓力	压力	yālì	n	pressure
4.	受到		shòu dào	vc	to receive
5.	良好		liánghǎo	adj	good
6.	教育		jiàoyù	n/v	education; to educate
7.	生		shēng	v	to give birth to; to be born
8.	存		cún	v	to save up
9.	不斷	不断	búduàn	adv	continuously
10.	大人		dàren	n	adult
11.	掙錢	挣钱	zhèng qián	vo	to earn money; to make money
12.	減輕	减轻	jiǎnqīng	v	to lessen
13.	負擔	负担	fùdān	n	burden
14.	適合	适合	shìhé	v	to suit
15.	影響	影响	yǐngxiǎng	v/n	to influence; to have an impact; influence
16.	家庭		jiātíng	n	family (unit); household
17.	取得		qǔdé	v	to obtain; to gain; to acquire
18.	零用錢	零用钱	língyòngqián	n	allowance; spending money
19.	獎學金	奖学金	jiǎngxuéjīn	n	scholarship money
20.	交		jiāo	v	to hand over
21.	政府		zhèngfǔ	n	government
22.	貸款	贷款	dàikuǎn	n/v	loan; to provide a loan
23.	農村	农村	nóngcūn	n	countryside; village; rural area

24.	工資	工资	gōngzī	n	wages; pay
25.	低		dī	adj	low
26.	家教		jiājiào	n	tutor
27.	讀書	读书	dú shū	vo	to attend school; to study; to read aloud
28.	借		jiè	v	to borrow; to lend
29.	嫌		xián	v	to dislike; to mind; to complain of
30.	難吃	难吃	nánchī	adj	not tasty
31.	欠		qiàn	v	to owe
32.	銀行	银行	yínháng	n	bank
33.	事情		shìqing	n	thing; matter
34.	乖		guāi	adj	(of children) obedient; well-behaved

Proper Noun

| 35. | 英語 | 英语 | Yīngyǔ | | English language |

Enlarged Characters

| 壓 | 斷 | 擔 | 響 | 獎 | 農 | 讀 |
| 压 | 断 | 担 | 响 | 奖 | 农 | 读 |

Culture Highlights

❶ Higher education in China used to be free. Beginning in the late 1980s, the state started to charge tuition. Surveys in recent years have repeatedly shown that educational expenses are the largest expense in the average household's annual budget, more than savings for retirement or housing expenditures. Both need- and merit-based scholarships are available. Parents, however, remain the main source of financial support for Chinese college students.

❷ Increasingly, Chinese college students work on or off campus to offset living expenses. The most popular form of part-time employment is tutoring elementary and middle school students. Depending on the subject, the work can be quite lucrative, especially musical instrument instruction. Some college students work in sales, do creative work such as graphic design, or engage in translation services.

你會申請這份工作嗎？
你会申请这份工作吗？

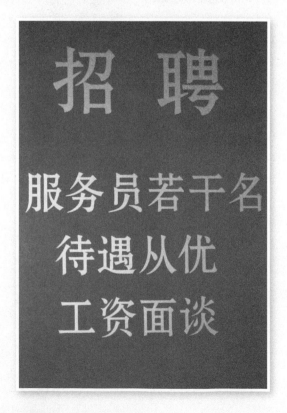

這份工作適合你嗎？
这份工作适合你吗？

Grammar

1. Directional Complements Suggesting Result

By definition, directional complements have to do with direction. For instance, 來/来 signifies movement toward the speaker; 上 indicates upward movement, and so on. However, many directional complements do not actually deal with direction in a literal sense, but rather suggest a result or state of being. In this lesson, we have directional complements that express result.

❶ 他們希望兩個孩子能受到良好的教育，所以孩子一生下來就開始給他們存教育費。

他们希望两个孩子能受到良好的教育，所以孩子一生下来就开始给他们存教育费。

(They hoped that their two children would get a good education. Therefore, they started to save for their educational expenses as soon as the children were born.)

Here, 下來/下来 implies detachment or separation of one thing from another. Similarly, we say 從本子上撕 (sī) 下一張紙來/从本子上撕 (sī) 下一张纸来 (tear a piece of paper from a notebook), 把西瓜切 (qiē) 下來一塊/把西瓜切 (qiē) 下来一块 (cut a slice off a watermelon), etc.

❷ 每年開學的時候，家裏還是得拿出很多錢來。

每年开学的时候，家里还是得拿出很多钱来。

(Every year at the beginning of the school year, [my] family still has to come up with a lot of money.)

出來/出来 signifies the emergence of something from a hidden place into the open or a change from having nothing to having something:

❸ 把你的問題説出來，我們大家幫你解決。

把你的问题说出来，我们大家帮你解决。

(Tell us your problem; get it out in the open. We will help you solve it.)

❹ 我看出來他生氣了。

我看出来他生气了。

(I could tell that he got angry.)

❺   給孩子想出來一個好名字。

給孩子想出来一个好名字。

(Come up with a good name for the child.)

上, 上來/上来, 上去, 下, 下來/下来, 下去, 出, 出來/出来, 過/过,
過來/过来, 過去/过去, 起, 起來/起来, 開/开, etc., all can convey result.
It is important to understand the meaning of these directional complements when they are
used in this sense. Try to memorize them together with their preceding verbs.

2. 來/来 Connecting Two Verb Phrases

When 來/来 connects two verb phrases with the second phrase indicating a purpose, it is
similar to "to," or "in order to" in English.

❶   大家決定開一個舞會來給他過生日。

大家决定开一个舞会来给他过生日。

(Everybody decided to throw a dance party to celebrate his birthday.)

❷   我覺得自己已經長大了，應該做一些工作來減輕父母的
負擔。

我觉得自己已经长大了，应该做一些工作来减轻父母的
负担。

(I feel I'm all grown up already. I should get a job to ease my parents' burden.)

❸   我妹妹告訴我應該用聽錄音的辦法來提高漢語水平。

我妹妹告诉我应该用听录音的办法来提高汉语水平。

(My younger sister tells me I should listen to recordings to improve my Chinese.)

3. The Dynamic Particle 了 (II)

We have already learned that 了 can indicate the realization of an action or the emergence
of a state. However, that does not mean that 了 is always required with completed
actions, as in this lesson:

❶   張天明的父母收入雖然不少，但是供天明和姐姐上大
學，經濟上還是有些壓力。他們希望孩子們能受到良好
的教育，所以孩子一生下來就開始給他們存教育費。
張天明的父母收入虽然不少，但是供天明和姐姐上大
学，经济上还是有些压力。他们希望孩子们能受到良好
的教育，所以孩子一生下来就开始给他们存教育费。
(Although Zhang Tianming's parents' income is not inconsiderable, sending Tianming
and his sister to college creates some financial pressure. They hope that their children
will receive a good education. Therefore, from the time the children were born they
started saving for their education.)

In the above passage,

他們希望孩子們能受到良好的教育，所以孩子一生下來
就開始給他們存教育費。
他们希望孩子们能受到良好的教育，所以孩子一生下来
就开始给他们存教育费。

is a completed event. However, it is presented as part of the background information to the
main narrative, 這時候麗莎和雪梅走了進來/这时候丽莎和雪梅走了
进来. That is why the verb 存 does not take 了.

4. Rhetorical Questions

Rhetorical questions are interrogative in form, but the speaker is really emphasizing a
point rather than asking a real question for which an answer is expected, for example,

❶   他昨天根本沒復習，怎麼能考100分呢？
他昨天根本没复习，怎么能考100分呢？
(He didn't review at all yesterday. How could he get a hundred on the test?)

The speaker is saying of course there's no way he could get a full score. The sentence is
affirmative in form but negative in meaning.

❷ 他已經學了三年化學了，這麼簡單的問題難道他
不會嗎？

他已经学了三年化学了，这么简单的问题难道他
不会吗？

(He's been studying chemistry for three years. Are you telling me he can't solve such a simple problem?)

The sentence is negative in form, but emphatically positive in meaning: "Surely, he should know how to solve the problem!"

Generally speaking, rhetorical questions that are affirmative in form carry an emphatically negative meaning; rhetorical questions that are negative in form carry an emphatically positive meaning. For more examples, see the following two sentences from this lesson:

❸ 她怎麼不想想，父母掙錢多不容易啊？

她怎么不想想，父母挣钱多不容易啊？

(How come she doesn't give any thought to how hard it is for her parents to earn money?)

The speaker means that she should think about this issue.

❹ 誰不知道你是父母的乖孩子！

谁不知道你是父母的乖孩子！

(Who doesn't know you are an exemplary child?)

[Everyone knows that you're an exemplary child.]

5. Adverb 可

可 is employed in colloquial speech to lend force to a statement. You can leave out 可 without changing the meaning, but the tone of voice will be weakened:

❶ 我可做不出這樣的事情。

我可做不出这样的事情。

(I would never be able to do a thing like that, not me.)

❷ A: 下個月有一個說中文的比賽，老師讓你去。
　　下个月有一个说中文的比赛，老师让你去。
　　(Next month there will be a Chinese speech contest. The teacher is asking you to go.)

B: 我可不行，一看見人多就緊張得說不出話來。
　　我可不行，一看见人多就紧张得说不出话来。
　　(Not me! I get tongue-tied as soon as I get in front of a crowd.)

❸ A: 你是不是說過這門課不必準備也能考100分？
　　你是不是说过这门课不必准备也能考100分？
　　(Didn't you say that you would be able to ace this class without any preparation?)

B: 你別亂說。我可沒說過。
　　你别乱说。我可没说过。
　　(Nonsense. Not me, I never said that.)

Words & Phrases

A. 壓力/压力 (pressure)

壓力/压力 is a noun, often appearing in patterns such as 有壓力/有压力, 給⋯壓力/给⋯压力, or 對⋯的壓力/对⋯的压力.

❶   考試考得不好，怕媽媽生氣，我覺得有壓力。
考试考得不好，怕妈妈生气，我觉得有压力。
(I didn't do well on the exam and I'm worried that my mom will be mad. I feel a lot of pressure.)

❷   這次考研究生，我的指導教授給我很大的壓力。
这次考研究生，我的指导教授给我很大的压力。
(This time I'm taking the entrance exam for graduate school and my advisor has given me a lot of pressure.)

❸   今年經濟很糟糕，我一直找不到工作，這對我的壓力很大。
今年经济很糟糕，我一直找不到工作，这对我的压力很大。
(The economy is doing really badly this year. I can't find a job and this puts a lot of pressure on me.)

B. 受到 (to receive)

受到 is often followed by the below abstract nouns, which are usually qualified as indicated by brackets below, e.g., 受到(大家的)歡迎/欢迎 (receive [everyone's] welcome); 受到(良好的)教育 (receive [a very good] education); 受到(老師的)影響/(老师的)影响 (receive [the teacher's] influence).

C. 減輕/减轻 (to lessen)

減輕/减轻 is generally followed by an abstract noun, e.g., 減輕負擔/减轻负担 (to lessen the burden), 減輕壓力/减轻压力 (to alleviate the pressure), 減輕痛苦/减轻痛苦 (to lessen the pain).

❶   學生希望老師少給一些功課，減輕他們的負擔。

學生希望老师少给一些功課，减轻他们的负担。

(The students wish that the teacher would assign them less homework so as to lighten their burden.)

❷   找到工作了，他的壓力減輕了不少。

找到工作了，他的压力减轻了不少。

(Now that he's found a job, he feels a load has been taken off his shoulders.)

❸   醫生想了很多辦法來減輕他的痛苦 (tòngkǔ)。

医生想了很多办法来减轻他的痛苦 (tòngkǔ)。

(The doctor tried many different ways to ease his pain.)

D. 適合/适合 (to suit) and 合適/合适 (suitable)

In Level 1 we learned 合適/合适 as an adjective meaning "suitable." In this lesson we have 適合/适合, meaning "to suit." 適合/适合 is a transitive verb; in other words, it must be followed by a noun or occur in a "pivotal sentence" in which the object also serves as the subject of the following clause.

Note the contrasting functions of these two words in the following sentences:

❶   這條牛仔褲不適合你穿，你媽媽穿可能合適。

这条牛仔裤不适合你穿，你妈妈穿可能合适。

(These jeans don't suit you. They might be suitable for your mom.)

❷   這種傢具適合家裏用，放在辦公室不合適。

这种家具适合家里用，放在办公室不合适。

(This kind of furniture suits home use [more]. It's not suitable to be put in an office.)

❸ 這個專業不適合你，你還是選別的專業吧。

这个专业不适合你，你还是选别的专业吧。

(This major doesn't suit you. You'd better pick another major.)

E. 影響/影响 (to influence or affect; influence)

影響/影响 can be a verb:

❶ 睡覺的時間不夠會影響健康。 [verb]

睡觉的时间不够会影响健康。

(Not having enough time to sleep will affect one's health.)

❷ 你看書吧，我坐在這兒不説話，不會影響你。 [verb]

你看书吧，我坐在这儿不说话，不会影响你。

(Why don't you study? I'll sit here quietly and won't distract you.)

影響/影响 can also be a noun and often appears in the pattern of A 對/对 B 有影響/影响 (A has an influence on B) as seen in ❸:

❸ 你不去開這個會，對你找工作會有影響。 [noun]

你不去开这个会，对你找工作会有影响。

(If you don't go to the meeting, it'll affect your chances of getting a job.)

F. 取得 (to obtain)

取得 is also followed by abstract nouns such as 經驗/经验, 同意, 好成績/好成绩 (hǎo chéngjì, success; a good grade), 進步/进步 (jìnbù, progress).

G. 說到/说到 (speaking of)

To expand on a topic already mentioned, we can say 說到/说到…

❶ 說到錢，我的同屋今天跟我說，她媽媽生氣了，不給她
錢了。

说到钱，我的同屋今天跟我说，她妈妈生气了，不给她
钱了。

(Speaking of money, my roommate told me that her mom got angry and wouldn't give her any more money.)

❷ **A:** 你想什麼呢？

你想什么呢？

(What are you thinking?)

B: 我在想下個學期選什麼課呢。

我在想下个学期选什么课呢。

(I'm thinking about what classes I should take next semester.)

A: 說到下個學期的課，我們可以不選我們學校的課嗎？

说到下个学期的课，我们可以不选我们学校的课吗？

(Speaking of next semester's classes, can we choose not to take our school's classes?)

B: 那你選哪兒的課？

那你选哪儿的课？

(Then where will you take classes?)

A: 我想去中國留學。

我想去中国留学。

(I want to go to China to study abroad.)

B: 我不知道行不行，可能得取得指導教授的同意，你去
問問吧。

我不知道行不行，可能得取得指导教授的同意，你去
问问吧。

(I don't know if you can or not. You probably have to get permission from your advisor. You should go ask.)

❸ A: 聽說張天明的表哥打球打得很棒。

听说张天明的表哥打球打得很棒。

(I hear Zhang Tianming's cousin is a great ballplayer.)

B: 說到打球，我們這個週末去打籃球好嗎？

说到打球，我们这个周末去打篮球好吗？

(Speaking of playing ball, should we go play basketball this weekend?)

H. 嫌 (to dislike)

嫌 is a verb meaning "to dislike, to detest." It is usually followed by a clause.

❶ 我妹妹嫌這個餐館兒的菜太油太鹹。

我妹妹嫌这个餐馆儿的菜太油太咸。

(My little sister dislikes the fact that the food at this restaurant is so greasy and salty.)

❷ 小林嫌她男朋友做事太馬虎，所以跟他分手了。

小林嫌她男朋友做事太马虎，所以跟他分手了。

(Xiao Lin didn't like the fact that her boyfriend was so careless. That was why she broke up with him.)

❸ 我同屋嫌在餐館兒打工太累，掙錢太少，決定另外找
工作。

我同屋嫌在餐馆儿打工太累，挣钱太少，决定另外找
工作。

(My roommate thought that working at the restaurant was too exhausting and the pay was too little, so he decided to look for a job elsewhere.)

I. 不是 A, 就是 B (if it's not A, it's B; either A or B)

This pattern is often used to enumerate two predictable scenarios:

1　她嫌學校餐廳的菜不好吃，不是叫外賣，就是跟同學去飯館。

　　她嫌学校餐厅的菜不好吃，不是叫外卖，就是跟同学去饭馆。

(She finds the food at the school cafeteria unappetizing, so she either orders takeout or goes out to restaurants with her classmates.)

2　現在租房子很不容易，不是價錢太貴，就是房子不好，麻煩得很。

　　现在租房子很不容易，不是价钱太贵，就是房子不好，麻烦得很。

(It's really difficult to rent an apartment now. Either the rent is too expensive, or the rooms are bad. It's a real hassle.)

3　昨天的晚會來的不是同學，就是朋友，他都認識。

　　昨天的晚会来的不是同学，就是朋友，他都认识。

(Those who came to the party were either classmates or friends. He knew them all.)

4 **A:**　你們常常吃牛肉嗎？

　　你们常常吃牛肉吗？

(Do you often eat beef?)

B:　不，我們平常不是吃雞，就是吃魚，不吃牛肉。

　　不，我们平常不是吃鸡，就是吃鱼，不吃牛肉。

(No, we usually have either chicken or fish. We don't eat beef.)

J. 多 (How...it is!)

This is an adverb used as an intensifier in exclamatory sentences:

❶   父母掙錢多不容易啊！
父母挣钱多不容易啊！

(What a difficult thing for parents to make (enough) money!)

❷   小明，外邊多冷呀，乖乖待在屋子裏，別出去亂跑。
小明，外边多冷呀，乖乖待在屋子里，别出去乱跑！

(Little Ming, it's really cold out. Be a good boy and stay indoors. Don't go out.)

❸   這套運動服多難看，誰買呀？送我都不要。
这套运动服多难看，谁买呀？送我都不要。

(This sweatsuit is so ugly! Who'd buy it? I wouldn't take it even as a gift.)

日 期 DATE	币 种 CURR.	钞/汇 C/E	注 释 NOTES	支出(－)或存入(＋) WITHDRAWAL OR DEPOSIT	结　　余 BALANCE	网点号 S.N.	操 作 OPER.
51							
52							
53							
54							
55							
56							
57							
58							
59							
60							

This is a page of a bank deposit book.

Language Practice

A. Be Your Own Bookkeeper

It's a good practice to list your monthly income and expenses and see if you can balance your monthly budget. Put together a hypothetical budget using the following chart.

收入

1. 工資/工资：　　$_____
2. 父母給的零用錢/
   父母给的零用钱：$_____
3. 獎學金/奖学金：　$_____
4. 其他：　　　　　$_____

支出(zhīchū)

1. 生活費/生活费
   a. 房租：　　　　$_____
   b. 水電費/水电费：$_____
   c. 飯錢、菜錢/
      饭钱、菜钱：　$_____
   d. 車錢/车钱：　　$_____
   e. 手機費/手机费：$_____
   f. 其他：　　　　$_____
2. 教育費/教育费
   a. 書錢/书钱：　　$_____
   b. 文具：　　　　$_____
   c. 網絡費/网络费：$_____
   d. 其他：　　　　$_____

After filling out your own budget, work with a partner and ask each other if you can pay for your monthly expenses without going into debt.

A: 你每個月的錢夠不夠
付你的生活費和教育費?

A: 你每个月的钱够不够
付你的生活费和教育费?

B: _____ 。

B: _____ 。

If the answer is negative, ask for possible solutions.

A: 那你打算怎麼辦?

A: 那你打算怎么办?

Here are some suggestions, and you can add your own two cents in #7 and #8.

1. 跟銀行借錢	1. 跟银行借钱
2. 跟父母借錢	2. 跟父母借钱
3. 申請新的信用卡	3. 申请新的信用卡
4. 多打工	4. 多打工
5. 不亂花錢	5. 不乱花钱
6. 搬回家住,把房租、饭錢省下來	6. 搬回家住,把房租、饭钱省下来
7. _____	7. _____
8. _____	8. _____

Pick the ones that suit your situation, and tell your partner what you plan to do.

B: _____ 。

B. Part-Time Jobs

a. Locations: Work with a partner to identify some of the places where you may be able to find a part-time job. Add your own pick to #6.

1.

2.

3.

4.

5.

6. 其他地方？

Ask each other if you have worked in those places.

EXAMPLE:

A: 你在咖啡館打過工嗎？　A: 你在咖啡馆打过工吗？
B: 我在咖啡館打過工。　B: 我在咖啡馆打过工。

or

B: 我沒在咖啡館打過工。　B: 我没在咖啡馆打过工。

b. Job titles: Work with your partner to identify the following part-time jobs.

1. 咖啡館服務員　1. 咖啡馆服务员
2. 餐館師傅　2. 餐馆师傅
3. 商店售貨員　3. 商店售货员

4. 書店店員　　　　　　　　　4. 书店店员
5. 出版公司翻譯　　　　　　　5. 出版公司翻译
6. 旅行社導遊　　　　　　　　6. 旅行社导游
7. 網絡公司網站管理員　　　　7. 网络公司网站管理员

Tell each other if you have done such work before.

EXAMPLE:

我在咖啡館當過服務員。　　我在咖啡馆当过服务员。

or

我没在咖啡館當過服務員。　我没在咖啡馆当过服务员。

Poll your class and see what kinds of part-time jobs your classmates have done.

C. Are You Easily Distracted?

Ask three to five of your classmates what may have a negative impact on their studies.

EXAMPLE:

You:　什麼會影響你學習？　　　You:　什么会影响你学习？
Jerry:　睡不好覺會影響我學習。　Jerry:　睡不好觉会影响我学习。

Record their answers here:

| Jerry | 睡不好覺 | Jerry | 睡不好觉 |
| Naomi | 生病 | Naomi | 生病 |

Classmate #1_____

Classmate #2_____

Classmate #3_____

…

Share your list with a partner and see if any of the answers collected are the same. Then rank the answers and report back to the class.

D. Picky! Picky! Picky!

Zhang Tianming can be picky. In Lesson 2, he dislikes his bedroom being too hot, his bathroom being too small, and possibly the food in the cafeteria being unappetizing.

EXAMPLE:　Lesson 2

張天明嫌房間裏沒有空調，
衛生間太小，學校餐廳的飯
不怎麼樣。

张天明嫌房间里没有空调，
卫生间太小，学校餐厅的饭
不怎么样。

Now think back to Lesson 4 and Lesson 5. With the help of a partner, investigate why Zhang Tianming is not satisfied with his wardrobe and future job prospects.

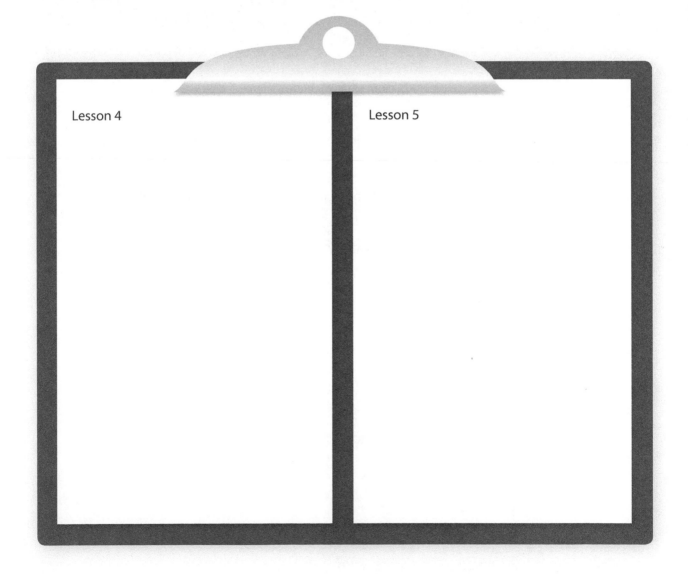

Lesson 4

Lesson 5

E. So Predictable!

Some people always do the same things, eat the same food, buy the same clothes, etc.

Working with a partner, see how predictable Tianming, Lisa, Ke Lin, and Xuemei are.

EXAMPLE: free time   blogging/playing computer games

→ **A:** 張天明有空兒的時候　　　　　**A:** 张天明有空儿的时候
　　做什麼？　　　　　　　　　　　做什么？

B: 張天明有空兒的時候，　　　　**B:** 张天明有空儿的时候，
　　不是寫博客，就是玩　　　　　不是写博客，就是玩
　　電腦遊戲。　　　　　　　　　电脑游戏。

1.   shopping for shoes   black/brown

2.   ordering in restaurants   steamed fish/beef with Chinese broccoli

3.   out on the town   concert/karaoke

4.   watching TV   basketball game/soccer game

How about you? Are there any routines in your daily life that you wish to share?

F. Get to Work!

Ask yourself what possible reasons would make you look for a part-time job: to earn some spending money, to get work experience, to help out your family, etc. Write them down in Chinese, and mark the most important reason with an asterisk:

1. _____

2. _____

…

*. _____

Then tell your teacher and classmates why you would work part time:

我想打工，除了為了/为了 _____1._____，

_____2._____

____…____，以外，最重要的是_____*____

_____○

G. Work vs. Study

Discuss with a partner the good and the bad aspects of working while studying in school, and list them below.

你覺得一邊讀書一邊打工掙錢
有什麼好處？有什麼壞處？

你觉得一边读书一边打工挣钱
有什么好处？有什么坏处？

好處/好处

1. _____

2. _____

3. _____

…

壞處/坏处

1. _____

2. _____

3. _____

…

Based on the lists, compose a short report. Try to make it as smoothly connected as you can.

我們覺得一邊讀書一邊打工
掙錢對___Good 1/2/3___
很有幫助。
但我們也覺得一邊讀書一邊
打工掙錢可能對___Bad 1/2/3___
有不好的影響。

我们觉得一边读书一边打工
挣钱对___Good 1/2/3___
很有帮助。
但我们也觉得一边读书一边
打工挣钱可能对___Bad 1/2/3___
有不好的影响。

Pinyin Text

Zhāng Tiānmíng de fùmǔ shōurù suīrán bù shǎo, dànshì gōng❶ Tiānmíng hé jiějie shàng dàxué, jīngjì shang háishi yǒu xiē yālì. Tāmen xīwàng háizi men néng shòu dào liánghǎo de jiàoyù, suǒyǐ háizi yì shēng xia lai❶ jiù kāishǐ gěi tāmen cún❷ jiàoyù fèi. Kěshì yīnwèi xué fèi hé shēnghuó fèi búduàn tígāo, jiā li měinián hái děi lìngwài ná chu hěn duō qián lai. Zhāng Tiānmíng juéde zìjǐ yǐjīng shì dàren le, yīnggāi zhǎo gōngzuò zhèng qián lái❷ jiǎnqīng fùmǔ de fùdān, suǒyǐ jiù shàng wǎng kàn kan yǒu méiyǒu shìhé zìjǐ de gōngzuò❸. Zhè shíhou Lìshā hé Xuěméi zǒu le jìn lai.

Xuěméi:	Tiānmíng, nǐ zài wǎng shang kàn shénme ne?
Zhāng Tiānmíng:	Wǒ xiǎng dǎ diǎnr gōng, shǎo huā yì diǎnr jiā li de qián.
Xuěméi:	Nǐ fùmǔ de gōngzuò dōu hěn hǎo, xūyào nǐ qù dǎ gōng zhèng qián ma? Dǎ gōng huì bú huì yǐngxiǎng xuéxí?
Zhāng Tiānmíng:	Wǒ xiǎng dǎ gōng, chúle wèile jiǎnqīng jiātíng jīngjì fùdān yǐwài, gèng zhòngyào de shì xiǎng qǔdé yì xiē gōngzuò jīngyàn. Rúguǒ dǎ gōng shíjiān bú tài duō, bú huì yǐngxiǎng xuéxí.
Lìshā:	Wǒ yě xiǎng dǎ gōng zhèng diǎnr língyòng qián.
Xuěméi:	Nǐ bú shì yǒu jiǎngxuéjīn ma?
Lìshā:	Jiǎngxuéjīn bú gòu jiāo xuéfèi, wǒ hái shēnqǐng le zhèngfǔ de xuéshēng dàikuǎn. Āi, Xuěméi, Zhōngguó dàxuéshēng yě dǎ gōng ma?
Xuěméi:	Yǐqián búyòng, yīnwèi nà shíhou shàng dàxué búyòng jiāo xuéfèi. Xiànzài dàxué shōu fèi le, suǒyǐ bù shǎo dàxuéshēng yě xiǎng bànfǎ dǎ gōng zhèng qián.
Lìshā:	Zhōngguó dàxuéshēng yìbān zài nǎr dǎ gōng? Zài cānguǎnr dāng fúwùyuán ma?
Xuěméi:	Zài cānguǎnr dǎ gōng de dàxuéshēng yě yǒu, dànshì hěn shǎo. Zhōngguó chéngshì li yǒu hěn duō cóng nóngcūn lái zhǎo gōngzuò de rén, fànguǎnr xǐhuan zhǎo tāmen, yīnwèi gōngzī❸ bǐjiào dī.
Lìshā:	Nǐ dǎ guo gōng ma?
Xuěméi:	Dǎ guo, wǒ zuò guo jiājiào❹, jiāo Yīngyǔ. Wǒ de tóngxué yǒude zuò fānyì, yǒude guǎnlǐ diànnǎo.

Zhāng Tiānmíng:	Kàn qi lai bù shǎo xuésheng dōu shì yìbiān dú shū yìbiān dǎ gōng zhèng qián.
Lìshā:	Shuō dào qián, wǒ de tóngwū jīntiān gēn wǒ jiè qián⑤. Tā shuō tā māma shēng qì le, bù gěi tā qián le.
Xuěméi:	Wèishénme?
Lìshā:	Tā fùmǔ bǎ tā zhè ge xuéqī de fàn qián dōu jiāo le, kěshì tā xián xuéxiào cāntīng de cài nánchī, bú shì jiào wàimài, jiù shì gēn tóngxué qù fànguǎnr, hái jīngcháng luàn mǎi dōngxi, luàn huā qián, qiàn le yínháng hé xìnyòngkǎ gōngsī hěn duō qián. Shàng ge yuè fùmǔ gěi de língyòng qián, tā bú dào⑥ shí tiān jiù huā wán le, yòu gēn māma yào le yì xiē, hái shì bú gòu.
Xuěméi:	Nánguài tā māma shēngqì. Tā zěnme bù xiǎng xiang④, fùmǔ zhuàn qián duō bù róngyì a?
Zhāng Tiānmíng:	Wǒ kě⑤ zuò bù chū zhèyàng de shìqing.
Lìshā:	Shéi bù zhīdào④ nǐ shì fùmǔ de guāi háizi! Hǎo ba, nǐ màn mānr zhǎo, wǒmen zǒu le.

English Text

Although Zhang Tianming's parents' income is not inconsiderable, sending Tianming and his sister to college creates some financial pressure for them. They [Tianming's Mom and Dad] hope that their children will receive a good education. Therefore, from the time their children were born they started saving for their educational expenses. However, because tuition and living expenses keep rising, the family still has to come up with a lot of extra money. Zhang Tianming feels that he is already an adult and should find a job to alleviate his parents' burden, so he goes online to see if there are any suitable jobs for him. As he is doing that, Lisa and Xuemei walk in.

Lisa:	Tianming, what are you searching online?
Zhang Tianming:	I want to work so that I can spend less of my family's money.
Xuemei:	Your parents have good jobs. Do you need to work in order to make money? Wouldn't working affect your studies?

Zhang Tianming:	I want to work. Besides wanting to ease my family's financial burden, I also want to gain some working experience. If I don't spend too much time working, it shouldn't affect my studies.
Lisa:	I also want to work to make some spending money.
Xuemei:	Don't you have a scholarship?
Lisa:	The scholarship isn't enough to cover tuition. I also applied for a government student loan. Xuemei, do Chinese college students also work?
Xuemei:	They didn't have to before. Because then they didn't have to pay for college tuition. Now universities charge tuition, so many students also try to find jobs to make some money.
Lisa:	Where do Chinese students usually work? In restaurants as waiters?
Xuemei:	There are some students who work in restaurants, but not many. In Chinese cities there are many people from rural areas looking for jobs. Restaurants like to hire them because their wages are relatively low.
Lisa:	Have you worked before?
Xuemei:	Yes, I have. I tutored. I taught English. Some of my classmates worked as translators or managed computers.
Zhang Tianming:	Seems many students go to school and work part-time to make money at the same time.
Lisa:	Speaking of money, today my roommate wanted to borrow money from me. She said her mom was upset and stopped giving her any money.
Xuemei:	Why?
Lisa:	Her parents paid for her food this semester, but she found the school cafeteria's food inedible. She ordered takeout or she went to restaurants with classmates. She also spent money recklessly on other things, and owes the bank and credit companies a lot of money. Last month she spent the allowance that her parents had given her in less than ten days, and then asked for some more from her mother. That still wasn't enough.
Xuemei:	No wonder her mother is angry. Why doesn't she give any thought to how hard it is for her parents to make money?
Zhang Tianming:	I would never be able to do [what she did].
Lisa:	We all know you're such a model child! All right, you take your time looking. We're leaving.

SELF-ASSESSMENT

How well can you do these things? Check (✔) the boxes to evaluate your progress and see which areas you may need to practice more.

I can	Very Well	OK	A Little
Itemize my monthly income and expenses	☐	☐	☐
Describe my spending habits and assess whether I'm in good financial shape	☐	☐	☐
State some possible reasons for students to work part-time	☐	☐	☐
Present the pros and cons regarding working while in school	☐	☐	☐
Complain about things that I dislike	☐	☐	☐

第九课
教育

第九课
教育

9

 LEARNING OBJECTIVES

In this lesson, you will learn to use Chinese to

1. Comment if you had a stress-free childhood;
2. Name some typical classes offered in after-school programs;
3. Indicate agreement or disagreement;
4. Present your opinions;
5. Talk about parents' aspirations for their children.

 RELATE AND GET READY

In your own culture/community—

- Is it common for parents to enroll their children in after-school programs?
- Do many people pursue graduate degrees?
- Do children have a say in family decisions?
- Is it common for both parents to be equally involved in their children's upbringing?

Before You Study

Check the statements that apply to you.

☐ 1. I talk to my friends online.
☐ 2. I attended after-school programs as a child.

When You Study

Listen to the audio recording and scan the text. Ask yourself the following questions before you begin a close reading of the text.

1. What is the source of friction between Li Zhe's brother and sister-in-law?

 李哲的父母是墨西哥移民，他和他哥哥都是在加州出生、長大的。哥哥是電腦博士❶，自己設計、管理網站。李哲的嫂子十五年前從香港來美國留學，拿到碩士學位以後找到工作，就在美國住了下來。哥哥和嫂子結婚十

LANGUAGE NOTES
❶ 1. A bachelor's degree is 學士學位/学士学位.

3. I enjoy my foreign language studies.

4. I have someone to talk with if I need to vent.

5. I don't feel pressured by my family regarding my academic achievement and future career plans.

2. Why was Li Zhe chatting online?

3. What does Lisa wish her parents had done when she was little?

4. Why does Lisa empathize with Li Zhe's sister-in-law?

李哲的父母是墨西哥移民，他和他哥哥都是在加州出生、长大的。哥哥是电脑博士❶，自己设计、管理网站。李哲的嫂子十五年前从香港来美国留学，拿到硕士学位以后找到工作，就在美国住了下来。哥哥和嫂子结婚十年了，生活一直很美滿，可是最近兩年在女兒的教育問題上，意見常常不同，有時甚至吵得很厲害。一天，李哲正在線上跟姪女聊天兒，看見麗莎走了進來。

(李哲下綫…)

李哲：　麗莎，有事兒嗎？

麗莎：　沒什麼事兒，我找天明，以為他在你這兒呢。對不起，害得你把電話掛了。

李哲：　坐，坐，坐。剛才是我姪女給我打電話，我們正好說完了。

麗莎：　你有姪女？今年多大了？

李哲：　今年剛八歲。

麗莎：　她給你打電話有什麼事啊？

李哲：　說來話長❷。我姪女才①小學三年級，我嫂子就把她的時間安排得②滿滿的：星期一學鋼琴❸，星期二學畫畫兒，星期三學游泳，星期四學滑冰，星期五好不容易休息一天，星期六又叫她去上中文學校。她不喜歡學中文，於是就打電話到我這兒來，一邊哭一邊抱怨。

麗莎：　沒那麼嚴重吧？她只是個孩子，能抱怨些什麼啊？

李哲：　她說兒童❹也是人，有自己的愛好和興趣，家長應該尊重孩子自己的選擇。

麗莎：　她說話怎麼像個小大人一樣？

LANGUAGE NOTES

❷ 說來話長/说来话长 is a cliché. The expression literally means, "if one wants to talk about it, it's a long story."

❸ Pianos are 鋼琴/钢琴, literally, "a steel musical instrument." Violins are 小提琴 (xiǎotíqín: "a small hand-carried musical instrument"). What do you think 中提琴 and 大提琴 are?

年了，生活一直很美满，可是最近两年在女儿的教育问题上，意见常常不同，有时甚至吵得很厉害。一天，李哲正在线上跟侄女聊天儿，看见丽莎走了进来。

(李哲下线…)

李哲：　丽莎，有事儿吗？

丽莎：　没什么事儿，我找天明，以为他在你这儿呢。对不起，害得你把电话挂了。

李哲：　坐，坐，坐。刚才是我侄女给我打电话，我们正好说完了。

丽莎：　你有侄女？今年多大了？

李哲：　今年刚八岁。

丽莎：　她给你打电话有什么事啊？

李哲：　说来话长❷。我侄女才①小学三年级，我嫂子就把她的时间安排得②满满的：星期一学钢琴❸，星期二学画画儿，星期三学游泳，星期四学滑冰，星期五好不容易休息一天，星期六又叫她去上中文学校。她不喜欢学中文，于是就打电话到我这儿来，一边哭一边抱怨。

丽莎：　没那么严重吧？她只是个孩子，能抱怨些什么啊？

李哲：　她说儿童❹也是人，有自己的爱好和兴趣，家长应该尊重孩子自己的选择。

丽莎：　她说话怎么像个小大人一样？

---

❹ 兒童/儿童 and 孩子 both mean "children," but 兒童/儿童 is formal and literary whereas 孩子 is spoken and casual. Therefore, children's hospitals are 兒童醫院/儿童医院, not *孩子醫院/孩子医院; Children's Day (June 1 in China) is 兒童節/儿童节, not *孩子節/孩子节.

李哲：　這些話一定是跟我哥哥學的。我嫂子整天要她學
　　　　這學那，可是我哥哥反對給孩子太大的壓力，他
　　　　認為⑤對孩子來說，最重要的是有一個快樂的童年。

麗莎：　我的童年可以説很快樂。可是現在，每次上中文課
　　　　我就想，要是我小時候父母就讓我學中文，我現在
　　　　就輕鬆多了。

李哲：　没想到這兒有我嫂子的一個知音！這麼説你同意我
　　　　嫂子的做法？

麗莎：　我並③不完全同意，但我能理解。

李哲：　很多家長望子成龍，望女成鳳，都希望自己的孩子
　　　　小時候好好學習，將來能做出一番大事業。可是到
　　　　現在我也想不清楚，孩子到底是將來"成龍""成
　　　　鳳"好④，還是有一個快樂的童年好？

麗莎：　我的看法是兩個都重要。一個人當然應該有快樂的
　　　　童年，但是也應該成為社會需要的人材，所以孩子
　　　　最好還是在學校多學一些知識。

李哲：　可是你別忘了，有些知識不是在學校裏或者從書本⑥
　　　　上學的，而是⑤從社會、從生活中學的。

麗莎：　哎，李哲，你真成了哲學家⑦了。

After You Study

Challenge yourself to complete the following tasks in Chinese.
1. Give a brief description of Li Zhe's brother.
2. Give a brief description of Li Zhe's sister-in-law.

LANGUAGE NOTES

❺ 認為/认为 is different from 對⋯來説/对⋯来説. While 對⋯來説/对⋯来説 can only convey the speaker's opinion, 認為/认为 may express either the opinion of the speaker or the opinion of the person being spoken about.

李哲：　这些话一定是跟我哥哥学的。我嫂子整天要她学
　　　　这学那，可是我哥哥反对给孩子太大的压力，他
　　　　认为⑤对孩子来说，最重要的是有一个快乐的童年。

丽莎：　我的童年可以说很快乐。可是现在，每次上中文课
　　　　我就想，要是我小时候父母就让我学中文，我现在
　　　　就轻松多了。

李哲：　没想到这儿有我嫂子的一个知音！这么说你同意我
　　　　嫂子的做法？

丽莎：　我并③不完全同意，但我能理解。

李哲：　很多家长望子成龙，望女成凤，都希望自己的孩子
　　　　小时候好好学习，将来能做出一番大事业。可是到
　　　　现在我也想不清楚，孩子到底是将来"成龙""成
　　　　凤"好④，还是有一个快乐的童年好？

丽莎：　我的看法是两个都重要。一个人当然应该有快乐的
　　　　童年，但是也应该成为社会需要的人材，所以孩子
　　　　最好还是在学校多学一些知识。

李哲：　可是你别忘了，有些知识不是在学校里或者从书本❻
　　　　上学的，而是⑤从社会、从生活中学的。

丽莎：　哎，李哲，你真成了哲学家❼了。

---

3. List the classes that Li Zhe's niece takes outside of school hours.

4. According to Li Zhe, where does learning take place?

---

❻ 書本/书本 is a collective noun for books in general.

❼ 家 can be used as a suffix to mean an expert or established scholar in a particular field: 畫家/画家, 哲學家/哲学家, 文學家/文学家, 歷史學家/历史学家, 化學家/化学家, etc.

VOCABULARY

1.	移民		yímín	n/v	immigrant; to immigrate
2.	博士		bóshì	n	Ph.D.; doctor [academic degree]
3.	設計	设计	shèjì	v/n	to design; design
4.	嫂子		sǎozi	n	older brother's wife
5.	留學	留学	liú xué	vo	to study abroad
6.	碩士	硕士	shuòshì	n	master's degree
7.	結婚	结婚	jié hūn	vo	to get married; to marry
8.	美滿	美满	měimǎn	adj	happy and satisfying
9.	厲害	厉害	lìhai	adj	terrible; formidable
10.	侄女		zhínǚ	n	brother's daughter
11.	小學	小学	xiǎoxué	n	elementary school; grade school
12.	安排		ānpái	v	to arrange
13.	滿	满	mǎn	adj	full
14.	鋼琴	钢琴	gāngqín	n	piano
15.	畫畫兒	画画儿	huà huàr	vo	to draw; to paint
16.	抱怨		bàoyuàn	v	to complain
17.	兒童	儿童	értóng	n	children
18.	家長	家长	jiāzhǎng	n	parents; guardian of a child
19.	尊重		zūnzhòng	v	to respect
20.	選擇	选择	xuǎnzé	n/v	choice; to choose
21.	反對	反对	fǎnduì	v	to oppose
22.	認為	认为	rènwéi	v	to think; to consider

23.	童年	tóngnián	n	childhood
24.	知音	zhīyīn	n	someone who truly understands; soulmate
25.	做法	zuòfǎ	n	way of doing things; course of action
26.	並　　并	bìng	adv	actually; definitely [See Grammar 3.]
27.	完全	wánquán	adv/adj	completely; fully; complete; whole
28.	理解	lǐjiě	v	to understand
29.	望子成龍　望子成龙	wàng zǐ chéng lóng		to hope that one's son will become a dragon; to hope that one's son will become successful
30.	望女成鳳　望女成凤	wàng nǔ chéng fèng		to hope that one's daughter will become a phoenix; to hope that one's daughter will become successful
31.	番	fān	m	(measure word for type or kind)
32.	事業　事业	shìyè	n	career; undertaking
33.	看法	kànfǎ	n	point of view
34.	社會　社会	shèhuì	n	society
35.	人材	réncái	n	person of ability, integrity, and talent
36.	知識　知识	zhīshi	n	knowledge
37.	書本　书本	shūběn	n	books
38.	不是…而是…	búshì… érshì…		it's not...but... [See Grammar 5.]

Proper Noun

39.	墨西哥	Mòxīgē		Mexico

Enlarged Characters

厲	畫	擇	龍	鳳
厉	画	择	龙	凤

教育硕士招生

誰會對這個廣告有興趣?
谁会对这个广告有兴趣?

Culture Highlights

❶ The term 知音 comes from a well-known story about the friendship between the 琴 (a classical Chinese seven-stringed plucked instrument) virtuoso Yu Boya 俞伯牙 and Zhong Ziqi 鐘子期/钟子期, a humble woodcutter. Once when Boya was playing the 琴, a string broke. Zhong commented, "That was superb playing about Confucius praising his disciple Yan Hui. It's a pity that the string broke at the fourth phrase." Boya was amazed at having found such a 知音, or someone genuinely capable of understanding his music. When Zhong Ziqi died, Boya was so distraught that he smashed his instrument and stopped playing. That's why 知音 has now come to mean a "soul-mate" or "kindred spirit."

❷ 龍/龙 is an animal with magical powers in ancient Chinese mythology and a symbol of imperial power. 鳳/凤, short for 鳳凰/凤凰 (fènghuáng), is the sovereign of all birds in Chinese legends. The dragon and phoenix in 望子成龍/望子成龙 and 望女成鳳/望女成凤 are metaphors for outstanding talents.

左邊是龍，右邊是鳳凰。
左边是龙，右边是凤凰。

Grammar

1. Adverb 才

才 is used before numbers to express a small quantity:

❶   我每天上網才三個小時，時間不多。

我每天上网才三个小时，时间不多。

(I go online for only three hours a day. That's not much time.)

❷   現在才六點，球賽八點開始，不用這麼早去。

现在才六点，球赛八点开始，不用这么早去。

(It's only six o'clock. The ballgame starts at eight. There's no need to go so early.)

❸   你今年才二十歲，就想結婚？

你今年才二十岁，就想结婚？

(You are just twenty years old, and you already want to get married?)

When 才 is used after numbers and measure words and before verbs, it expresses slowness or lateness, as we have already learned.

❹   我大哥二十歲就念完博士了，我二十歲才上大學。

我大哥二十岁就念完博士了，我二十岁才上大学。

(My older brother finished his doctorate at the tender age of twenty. I didn't even start college until twenty.)

2. Descriptive Complements

Descriptive complements can also indicate the result of an action. In terms of structure and meaning, descriptive complements are quite complicated. Like resultative complements, descriptive complements can be divided into different categories. Some are related to the verb in meaning, some to the subject, and some to the object.

A. Complements that are related to the verb in meaning:

❶   我每天起床起得很早。
(I get up very early every morning.)
(起床—早)

❷   他跑步跑得很快。
(He runs very quickly.)
(跑—快)

B. Complements that are related to the subject in meaning:

❸   他高興得笑了起來。
他高兴得笑了起来。
(He was so happy that he started to laugh.)
(他—高興/高兴，他—笑了起來/来)

❹   聽了她的話，我笑得肚子都疼了。
听了她的话，我笑得肚子都疼了。
(When I heard her words, I laughed until my stomach began to hurt.)
(我—笑，我—肚子疼了)

C. Complements that are related to the object in meaning:

❺   我侄女才小學三年級，我嫂子就把她的時間安排得
滿滿的。
我侄女才小学三年级，我嫂子就把她的时间安排得
满满的。
(My niece is just a third grader. My sister-in-law is already making her schedule extremely busy.)
(嫂子—安排時間/安排时间，時間/时间—滿滿的/
满满的)

❻ 老師說我太懶，不用功，說得我很不好意思。

老师说我太懒，不用功，说得我很不好意思。

(My teacher said I was too lazy and didn't work hard enough. I was very embarrassed.)

(老師/老师—說/说—我，我—不好意思。)

If the descriptive complement is related in meaning to the subject or the object, the verb or the adjective that takes the descriptive complement is often the cause, and the complement indicates the result, as seen in ❸, ❹, ❺ and ❻.

3. Adverb 並/并

並/并 is used before 不, 沒 or other similar adverbs to make an emphatic point, often to refute a specific statement and point out the truth:

❶ 李哲：沒想到這兒有我嫂子的一個知音！這麼說你同意我嫂子的做法？

李哲：没想到这儿有我嫂子的一个知音！这么说你同意我嫂子的做法？

(Li Zhe: Who knew? My sister-in-law has an appreciative audience here. Do you mean to say that you agree with my sister-in-law's method?)

麗莎：我並不完全同意，但我能理解。

丽莎：我并不完全同意，但我能理解。

(Lisa: Actually, I don't agree completely, but I can understand her.)

❷ A: 你要上醫學院，這麼說，你喜歡當醫生。

你要上医学院，这么说，你喜欢当医生。

(You want to go to medical school. Does that mean you'd like being a doctor?)

B: 實際上我並不想當醫生，可是我父母非讓我上醫學院
不可。

实际上我并不想当医生，可是我父母非让我上医学院
不可。

(Actually, I don't really want to be a doctor, but my parents insist that I go to
medical school.)

❸ A: 小李告訴我，你說你的手機在我這兒？

小李告诉我，你说你的手机在我这儿？

(Little Li told me that you said your cell phone was here with me?)

B: 這個小李，我只說你借過我的手機，並沒說我的手機在
你那兒。

这个小李！我只说你借过我的手机，并没说我的手机在
你那儿。

(That Little Li! All I said was you had borrowed my cell phone. I never said that you
had my cell phone.)

4. Adjectives as Predicates

When an adjective is used as a predicate, the subject of the sentence can be a "subject +
predicate" phrase:

❶ 你說，我們寒假去哪兒旅行好？

你说，我们寒假去哪儿旅行好？

(Say, where should we travel during the winter break?)

❷ 今天晚上有一個生日舞會，我不知道穿什麼衣服合適。

今天晚上有一个生日舞会，我不知道穿什么衣服合适。

(Tonight there is a birthday party. I don't know what to wear.)

❸ 你現在讀書最重要，交女朋友不用着急。

你现在读书最重要，交女朋友不用着急。

(The most important thing for you now is studying. There's no need for you to rush to
find a girlfriend.)

5. 不是A, 而是B

When responding to a statement or situation, the speaker wishes to negate A and strongly affirm B.

1 麗莎，你知道有些知識不是在學校裏或者從書本上學的，而是從社會、從生活中學的。

丽莎，你知道有些知识不是在学校里或者从书本上学的，而是从社会、从生活中学的。

(Lisa, you know some knowledge can't be learned in school or from books. Rather one learns it from society, from life.)

2 我不是不希望孩子將來有一番大事業，而是不想給他太大的壓力。

我不是不希望孩子将来有一番大事业，而是不想给他太大的压力。

(It's not that I don't want my child to have a great career in the future. It's just that I don't want to put too much pressure on him.)

3 你這樣做不是為他好，而是給他找麻煩。

你这样做不是为他好，而是给他找麻烦。

(What you're doing won't do him any good; on the contrary, it will bring him trouble.)

4 **A:** 你不叫我買這件襯衫，是怕我的錢不夠，跟你借錢嗎？

你不叫我买这件衬衫，是怕我的钱不够，跟你借钱吗？

(You don't want me to buy this shirt. Is it because you're afraid that I don't have enough money, and I'll borrow money from you?)

B: 你想錯了，我不是怕你跟我借錢，而是覺得這件襯衫質量不好，你不應該買。

你想错了，我不是怕你跟我借钱，而是觉得这件衬衫质量不好，你不应该买。

(You're wrong. I'm not afraid that you'll borrow money from me. Rather I feel that the quality of the shirt is not great. You shouldn't get it.)

5 **A:** 剛才找你的人是你的女朋友吧?

刚才找你的人是你的女朋友吧?

(Was that person who came looking for you just now your girlfriend?)

B: 別亂說，她不是我的女朋友，而是我的嫂子。

别乱说，她不是我的女朋友，而是我的嫂子。

(Don't talk nonsense. She's not my girlfriend, she is my sister-in-law.)

這位老師教什麼? 化學、英語、還是音樂?
他拿到的是什麼樣的學位?
这位老师教什么? 化学、英语、还是音乐?
他拿到的是什么样的学位?

Words & Phrases

A. 一直 **(all along; continuously)**

❶ 開學已經兩個多月了，張天明一直住在學生宿舍裏。
開学已经两个多月了，张天明一直住在学生宿舍里。
(School started two months ago. Zhang Tianming has been living in student housing since then.)

❷ 她搬進新房子後，一直沒交房租。
她搬进新房子后，一直没交房租。
(Since she moved into her new apartment, she hasn't been paying her rent.)

❸ 小林的專業是金融，畢業以後，一直在銀行工作。
小林的专业是金融，毕业以后，一直在银行工作。
(Xiao Lin's major was finance. Ever since he graduated, he's been working in the banking industry.)

這是什麼廣告？
这是什么广告？

❹　小張有兩條毯子，只用了一條，另外的一條一直放在櫃
子裏。

小张有两条毯子，只用了一条，另外的一条一直放在柜
子里。

(Xiao Zhang has two blankets. She is only using one of them. The other one is stored
in the cabinet.)

B. 好(不)容易 (with a lot of difficulty)

Both 好不容易 and 好容易 mean 很不容易, "with a lot of difficulty."

❶　演唱會的票很難買，我好不容易才買到一張。

演唱会的票很难买，我好不容易才买到一张。

(It was really hard to get tickets for this concert. It took me a lot of trouble to get
one.)

❷　今天的功課真多，我好容易才做完。

今天的功课真多，我好容易才做完。

(There was so much homework today. It took me forever to get it done.)

❸　這個生詞昨天我好不容易才記住了，可是今天又忘了。

这个生词昨天我好不容易才记住了，可是今天又忘了。

(I finally managed to remember this new word yesterday, but I forgot it again today.)

C. 像…一樣/像…一样 (as if)

❶　她說話怎麼像個小大人一樣？

她说话怎么像个小大人一样？

(How come she talks like she's an adult?)

❷　這碗湯一點兒味道都沒有，像是沒放鹽一樣。

这碗汤一点儿味道都没有，像是没放盐一样。

(This soup is so bland, as if it has no salt in it.)

❸   那個孩子像個小狗一樣跟在他後邊。

那个孩子像个小狗一样跟在他后边。

(That kid follows him like a puppy.)

D. 可以說/可以说 (you could say)

This expression means "it could be said," or "you could say." Sometimes it is followed by a second clause offering a contrary view or scenario.

❶   我的童年可以說很快樂。可是…

我的童年可以说很快乐。可是…

(You could say that I had a happy childhood, but ...)

❷   小高可以說是我們這裏最聰明的人了。

小高可以说是我们这里最聪明的人了。

(You could say that Little Gao is the smartest guy among us.)

❸   小林在我們班可以說是最用功的了，可是考試並不是最
好的。

小林在我们班可以说是最用功的了，可是考试并不是最
好的。

(Little Lin could be said to be the most diligent student in our class, but his test scores are not the best.)

E. 這麼說/这么说 (so that means)

This phrase introduces a conclusion that a speaker draws from what has just been said.

❶ A: 明天我很忙，那個演唱會…

明天我很忙，那个演唱会…

(Tomorrow I'll be very busy. That concert...)

B: 這麼説，你明天不去聽演唱會了。

这么说，你明天不去听演唱会了？

(So that means you won't be going to the concert tomorrow?)

A: 對。

对。

(Correct.)

❷ **A:** 小張已經去中國了。

小张已经去中国了。

(Little Zhang has already left for China.)

B: 這麼説，他不考試就走了？

这么说，他不考试就走了？

(Does that mean he left without taking the exam?)

A: 是的。他説回來再考。

是的。他说回来再考。

(Yes. He said he'll take it when he comes back.)

❸ **A:** 小張和他的女朋友最近吵架吵得很屬害，兩個人決定分手。

小张和他的女朋友最近吵架吵得很厉害，两个人决定分手。

(Little Zhang and his girlfriend have been having terrible arguments recently. They decided to call it quits.)

B: 這麼説，他們不打算結婚了？他們的父母知道嗎？

这么说，他们不打算结婚了？他们的父母知道吗？

(Does that mean they aren't getting married? Do their parents know?)

A: 知道，他們都理解。

知道，他们都理解。

(Yes, and they understand.)

F. 最好 (had better; it's best)

❶　吃完飯後，最好不要馬上運動。

吃完饭后，最好不要马上运动。

(It's best not to exercise right after you eat.)

❷　**A:** 我想學化學專業，將來好找工作。

我想学化学专业，将来好找工作。

(I'd like to major in chemistry so that I can get a job easily.)

　　B: 你喜歡化學嗎？如果不喜歡，最好別學。

你喜欢化学吗？如果不喜欢，最好别学。

(Do you like chemistry? If you don't, you'd better not major in it.)

❸　這部電影很受歡迎，看的人多，如果想看，最好早點買票。

这部电影很受欢迎，看的人多，如果想看，最好早点买票。

(This film is very popular. Many people want to see it. If you want to see it, you'd better get a ticket as soon as you can.)

碩士班:
教育、人文藝術、理學等22個班別
（98年1月12日起繳費報名）

大學部重點運動項目績優學生單獨招生:
籃球(女)、游泳、羽球(女)、網球(女)
跆拳道、鐵人三項等6個項目
（98年2月23日起繳費報名）

在職進修碩士班:
教育、人文藝術、理學等13個班別
（98年3月2日起繳費報名）

博士班:
教育、中國語文、教育行政與評鑑研究所
（98年3月11日起繳費報名）

What degrees do they offer?

Language Practice

A. The Early Years

For this exercise, take on the persona of your favorite actor, athlete, politician, or other role model. Pretend you are being interviewed for a new biography. On a scale of 1-5, rate your childhood.

	not at all				extremely
happy	1	2	3	4	5
pressured	1	2	3	4	5

Go around the class and ask your classmates (in the roles of their new personas):

1. 你的童年快樂嗎？
2. 你的童年壓力大嗎？

1. 你的童年快乐吗？
2. 你的童年压力大吗？

Record and sum up their answers.

EXAMPLE:

Kayla, Jennifer, Matt 覺得他們的
童年一點都不快樂，
壓力大得不得了。

Kayla, Jennifer, Matt 觉得他们的
童年一点都不快乐，
压力大得不得了。

or

Kaitlin, Steve, Rosa 覺得他們的
童年非常快樂，
一點壓力都沒有。

Kaitlin, Steve, Rosa 觉得他们的
童年非常快乐，
一点压力都没有。

B. Extracurricular Experiences

List Li Zhe's niece's extracurricular activities in Chinese. In addition, list any other common ones that you can think of.

_____

_____

_____

_____

Work with a partner, and ask each other

    a. if you participated in any of the ones listed when you were growing up;

    b. if any of the ones you participated in were your own choices;

    c. if any of the ones you participated in were arranged by your parents;

    d. if you enjoyed the activities, regardless of who arranged them.

C. Helicopter Parents?

If you were a parent, what kind of after-school schedule would you establish for your children to prepare them for the future?

	星期一	星期二	星期三	星期四	星期五	星期六	星期日
下午							
晚上							

Pair up with a partner, and take turns to go over your schedules. Then comment on what you think of each other's schedule. Would it be too much for the children? Do they need some breathing room? Would the children complain? How much say would the children have in choosing their own activities?

┌───┐
│ ⬤ 班　別 │
├───┤
│ ☆ 兒 童 英 語 班：按英語程度分班，8人精致小班，每週上課三天 │
│ 　　　　　　　　　(一、三、四，下午班：1:30 - 3:30、或傍晚班：4:30 - 6:30)。 │
│ ☆ 兒童中文作文班：每週上課二次，(每週三、四)。 │
└───┘

父母可以送孩子來這兒學什麼？
父母可以送孩子来这儿学什么？

D. Expectations and Accomplishments

a. List the things that your parents hope you will have accomplished after completing your education.

1._____

2._____

3._____

•••

b. List the things that you expect yourself to accomplish after graduation.

1._____

2._____

3._____

•••

c. List the things that you hope your future children/nephews/nieces will accomplish when they grow up.

1._____

2._____

3._____

•••

Look at the three lists and discuss with a partner if you can live up to your parents' expectations, how your own expectations for yourself are similar to or different from your parents' expectations for you, and whether you will be like your parents in your expectations of the next generation. Jot down what you have been discussing on the clipboard below and pay attention to the use of time phrases and pronouns/nouns as connectors and other conjunctions to build a more coherent and cohesive narrative. Then present your narrative to your class.

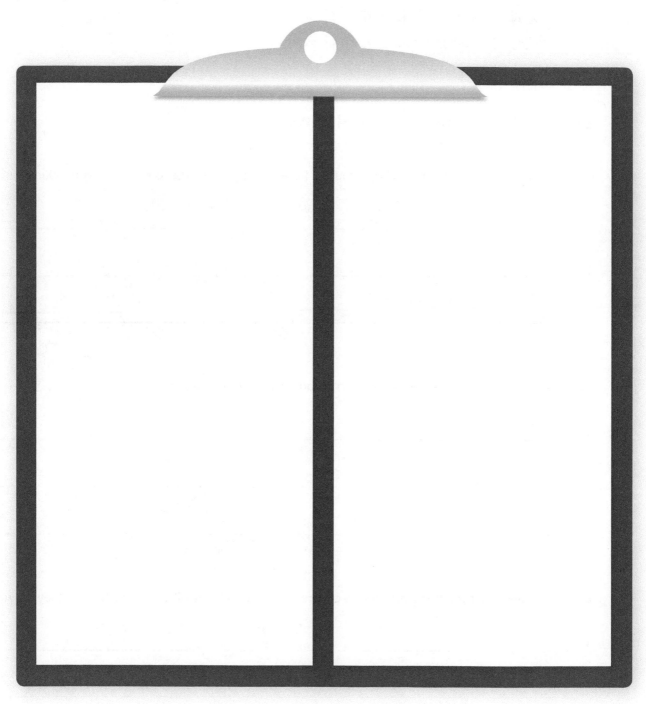

望女成鳳
望女成凤

E. Check Your Facts!

Pair up with a partner and get your facts straight based on the text of this lesson.

EXAMPLE:　李哲的父母是加拿大移民。

A: 我聽説李哲的父母是
加拿大移民。

B: 李哲的父母不是加拿大
移民，而是墨西哥移民。

A: 我听说李哲的父母是
加拿大移民。

B: 李哲的父母不是加拿大
移民，而是墨西哥移民。

1. 李哲的哥哥是電腦碩士
2. 李哲的哥哥同意給孩子
很大的壓力
3. 麗莎同意李哲嫂子的做法

1. 李哲的哥哥是电脑硕士
2. 李哲的哥哥同意给孩子
很大的压力
3. 丽莎同意李哲嫂子的做法

4. 李哲的哥哥和嫂子在家庭經濟問題上意見不同

4. 李哲的哥哥和嫂子在家庭经济问题上意见不同

F. Taking Sides

How do you state your agreement or disagreement with others? Here are some options:

1. 我同意/反對⋯
2. 我(不)同意___的看法/做法/意見。我認為/覺得⋯
3. 我覺得___說的話很有道理/沒有道理。
4. 我不完全同意/反對⋯

1. 我同意/反对⋯
2. 我(不)同意___的看法/做法/意见。我认为/觉得⋯
3. 我觉得___的话很有道理/没有道理。
4. 我不完全同意/反对⋯

Use at least three of the above four options to state your opinions in the following exercises.

a. 李哲的侄女認為兒童也是人，有自己的愛好和興趣，家長應該尊重孩子自己的選擇。你同意嗎？

b. 李哲的哥哥反對給孩子太大的壓力。你覺得呢？

c. 麗莎覺得孩子應該有個快樂的童年，也應該好好學習。你的看法呢？

a. 李哲的侄女认为儿童也是人，有自己的爱好和兴趣，家长应该尊重孩子自己的选择。你同意吗？

b. 李哲的哥哥反对给孩子太大的压力。你觉得呢？

c. 丽莎觉得孩子应该有个快乐的童年，也应该好好学习。你的看法呢？

G. Your Opinions, Please!

Answer the following questions according to your own perspective.

a. 柯林對大一新生住在校內的看法是什麼？
你同意嗎？為什麼？

b. 張天明買衣服的標準是什麼？你的看法呢？

c. 李哲大學畢業以後，打算念研究生。你有什麼建議？

d. 雖然張天明常常忘這忘那，讓麗莎生氣，但麗莎並沒跟天明分手。你對麗莎的決定有什麼看法？

a. 柯林对大一新生住在校内的看法是什么？
你同意吗？为什么？

b. 张天明买衣服的标准是什么？你的看法呢？

c. 李哲大学毕业以后，打算念研究生。你有什么建议？

d. 虽然张天明常常忘这忘那，让丽莎生气，但丽莎并没跟天明分手。你对丽莎的决定有什么看法？

Pinyin Text

Lǐ Zhé de fùmǔ shì Mòxīgē yímín, tā hé tā gēge dōu shì zài Jiāzhōu chūshēng, zhǎng dà de. Gēge shì diànnǎo bóshì❶, zìjǐ shèjì, guǎnlǐ wǎngzhàn. Lǐ Zhé de sǎozi shíwǔ nián qián cóng Xiānggǎng lái Měiguó liú xué, ná dào shuòshì xuéwèi yǐhòu zhǎo dào gōngzuò, jiù zài Měiguó zhù le xia lai. Gēge hé sǎozi jié hūn shí nián le, shēnghuó yìzhí hěn měimǎn, kěshì zuìjìn liǎng nián zài nǚ'ér de jiàoyù wèntí shang, yìjiàn chángcháng bù tóng, yǒu shí shènzhì chǎo de hěn lìhai. Yì tiān, Lǐ Zhé zhèngzài xiàn shang gēn zhínǚ liáo tiānr, kàn jiàn Lìshā zǒu le jin lai.

(Lǐ Zhé xià xiàn …)

Lǐ Zhé: Lìshā, yǒu shìr ma?

Lìshā: Méi shénme shìr, wǒ zhǎo Tiānmíng, yǐwéi tā zài nǐ zhèr ne. Duìbuqǐ, hài de nǐ bǎ diànhuà guà le.

Lǐ Zhé: Zuò, zuò, zuò. Gāngcái shì wǒ zhínǚ gěi wǒ dǎ diànhuà, wǒmen zhènghǎo shuō wán le.

Lìshā: Nǐ yǒu zhínǚ? Jīnnián duō dà le?

Lǐ Zhé: Tā jīnnián gāng bā suì.

Lìshā: Tā gěi nǐ dǎ diànhuà yǒu shénme shì a?

Lǐ Zhé: Shuō lái huà cháng❷. Wǒ zhínǚ cái① xiǎoxué sān niánjí, wǒ sǎozi jiù bǎ tā de shíjiān ānpái de② mǎn mǎn de: xīngqīyī xué gāngqín❸, xīngqī'èr xué huà huàr, xīngqīsān xué yóu yǒng, xīngqīsì xué huá bīng, xīngqīwǔ hǎobù róngyì xiūxi yì tiān, xīngqīliù yòu jiào tā qù shàng Zhōngwén xuéxiào. Tā bù xǐhuan xué Zhōngwén, yúshì jiù dǎ diànhuà dào wǒ zhèr lái, yìbiān kū yìbiān bàoyuàn.

Lìshā: Méi nàme yánzhòng ba? Tā zhǐ shì ge háizi, néng bàoyuàn xiē shénme a?

Lǐ Zhé: Tā shuō értóng❹ yě shì rén, yǒu zìjǐ de àihào hé xìngqù, jiāzhǎng yīnggāi zūnzhòng háizi zìjǐ de xuǎnzé.

Lìshā: Tā shuō huà zěnme xiàng ge xiǎo dàren yíyàng?

Lǐ Zhé: Zhè xiē huà yídìng shì gēn wǒ gēge xué de. Wǒ sǎozi zhěngtiān yào tā xué zhè xué nà, kěshì wǒ gēge fǎnduì gěi háizi tài dà de yālì, tā rènwéi❺ duì háizi lái shuō, zuì zhòngyào de shì yǒu yí ge kuàilè de tóngnián.

Lìshā: Wǒ de tóngnián kěyǐ shuō hěn kuàilè. Kěshì xiànzài, měi cì shàng Zhōngwén kè wǒ jiù xiǎng, yàoshi wǒ xiǎoshíhou fùmǔ jiù ràng wǒ xué Zhōngwén, wǒ xiànzài jiù qīngsōng duō le.

Lǐ Zhé:	Méi xiǎng dào zhèr yǒu wǒ sǎozi de yí ge zhīyīn! Zhème shuō nǐ tóngyì wǒ sǎozi de zuòfǎ?
Lìshā:	Wǒ bìng③ bù wánquán tóngyì, dàn wǒ néng lǐjiě.
Lǐ Zhé:	Hěn duō jiāzhǎng wàng zǐ chéng lóng, wàng nǚ chéng fèng, dōu xīwàng zìjǐ de háizi xiǎoshíhou hǎo hāo xuéxí, jiānglái néng zuò chū yì fān dà shìyè. Kěshì dào xiànzài wǒ yě xiǎng bu qīngchu, háizi dàodǐ shì jiānglái "chéng lóng" "chéng fèng" hǎo④, háishi yǒu yí ge kuàilè de tóngnián hǎo?
Lìshā:	Wǒ de kànfǎ shì liǎng ge dōu zhòngyào. Yí ge rén dāngrán yīnggāi yǒu kuàilè de tóngnián, dànshì yě yīnggāi chéngwéi shèhuì xūyào de réncái, suǒyǐ háizi zuìhǎo háishì zài xuéxiào duō xué yì xiē zhīshi.
Lǐ Zhé:	Kěshì nǐ bié wàng le, yǒu xiē zhīshi bú shì zài xuéxiào li huòzhě cóng shūběn⑥ shang xué de, ér shì④ cóng shèhuì, cóng shēnghuó zhōng xué de.
Lìshā:	Āi, Lǐ Zhé, nǐ zhēn chéng le zhéxuéjiā⑦ le.

English Text

Li Zhe's parents are Mexican immigrants. He and his older brother were both born and grew up in California. His older brother has a doctorate in Computer Science. He designs and manages websites. Li Zhe's sister-in-law came from Hong Kong to the United States fifteen years ago to study. After she got a master's degree and found a job, she settled in America. Li Zhe's older brother and sister-in-law have been married for ten years. They have always been very happy, but in the last couple of years their opinions have differed over their daughter's education, sometimes causing big arguments. One day, Li Zhe is chatting with his niece online when he sees Lisa walk in.

(Li Zhe logs off.)

Li Zhe:	Lisa, what's up?
Lisa:	Nothing. I came to look for Tianming. I thought he was here with you. I'm sorry. I made you hang up.
Li Zhe:	Sit, please sit. Just now my niece called me but we had just finished talking.
Lisa:	You have a niece? How old is she?
Li Zhe:	She just turned eight this year.

Lisa: What did she want to talk about?

Li Zhe: It's a long story. My niece just started third grade. My sister-in-law is already cramming her schedule full of activities: Monday piano lesson; Tuesday painting lesson; Wednesday swimming; Thursday ice skating; Friday a rare break; Saturday Chinese lesson. She doesn't like studying Chinese. That's why she called me. She cried and complained.

Lisa: Is it that serious? She's just a kid. What does she have to complain about?

Li Zhe: She says even a kid is a person with her own interests and hobbies. Parents should respect their children's choices.

Lisa: She talks just like a little grownup!

Li Zhe: She must have learned it from my older brother. My sister-in-law is always wanting her to study this or that, but my older brother objects to putting too much pressure on her. He thinks that the most important thing for a kid is to have a happy childhood.

Lisa: I can say that I had a very happy childhood, but now every time I'm in my Chinese class I wish that my parents had made me learn Chinese when I was a child. I would have a much easier time.

Li Zhe: Who knew? My sister-in-law has a kindred spirit here. Does that mean you agree with my sister-in-law's method?

Lisa: I don't agree entirely, but I can understand.

Li Zhe: Many parents hope that their children will rise above the others. They all hope that their children study well when they are young so that they can have a successful career, but even now I still haven't figured it out whether it's better for children to become high achievers in the future or have a happy childhood.

Lisa: My view is that both are important. Of course, everyone should have a happy childhood, but he or she should also become an accomplished person who can make a contribution to society. So it's best for children to learn as much as they can in school.

Li Zhe: But don't forget: Some knowledge can't be learned in school or from books. It must be learned from society, from life.

Lisa: Oh, Li Zhe, you've really turned into a bona fide philosopher.

SELF-ASSESSMENT

How well can you do these things? Check (✔) the boxes to evaluate your progress and see which areas you may need to practice more.

I can	Very Well	OK	A Little
Talk about whether I had a carefree childhood	☐	☐	☐
List some commonly offered classes in after-school programs	☐	☐	☐
State whether I agree or disagree with others' point of view	☐	☐	☐
Begin presenting my viewpoints with appropriate wording	☐	☐	☐
Discuss parents' hopes and expectations for their children	☐	☐	☐

第十課　第十课
中國地理　中国地理

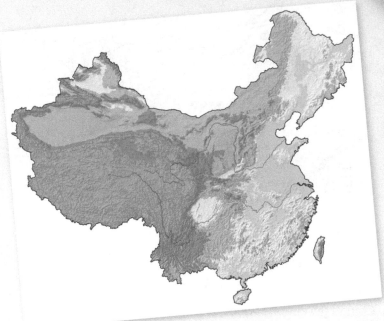

LEARNING OBJECTIVES

In this lesson, you will learn to use Chinese to

1. Locate major Chinese cities, provinces, and rivers on the map;
2. Give a brief introduction to the geographic features of China;
3. Compare some basic geographic aspects of China and the United States;
4. Describe features that may attract you to or deter you from visiting a tourist site;
5. Plan a trip to China.

RELATE AND GET READY

In your own culture/community—

* Can you name the major rivers and mountain ranges in your country?
* Do you know where your country's major cities are located, along the coasts or mostly inland?
* Can you give an account of the population and geographic location of your town/city?
* Do people consider your local town/city to be popular with tourists?

Before You Study

Check the statements that apply to you.

- ☐ 1. I know my country's geography well.
- ☐ 2. I know China's geography well.

When You Study

Listen to the audio recording and scan the text. Ask yourself the following questions before you begin a close reading of the text.

1. When will this trip take place?

寒假快到了，張天明這幾天一直在考慮旅行❶的事兒。
他的父母希望他去他們的家鄉南京看看，張天明也很想
當麗莎的導遊，帶她到中國的一些地方走走。除了南京
以外，還應該去什麼地方呢？為了決定旅行的路線，
張天明拿出一張中國地圖，研究了起來①。

LANGUAGE NOTES

❶ 旅行 and 旅遊/旅游 are more or less synonymous. 遊/游 means to wander, so 旅遊/旅游
specifically implies traveling for pleasure. To travel for business is 出差 (chū chāi). 旅行 by itself

- 3. I know which parts of China I would like to visit.
- 4. I am good at budgeting and setting up an itinerary for a trip.

2. What will be their first stop in China?

3. What are the two main factors determining their travel itinerary?

寒假快到了，张天明这几天一直在考虑旅行❶的事儿。
他的父母希望他去他们的家乡南京看看，张天明也很想
当丽莎的导游，带她到中国的一些地方走走。除了南京
以外，还应该去什么地方呢？为了决定旅行的路线，
张天明拿出一张中国地图，研究了起来❶。

doesn't state the purpose of travel. However, "travel agency" is always 旅行社. Tourists are 遊客/
游客 or 觀光客/观光客 (guānguāngkè) in Taiwan, where 觀光/观光 means "sightseeing."

張天明：　麗莎，你來看看中國地圖，看到哪兒去旅行好。

麗莎：　　看地圖？你這個主意不錯，我也正想學學中國地理呢。我對中國地理了解得太少了。

張天明：　我們先到南京，我父母的家鄉…在這裏，在中國的東南邊。然後你想去哪兒？

麗莎：　　哎，這是哈爾濱，對嗎？去哈爾濱吧。

張天明：　你一下子要從東南邊跑到最北邊去？

麗莎：　　昨天電視裏介紹哈爾濱的冰燈了，好看極了。

張天明：　冰燈好看是好看，可是哈爾濱現在冷得不得了，夏天再去吧。

麗莎：　　噢，好吧。不去北邊，那坐火車去西邊吧，聽説新疆是個很特別的地方。

張天明：　新疆在西北，十月就開始冷起來了①，現在去不合適。另外，坐火車太花時間，下次再去吧！

麗莎：　　你説坐火車太花時間，這麼説坐船也不行了，對嗎？要不然我真想坐船從東往西，看看長江或者黃河的風景。

張天明：　中國的河流②，大多是從西往東流，如果坐船從東往西走，肯定得花更長的時間。

麗莎：　　為什麼中國的河流大多從西往東流呢？

張天明：　因為中國西邊是高原，那兒有世界上最高的山。而②東邊是平原和大海。

LANGUAGE NOTES

❷ 河流 is a collective noun. It refers to rivers in general or all the rivers within a geographic area. 河 refers to a specific river or several rivers.

张天明：　丽莎，你来看看中国地图，看到哪儿去旅行好。

丽莎：　　看地图？你这个主意不错，我也正想学学中国地理呢。我对中国地理了解得太少了。

张天明：　我们先到南京，我父母的家乡…在这里，在中国的东南边。然后你想去哪儿？

丽莎：　　哎，这是哈尔滨，对吗？去哈尔滨吧。

张天明：　你一下子要从东南边跑到最北边去？

丽莎：　　昨天电视里介绍哈尔滨的冰灯了，好看极了。

张天明：　冰灯好看是好看，可是哈尔滨现在冷得不得了，夏天再去吧。

丽莎：　　噢，好吧。不去北边，那坐火车去西边吧，听说新疆是个很特别的地方。

张天明：　新疆在西北，十月就开始冷起来了[①]，现在去不合适。另外，坐火车太花时间，下次再去吧！

丽莎：　　你说坐火车太花时间，这么说坐船也不行了，对吗？要不然我真想坐船从东往西，看看长江或者黄河的风景。

张天明：　中国的河流[②]，大多是从西往东流，如果坐船从东往西走，肯定得花更长的时间。

丽莎：　　为什么中国的河流大多从西往东流呢？

张天明：　因为中国西边是高原，那儿有世界上最高的山。而[②]东边是平原和大海。

麗莎：　　好像大城市都靠海或者離海不遠。你看，在北邊，
　　　　　這是北京、天津；東南邊，這兒有上海、南京；
　　　　　南邊這裏，是廣州和深圳。

張天明：你説的没錯。中國的人口主要集中在沿海一帶。
　　　　　西南呢，高山、高原多，西北呢，沙漠多，自然
　　　　　條件不太好，所以人口比較少。

麗莎：　　我覺得中國的地形和美國有點兒像。

張天明：你説的有道理。還有，中國和美國的緯度❸接近，
　　　　　面積也差不多，可是你知道，人口是美國的四倍
　　　　　多。聽説，過節或者放假的時候，中國的旅遊景點
　　　　　到處都是人山人海，擠得很。

麗莎：　　是嗎？

張天明：還好，我們到中國的時候，學生還没放假，也不是
　　　　　過年過節。

麗莎：　　可是中國這麼大，我們的寒假那麼短，到底去哪兒
　　　　　旅遊好呢？

張天明：我覺得去雲南最好不過了❸。

麗莎：　　雲南在哪裏？…我找到了，在這兒，是一個省，
　　　　　在西南部❹。那兒冬天不冷嗎？

張天明：聽説雲南有些地方四季如春，一年四季都不冷
　　　　　不熱。

LANGUAGE NOTES

❸ 緯度/纬度 is latitude; longitude is 經度/经度.

❹ Whereas 中國的西南邊/中国的西南边 "the Southwest of China" or "southwest of China"

丽莎：　好像大城市都靠海或者离海不远。你看，在北边，这是北京、天津；东南边，这儿有上海、南京；南边这里，是广州和深圳。

张天明：　你说的没错。中国的人口主要集中在沿海一带。西南呢，高山、高原多，西北呢，沙漠多，自然条件不太好，所以人口比较少。

丽莎：　我觉得中国的地形和美国有点儿像。

张天明：　你说的有道理。还有，中国和美国的纬度❸接近，面积也差不多，可是你知道，人口是美国的四倍多。听说，过节或者放假的时候，中国的旅游景点到处都是人山人海，挤得很。

丽莎：　是吗？

张天明：　还好，我们到中国的时候，学生还没放假，也不是过年过节。

丽莎：　可是中国这么大，我们的寒假那么短，到底去哪儿旅游好呢？

张天明：　我觉得去云南最好不过了❸。

丽莎：　云南在哪里？…我找到了，在这儿，是一个省，在西南部❹。那儿冬天不冷吗？

张天明：　听说云南有些地方四季如春，一年四季都不冷不热。

can refer to an area either within or outside China, 中國的西南部/中国的西南部 (the southwestern part of China) always refers to the southwestern region within China.

麗莎：　　我記得電視裏說過④，雲南風景好，少數民族⑤多，
　　　　　是個旅遊的好地方。

張天明：　好，雲南，決定了，就去雲南。

麗莎：　　張教授，謝謝你今天給我上的中國地理課。

張天明：　行、行、行，別貧了。

After You Study

Challenge yourself to complete the following tasks in Chinese.

1. Name the two major rivers in China.

2. Identify in general terms where the major mountain ranges and plateaus in China are located.

圖　　例

⓵	賓館、飯店	㊝	郵局
⊠	餐館	⊛	學校
Ω	鐵路售票處	♫	電影院
⊕	飛機售票處	⊕	醫院
⊕	長途汽車站	●	遊覽點
🚗	出租汽車站	●	百貨商店
¥	銀行	●	其他
	幹線道路		繁華街
————	鐵路	══○══	地鐵

This is the legend from a Chinese city map. Can you recognize some of the terms?

LANGUAGE NOTES

⑤ 少數民族/少数民族 means "ethnic minority," literally, "minority nationality."

丽莎：　　我记得电视里说过④，云南风景好，少数民族❺多，
　　　　　是个旅游的好地方。

张天明：好，云南，决定了，就去云南。

丽莎：　　张教授，谢谢你今天给我上的中国地理课。

张天明：行、行、行，别贫了。

3. Name some of the geographical similarities that China and the United States share.
4. Name the places that Lisa and Tianming will visit on their trip.

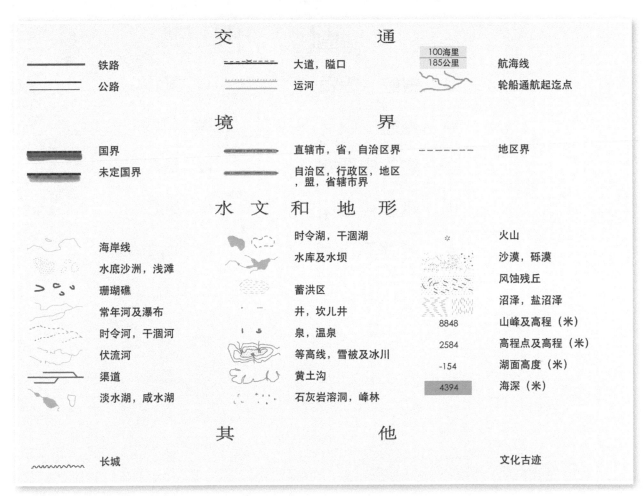

This is an example of a legend from a Chinese map. Can you locate some of the geographical terms introduced in this lesson?

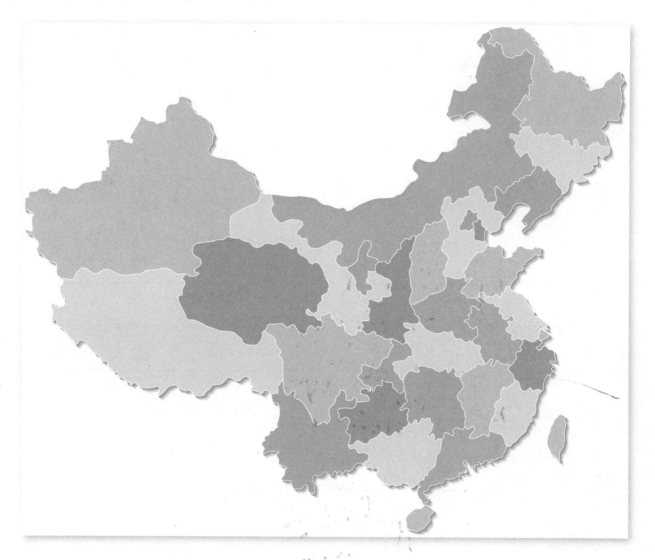

VOCABULARY

225 7694044

1.	地理		dìlǐ	n	geography
2.	家鄉	家乡	jiāxiāng	n	hometown
3.	路綫	路线	lùxiàn	n	route; itinerary
4.	研究		yánjiū	v/n	to study; to look into; research
5.	了解		liǎojiě	v	to understand; to know about; to be informed
6.	冰燈	冰灯	bīngdēng	n	ice lantern
7.	火車	火车	huǒchē	n	train
8.	船		chuán	n	boat; ship
9.	風景	风景	fēngjǐng	n	scenic landscape; scenery
10.	河流		héliú	n	river
11.	大多		dàduō	adv	mostly; for the most part
12.	高原		gāoyuán	n	plateau
13.	山		shān	n	mountain; hill
14.	而		ér	conj	(conjunction to connect two clauses) [See Grammar 2.]
15.	平原		píngyuán	n	plain
16.	海		hǎi	n	sea; ocean
17.	人口		rénkǒu	n	population
18.	主要		zhǔyào	adj	main; principal
19.	集中		jízhōng	v	to concentrate; to be concentrated
20.	沿海		yánhǎi	n	along the coast
21.	一帶	一带	yídài	n	the area around a particular place; the neighboring area

22.	沙漠	沙漠	shāmò	n	desert
23.	自然		zìrán	n/adj	nature; natural
24.	條件	条件	tiáojiàn	n	condition; requirement
25.	地形		dìxíng	n	terrain; topography
26.	緯度	纬度	wěidù	n	latitude
27.	接近		jiējìn	v	to be close to
28.	面積	面积	miànjī	n	area
29.	倍		bèi	m	(measure word for times by which something is multiplied)
30.	過節	过节	guò jié	vo	to celebrate a holiday
31.	旅遊	旅游	lǚyóu	v/n	to travel; travel
32.	景點	景点	jǐngdiǎn	n	scenic spot; tourist spot
33.	到處	到处	dàochù	adv	all around; all over
34.	人山		rén shān		huge crowds of people
	人海		rén hǎi		
35.	擠	挤	jǐ	adj/v	crowded; to push against; to squeeze
36.	短		duǎn	adj	short
37.	省		shěng	n	province
38.	部		bù		part; section
39.	四季		sìjì		spring-like all year around
	如春		rú chūn		
40.	少數	少数	shǎoshù	n	small number; few; minority
41.	民族		mínzú	n	ethnic group; people; nationality

Proper Nouns

| 42. | 南京 | | Nánjīng | | Nanjing |

43.	哈爾濱	哈尔滨	Hā'ěrbīn	Harbin
44.	新疆		Xīnjiāng	Xinjiang
45.	長江	长江	Cháng Jiāng	the Yangtze River
46.	黃河		Huáng Hé	the Yellow River
47.	天津		Tiānjīn	Tianjin
48.	廣州	广州	Guǎngzhōu	Guangzhou
49.	深圳		Shēnzhèn	Shenzhen
50.	雲南	云南	Yúnnán	Yunnan

到新疆吃什麼？吃烤羊肉串兒(kǎo yángròu chuànr)！
到新疆吃什么？吃烤羊肉串儿(kǎo yángròu chuànr)！

Enlarged Characters

| 鄉 | 緯 | 積 | 爾 | 濱 |
| 乡 | 纬 | 积 | 尔 | 滨 |

雲南的少數民族。
云南的少数民族。

雲南風景
云南风景

Culture Highlights

1 Harbin is the capital of Heilongjiang Province, which borders Russia. The city is well known for its long winters and historic Russian-style architecture. Since 1963, Harbin has hosted an annual ice and snow festival which draws many tourists from near and far. The festival includes an ice sculpting contest and numerous colorful ice lanterns.

哈爾濱的冰燈
哈尔滨的冰灯

2 The Yellow River is historically considered the cradle of Chinese civilization. Its middle reach is heavily silted with loess soil from the Yellow Earth Plateau, which elevates the riverbed far above ground.

哈爾濱的雪雕 (xuědiāo, snow sculpture)
哈尔滨的雪雕 (xuědiāo, snow sculpture)

3 The Yangtze River is the longest river in China and the third longest in the world. It is the traditional dividing line between the North and the South in China. Some of the most agriculturally productive land is found along the middle and lower parts of the river; these areas also include many of the country's most important cities such as Chongqing, Wuhan, Nanjing, and Shanghai. The Three Gorges Dam, one of the world's largest, is near Chongqing.

Part of the upper reaches of the Yangtze River in Yunnan.

4 Much of Yunnan is mountainous. Its climate varies from temperate to tropical. The rugged terrain and varied climate support a wide range of fauna and flora. Yunnan is what some scientists call an eco- or biodiversity hotspot. An estimated fifteen thousand plant species and almost half of China's birds and mammals are found in Yunnan.

5 There are fifty-six officially recognized nationalities in China. According to the Chinese National Statistics Bureau, as of November 2005, Han Chinese make up 90.56 percent of the total population. The Yunnan province is home to twenty-five distinct ethnic minorities, making it one of the country's most culturally diverse regions.

雲南景點一：麗江古城 (Lìjiāng gǔchéng)
云南景点一：丽江古城 (Lìjiāng gǔchéng)

雲南景點二：石林 (Shílín)
云南景点二：石林 (Shílín)

雲南景點三：元陽梯田 (Yuányáng tītián)
云南景点三：元阳梯田 (Yuányáng tītián)

6 The People's Republic of China is officially divided into twenty-three provinces (省, shěng), five autonomous regions (自治區/区, zìzhìqū), four provincial level municipalities (直轄市/直辖市, zhíxiáshì), and two special administrative regions (特別行政區/区, tèbié xíngzhèngqū). The four provincial level municipalities are Beijing (北京市), Tianjin (天津市), Shanghai (上海市) and Chongqing (重慶市/重庆市, Chóngqìngshì).

北京的兩個景點：鳥巢 (Niǎocháo)、水立方 (Shuǐlìfāng)
北京的两个景点：鸟巢 (Niǎocháo)、水立方 (Shuǐlìfāng)

上海浦東 (Pǔdōng)
上海浦东 (Pǔdōng)

Grammar

1. 起來/起来 Indicating the Beginning of an Action

起來/起来 can signify an action that starts to take place.

❶ 張天明拿出一張中國地圖，研究了起來。

张天明拿出一张中国地图，研究了起来。

(Zhang Tianming took out a map of China and started studying it.)

❷ 聽她說完那些話，大家都笑了起來。

听她说完那些话，大家都笑了起来。

(After listening to what she said, everybody began to laugh.)

❸ 你怎麼哭起來了？

你怎么哭起来了？

(How come you started crying?)

❹ 吃完晚飯，沒有什麼事兒，他就看起雜誌來。

吃完晚饭，没有什么事儿，他就看起杂志来。

(After dinner he had a free moment, so he began to flip through some magazines.)

When there is an object, it must be placed between 起 and 來/来 as in ❹. 起來/起来 can also be used after adjectives to indicate the start and continuation of a state:

❺ 六月了，天氣熱起來了。

六月了，天气热起来了。

(It's June now. The weather is starting to get hot.)

❻ 今天是週末，購物中心裏的人多起來了。

今天是周末，购物中心里的人多起来了。

(It's the weekend today. There are beginning to be more people in the shopping centers.)

❼ 他走進房間打開燈，房間裏一下子亮起來了。

他走进房间打开灯，房间里一下子亮起来了。

(He walked into the room and turned on the light. The room brightened up instantly.)

起來/起来 is often used with adjectives such as 亮, 大, 高, 多, 快, 長/长, etc., while 下來/下来 is often used with 暗 (àn), 小, 低, 少, 慢, and 短.

❽ 剛才他開車開得很快，進城以後，他開得慢下來了。

刚才他开车开得很快，进城以后，他开得慢下来了。

(Just now he was driving very fast. After he got into the city, he began to slow down.)

❾ 屋子裏的燈慢慢暗下來了。

屋子里的灯慢慢暗下来了。

(The light in the room started to dim slowly.)

夏天熱/夏天热, 冬天冷 and other seasonal weather changes can also be expressed with 起來/起来.

2. Conjunction 而

而 is used to connect two clauses that represent the different or contrasting characteristics or situations, often in literary language.

❶ 中國西邊是高原，那兒有世界上最高的山。而東邊是平原和大海。

中国西边是高原，那儿有世界上最高的山。而东边是平原和大海。

(In the western part of China there are plateaus. There you'll find the world's tallest mountain. In the eastern part of China, on the other hand, there are plains and oceans.)

❷ 小林畢業以後計劃回中國工作，而不準備留在美國。

小林毕业以后计划回中国工作，而不准备留在美国。

(Xiao Lin plans to go back to China to work, not to stay in the United States.)

❸ 我想去學校圖書館打工，而我的同屋想去校外打工。
我想去学校图书馆打工，而我的同屋想去校外打工。
(I want to work at the school library, but my roommate wants to work off campus.)

❹ 我哥哥已經拿到碩士學位了，而我才高中畢業。
我哥哥已经拿到硕士学位了，而我才高中毕业。
(My older brother has already gotten his master's degree. I, on the other hand, have just graduated from high school.)

3. 最 Adj 不過了 / 最 Adj 不过了

最 Adj 不過了 / 最 Adj 不过了 means 没有比⋯⋯更 Adj 的 (none can surpass). It is a rather strong expression, e.g.,

❶ 她過生日，買花送她最好不過了。
她过生日，买花送她最好不过了。
(Nothing would be a better gift for her birthday than flowers.)

❷ 這本書對世界经济的介紹最清楚不過了。
这本书对世界经济的介绍最清楚不过了。
(This book's presentation of the world economy surpasses all others in its clarity.)

❸ 這個實習工作對化學系的學生來说，最合適不過了。
这个实习工作对化学系的学生来说，最合适不过了。
(No internship is more appropriate for chemistry majors than this one.)

4. 過/过 Indicating Experience

To indicate that someone has had the experience of doing something, we use the dynamic particle 過/过. It differs from 了 in two ways:

A. 了 is descriptive in nature and is used to relate the occurrence of an action.

❶ 我去年去了一次中國，在北京實習了三個月，什麼地方都沒去，就回來了。

我去年去了一次中国，在北京实习了三个月，什么地方都没去，就回来了。

(Last year I went to China to intern in Beijing for three months. I came back without going anywhere else.)

❷ 第二天早上，我很早就起來了，起床後就去運動場跑步。

第二天早上，我很早就起来了，起床后就去运动场跑步。

(The following morning I got up really early. After I got up, I went jogging at the athletic field.)

❸ 客人們進來以後，找到了自己的位子，坐了下來。

客人们进来以后，找到了自己的位子，坐了下来。

(The guests walked in, found their seats, and sat down.)

過/过 is explanatory in nature. It is used to explain the reasoning for the following statement. In other words, the emphasis is on the impact a past action has had on the present situation:

❹ (以前)我們在一起學過英文，我知道他英文很好。

(以前)我们在一起学过英文，我知道他英文很好。

(We used to study English together. I know his English is very good.)

[Because we studied English together, I know his English is very good.]

❺ A: 你去過中國，請告訴我們去哪兒旅遊最好。

你去过中国，请告诉我们去哪儿旅游最好。

(You've been to China. Give us some tips on where some of the best places to go are.)

[Because you've been to China, you can give us some tips on where some of the best places to go are.]

B: 雲南的旅遊景點多，少數民族的文化也很有意思，是旅遊的好地方。

云南的旅游景点多，少数民族的文化也很有意思，是旅游的好地方。

(Yunnan has plenty of tourist sites, and the cultures of the minority ethnic groups are also intriguing. It's a good place to visit.)

❻ 他學過好幾年中文，都能看中文報紙、雜誌了。

他学过好几年中文，都能看中文报纸、杂志了。

(He's been studying Chinese for several years. He can even understand Chinese newspapers and magazines.)

[Because he's been studying Chinese for several years, he can understand Chinese newspapers and magazines.]

In the sentences above, the clauses containing 過/过 all serve as explanatory background to the clauses that follow. 過/过 indicates the impact or influence of a past action on the present.

B. 了 generally requires a specific time phrase, unless the sentence forms part of an extended narrative in which the temporal background has already been stated or is implicitly understood as in ❸ above; 過/过 does not. When we use 過/过, the time implied is often rather vague: "before," or "in the past." Only when we want to be more precise do we use a time phrase. Note that when 過/过 is used in the experiential sense, it usually cannot be followed by 了.

❼ A: 我聽説你沒去過別的國家，是真的嗎？

我听说你没去过别的国家，是真的吗？

(I heard that you have never been abroad. Is that true?)

B:　誰說的？我去年去過日本。
　　　谁说的？我去年去过日本。
(Who said that? I went to Japan last year.)

杭州西湖 (Xīhú)

Words & Phrases

> **A.** 為了/为了 (in order to) and 因為/因为 (because)

為了/为了 denotes purpose; 因為/因为 denotes cause.

❶　為了中文學得更好，我明年要去中國留學。
　　为了中文学得更好，我明年要去中国留学。
(In order to improve my Chinese, I'm going to study abroad in China next year.)

❷　因為在中國學中文條件更好，所以我明年去中國留學。
　　因为在中国学中文条件更好，所以我明年去中国留学。
(Because the conditions in China are even better for learning Chinese, I'm going to China to study next year.)

❸ 為了解決學費的問題，他一邊上學一邊打工。
为了解决学费的问题，他一边上学一边打工。
(In order to solve the problem of school tuition, he works part time.)

❹ 因為得交學費，所以他一邊上學一邊打工。
因为得交学费，所以他一边上学一边打工。
(Because he has to pay for school tuition, he works part time.)

❺ 因為這個學校很有名，所以我申請。
因为这个学校很有名，所以我申请。
(Because this school is very famous, I'm going to apply to it.)

❻ 我申請這個學校，是為了能跟我的女朋友在一起。
我申请这个学校，是为了能跟我的女朋友在一起。
(I'm applying to this school so that I can be with my girlfriend.)

B. 一下子 (in an instant)

一下子 is equivalent to 一下. It means "not much time has gone by," and it's often used to depict how fast or soon actions or things happen.

❶ 你一下子就要從南邊跑到最北邊去？
你一下子就要从南边跑到最北边去？
(All of a sudden, you want to go from the south to the northernmost part?)

❷ 你說的那個商店我一下子就找到了，不難找。
你说的那个商店我一下子就找到了，不难找。
(I found the store you mentioned right away. It wasn't difficult to find.)

❸ 媽媽給他的零用錢他一下子就花完了。
妈妈给他的零用钱他一下子就花完了。
(He went through the allowance that his mother had given him in no time.)

C. 大多 (mostly)

大多 is an adverb meaning "for the most part" or "mostly." It cannot be used before nouns.

❶   我們班的同學大多住在學校宿舍，差不多都沒有男朋友
或者女朋友。

我们班的同学大多住在学校宿舍，差不多都没有男朋友
或者女朋友。

(Most of our classmates live in the school dorms. Almost none of us have a boyfriend or girlfriend.)

❷   美國的大山和河流的名字，我弟弟大多說不對。

美国的大山和河流的名字，我弟弟大多说不对。

(My younger brother said the names of most of the big mountains and rivers of America incorrectly.)

❸   我們學校教授的研究，我大多都了解，你不用上網
看了。

我们学校教授的研究，我大多都了解，你不用上网
看了。

(I'm familiar with most of our school's professors' research. You don't need to go online to find out.)

D. 呢 (indicating a pause in speech)

This particle occurs after a subject or topic and is followed by a pause in speech. It usually appears in enumerative sentences suggesting contrast:

❶ **A:**   你們寒假準備做什麼？

你们寒假准备做什么？

(What do you plan to do over the winter break?)

B: 我呢，要回家，小張呢，要留在學校打工，小李要做
什麼，我不知道。

我呢，要回家，小张呢，要留在学校打工，小李要做
什么，我不知道。

(I'm going home. Little Zhang, on the other hand, has to stay at school and work.
I don't know what Little Li will do.)

❷ 選什麼專業好，我還沒想清楚。學醫呢，沒有意思，
學文學呢，怕以後不好找工作。

选什么专业好，我还没想清楚。学医呢，没有意思，
学文学呢，怕以后不好找工作。

(What'll be a good major to choose? I haven't figured it out. Studying medicine, on the
one hand, is boring. I'm worried that if I study literature, on the other hand, I won't
be able to find a job.)

❸ 你说的没錯兒，中國的人口主要集中在沿海一帶。
西南呢，高山、高原多，西北呢，沙漠多，自然條件
不太好，所以人口較少。

你说的没错儿，中国的人口主要集中在沿海一带。
西南呢，高山、高原多，西北呢，沙漠多，自然条件
不太好，所以人口较少。

(You put it correctly. China's population is concentrated along the coast. As for the
Southwest, there are numerous big mountains and plateaus. The Northwest, on the
other hand, has many deserts with unfavorable natural conditions. That's why the
population there is relatively sparse.)

Language Practice

A. Know Your Chinese Provinces?

1. Refer to a map of China to locate the following provinces:

四川省	四川省
廣東省	广东省
湖南省	湖南省
雲南省	云南省
山東省	山东省
A province of your choice	...

Work with a partner and describe to each other where these provinces are located in China.

_____在中國的_____部。　　_____在中国的_____部。

_____呢，在中國的　　　　_____呢，在中国的

_____部。　　　　　　　　　_____部。

...

B. From the North to the South

Refer to a map of China to find the following eight cities, and one additional city of your choice.

上海	北京	南京
天津	深圳	廣州
杭州	哈爾濱	

上海	北京	南京
天津	深圳	广州
杭州	哈尔滨	

Your choice _____

Then list them according to their latitude with the furthest north as #1:

1. Harbin
2. Beijing
3. _____
4. _____

5. Shanghai
6. Hangzhou
7. _____
8. _____

Work with a partner, and answer the following question:

Q: 哪些城市靠海或者離海不遠？ **Q:** 哪些城市靠海或者离海不远？

A: _____

南京的旅遊景點之一
南京的旅游景点之一

C. Geography Buff

1. Work with a partner and locate 長江/长江 and 黃河 on a map of China.
Then answer the following question:

Q: 長江在黃河的北邊還是南邊？ **Q:** 长江在黄河的北边还是南边？

A: _____

2. Work with a partner and locate a 高山, a 高原, and a 平原 on a map of China. Copy the names of the 高山, 高原, 平原, and ask your instructor to help you pronounce them. Then tell your class where they are located.

_____山在_____省的_____部。

or

_____高原在中國的_____部。　_____高原在中國的_____部。

or

_____平原在中國的_____部。　_____平原在中國的_____部。

D. Chinese Geography 101

Quiz yourself and check the boxes to indicate where most of China's major mountain ranges, deserts, plateaus, and plains are located.

	東南	西南	東北	西北
高山				
高原				
沙漠/沙漠				
平原				

a. State what you have checked in an organized short paragraph.

b. Then add to the paragraph information about which direction many major 河流 run.

c. The next step is to talk about population distributions along the coast vs. in the plateau areas.

Work with a partner to connect a, b, and c with appropriate cohesive devices, and discuss if there's anything else about Chinese geography that you can add. Then present your basic introduction of China's geography to your class. Your introduction can make use of PowerPoint slides or can be presented on YouTube if you wish. Include visual aids to enhance your presentation.

E. Research Time

Go online and find facts on the following:

	中國/中国	美國/美国 (or a different country of your choice)
1. 面積/面积		
2. 人口		
3. 緯度/纬度		
4. 首都		
5. 政治中心		
6. 經濟中心/经济中心		

7. 文化中心 ＿＿＿＿＿＿＿　＿＿＿＿＿＿＿

8. 最高的山 ＿＿＿＿＿＿＿　＿＿＿＿＿＿＿

Compare your search results with a partner and then prepare an oral or written report together. In your report, you will state and compare the sizes and the populations of the two countries, and where they are in the world according to latitude. Name their capitals, financial centers, cultural centers, and highest mountains, and then tell where these things are located within their respective countries.

F. Choose a Tourist Destination

a. Work with a partner to weigh the pros and cons of visiting the following places. Some things that can be taken into consideration are location, climate, transportation, cost, tourist population, tourist sites, etc.

	pros	cons
北京	＿＿＿＿＿	＿＿＿＿＿
上海	＿＿＿＿＿	＿＿＿＿＿
南京	＿＿＿＿＿	＿＿＿＿＿
杭州	＿＿＿＿＿	＿＿＿＿＿
深圳	＿＿＿＿＿	＿＿＿＿＿
香港	＿＿＿＿＿	＿＿＿＿＿
台北	＿＿＿＿＿	＿＿＿＿＿
哈爾濱/哈尔滨	＿＿＿＿＿	＿＿＿＿＿
Your Choice	＿＿＿＿＿	＿＿＿＿＿

b. Recommend one destination that you think would be ideal to visit:

夏天去＿＿＿＿＿旅遊最好，不過了，因為＿＿＿＿＿，＿＿＿＿＿＿＿＿；另外/再説，＿＿＿＿＿＿…

夏天去＿＿＿＿＿旅游最好不过了，因为＿＿＿＿＿，＿＿＿＿＿＿＿＿；另外/再说，＿＿＿＿＿＿…

or

冬天去＿＿＿＿＿旅遊最好
不過了，因為＿＿＿＿＿，
＿＿＿＿＿＿＿＿＿；
另外／再說，＿＿＿＿＿
＿＿＿＿＿＿＿＿…

冬天去＿＿＿＿＿旅游最好
不过了，因为＿＿＿＿＿，
＿＿＿＿＿＿＿＿＿；
另外／再说，＿＿＿＿＿
＿＿＿＿＿＿＿＿…

c. After listening to everyone's recommendations, group people who have the same recommendations together. Open the floor for a debate. Each group should defend its recommendations and point out why other places are not as good.

Words you can use to present your arguments in a coherent and cohesive manner include, but are not limited to:

認為	同意	反對	认为	同意	反对
看法	恐怕	不見得	看法	恐怕	不见得
比較	至於	不如	比较	至于	不如
難道	其實	實際上	难道	其实	实际上
甚至	結果	建議	甚至	结果	建议
考慮	比如		考虑	比如	
呢…呢…			呢…呢…		
要麼…要麼…			要么…要么…		
不是…而是…			不是…而是…		

d. The class should then vote on the best place in China that people can visit in summer or winter.

夏天去_____旅遊最好/合適。　夏天去_____旅游最好/合适。

冬天去_____旅遊最好/合適。　冬天去_____旅游最好/合适。

寒假春節
全面特價逢低搶GO
寒假春節年專區 敬請放心 保證出團

江南水鄉風情5/6日	1/23.26.27	13900起

桂林印象劉三姐龍勝梯田山水5日　21900起

1/26.27.28 贈送三項自費：按摩.野薑宵夜.魚鷹補魚秀價值1500元

五星北京龍慶峽冰雕美食6日　1/26 24900起

廣西南寧跨國德天瀑布精選6日 全程無購物 1/24 25900起

昆明大理麗江雙秀雙飛五星8日　1/23 1/26 26900起

貴州黃果樹羅平尊爵美食8日　1/23.26 全程無購物 27900起

中越祕境雙龍灣德天瀑布山水8日 1/23 1/25 32500起

湘西土家風情張家界鳳凰古城精選8日 全程無購物 32900起

1/26 特別加贈天門山纜車(價值2000元).白天無自費

冰雪大世界銀色東北精選8日　1/26 35900起

澳門威尼斯人+珠海+深圳主題樂園4日 4999起
1/13.15

寒假打算去哪兒旅遊？
寒假打算去哪儿旅游？

G. Be a Tour Consultant

Divide the class into two groups: one will be tour consultants and the other potential clients.

a. Training Session for the Consultants:

Imagine that you are a group of tour consultants in a travel agency specializing in trips to China, and most of your clients speak only Chinese. Work with your fellow consultants to make a comprehensive list of possible questions in Chinese that you will need to help your clients to plan their trips. The basic questions may include asking for travel dates, destinations, budgets, preferences for transportation, preferences for accommodations, etc.

1. _____

2. _____

3. _____

4. _____

5. _____

...

b. Brainstorming among the Clients

Team up with a travel companion to plan your travel itinerary, including travel dates, destinations, means of transportation, accommodation, budget, etc.

_____

_____

_____

_____

_____

_____

_____

_____

_____

Brainstorm questions that you may ask a travel consultant to get the best service and advice possible.

1._____

2._____

3._____

4._____

5._____

...

c. Now the consultants should pair up. Each pair sets up a stand to provide service, and the prospective clients take turns to visit each stand.

After visiting all the consultants, the clients have to rate and comment on the consultants' services. Comments may include if the consultants are able to 1) give suggestions based on their knowledge of the climate and geography of China, 2) remind them whether it's practical or realistic to travel to certain destinations with the given time frame, budget constraints, and personal preferences, and 3) show alternatives by pointing out the advantages of different options.

After listening to all the clients, the consultants have to decide which clients' questions are most challenging yet reasonable, and whose itinerary is most intriguing yet feasible in terms of time and budget.

云南 昆明 大理 丽江 品质双飞6日 **2750**
◆直飞丽江 ◆丽江古城三晚住宿 ◆送歌舞表演
昆明 大理 丽江＋香格里拉 双飞8日 **3180**
昆大理＋西双版纳 送野象谷 四飞8日 **3880**

长白山 吉林 长白山 天池 双卧5日 **1080**
＋镜泊湖 吊水楼瀑布 双卧5日 **1290**
扎龙 五大连池 镜泊湖 长白山 三卧7日 **2090**

新疆 丝绸之路 乌市 天山天池 **3980**
吐鲁番 敦煌 嘉峪关 兰州 双飞6日
乌市 布尔津 喀纳斯 魔鬼城 天山天池 双飞7日 **3880**

云南 昆明．大理．丽江／泸沽湖／香格里拉／版纳 双飞6/8/10／四飞8/10/12日 **2490**起

西藏 拉萨．布达拉宫．大昭寺／日喀则．林芝／江孜．雅鲁藏布江 双卧／单双飞6-12日 **2360**起

新疆 乌鲁木齐．吐鲁番．天池．敦煌．兰州／喀纳斯．魔鬼城／青海湖 单／双飞6/7/8/9/10日 **3720**起

江南山水

南京．无锡．杭州．苏州．上海＋水乡 双卧七日 三星送四星1晚 **820**
阅江楼．夫子庙．灵山大佛．木渎．周庄．西湖．寒山寺．外滩 无强制消费
上海半自助＋普陀山祈福 特快双卧六／单飞五日 **1460**起
杭州半自助＋秀水千岛湖 特快杭州往返双卧四日 **1260**
黄山观日出．西递古民居．千岛湖．杭州．上海＋水乡 双卧七日 **1780**
直达黄山 门票全含 三星住宿送1晚四星 北京成团
黄山观日出．西递古民居．千岛湖 双卧六日 三星送四星1晚 **1680**
南昌．道教仙山～三清山 空调快车往返 双卧四日 **1280**

這些是三家旅行社的廣告。你對哪條旅遊路線比較有興趣？
这些是三家旅行社的广告。你对哪条旅游路线比较有兴趣？

Pinyin Text

Hánjià kuài dào le, Zhāng Tiānmíng zhè jǐ tiān yìzhí zài kǎolǜ lǚxíng❶ de shìr. Tā de fùmǔ xīwàng tā qù tāmen de jiāxiāng Nánjīng kàn kan, Zhāng Tiānmíng yě hěn xiǎng dāng Lìshā de dǎoyóu, dài tā dào Zhōngguó de yì xiē dìfang zǒu zou. Chúle Nánjīng yǐwài, hái yīnggāi qù shénme dìfang ne? Wèile juédìng lǚxíng de lùxiàn, Zhāng Tiānmíng ná chu yì zhāng Zhōngguó dìtú, yánjiū le qi lai①.

Zhāng Tiānmíng:	Lìshā, nǐ lái kàn kan Zhōngguó dìtú, kàn dào nǎr qù lǚxíng hǎo.
Lìshā:	Kàn dìtú? Nǐ zhè ge zhúyi búcuò, wǒ yě zhèng xiǎng xué xue Zhōngguó dìlǐ ne. Wǒ duì Zhōngguó dìlǐ liǎojiě de tài shǎo le.
Zhāng Tiānmíng:	Wǒmen xiān dào Nánjīng, wǒ fùmǔ de jiāxiāng... Zài zhèli, zài Zhōngguó de dōngnánbian. Ránhòu nǐ xiǎng qù nǎr?
Lìshā:	Āi, zhè shì Hā'ěrbīn, duì ma? Qù Hā'ěrbīn ba.
Zhāng Tiānmíng:	Nǐ yíxiàzi yào cóng dōngnánbian pǎo dào zuì běibian qù?
Lìshā:	Zuótiān diànshì li jièshào Hā'ěrbīn de bīngdēng le, hǎokàn jí le.
Zhāng Tiānmíng:	Bīngdēng hǎokàn shì hǎokàn, kěshì Hā'ěrbīn xiànzài lěng de bù déliǎo, xiàtiān zài qù ba.
Lìshā:	Ō, hǎo ba. Bú qù běibian, nà zuò huǒchē qù xībian ba, tīngshuō Xīnjiāng shì ge hěn tèbié de dìfang.
Zhāng Tiānmíng:	Xīnjiāng zài xīběi, shíyuè jiù kāishǐ lěng qi lai le①, xiànzài qù bù héshì. Lìngwài, zuò huǒchē tài huā shíjiān, xiàcì zài qù ba!
Lìshā:	Nǐ shuō zuò huǒchē tài huā shíjiān, zhème shuō zuò chuán yě bù xíng le, duì ma? Yàobùrán wǒ zhēn xiǎng zuò chuán cóng dōng wǎng xī, kàn kan Cháng Jiāng huòzhě Huáng Hé de fēngjǐng.
Zhāng Tiānmíng:	Zhōngguó de héliú❷, dàduō shì cóng xī wǎng dōng liú, rúguǒ zuò chuán cóng dōng wǎng xī zǒu, kěndìng děi huā gèng cháng de shíjiān.
Lìshā:	Wèishénme Zhōngguó de héliú dàduō cóng xī wǎng dōng liú ne?
Zhāng Tiānmíng:	Yīnwèi Zhōngguó xībian shì gāoyuán, nàr yǒu shìjiè shang zuì gāo de shān. Ér② dōngbian shì píngyuán hé dà hǎi.
Lìshā:	Hǎoxiàng dà chéngshì dōu kào hǎi huòzhě lí hǎi bù yuǎn. Nǐ kàn, zài běibian, zhè shì Běijīng, Tiānjīn; dōngnánbian, zhèr yǒu Shànghǎi, Nánjīng, nánbian zhèli, shì Guǎngzhōu hé Shēnzhèn.

Zhāng Tiānmíng:	Nǐ shuō de méi cuò. Zhōngguó de rénkǒu zhǔyào jízhōng zài yánhǎi yídài. Xīnán ne, gāoshān, gāoyuán duō, xīběi ne, shāmò duō, zìrán tiáojiàn bú tài hǎo, suǒyǐ rénkǒu bǐjiào shǎo.
Lìshā:	Wǒ juéde Zhōngguó de dìxíng hé Měiguó yǒu diǎnr xiàng.
Zhāng Tiānmíng:	Nǐ shuō de yǒu dàoli. Hái yǒu, Zhōngguó hé Měiguó de wěidù③ jiējìn, miànjī yě chàbuduō, kěshì nǐ zhīdào, rénkǒu shì Měiguó de sì bèi duō. Tīngshuō, guò jié huòzhě fàng jià de shíhou, Zhōngguó de lǚyóu jǐngdiǎn dàochù dōu shì rén shān rén hǎi, jǐ de hěn.
Lìshā:	Shì ma?
Zhāng Tiānmíng:	Háihǎo, wǒmen dào Zhōngguó de shíhou, xuésheng hái méi fàng jià, yě bú shì guò nián guò jié.
Lìshā:	Kěshì Zhōngguó zhème dà, wǒmen de hánjià nàme duǎn, dàodǐ qù nǎr lǚyóu hǎo ne?
Zhāng Tiānmíng:	Wǒ juéde qù Yúnnán zuì hǎo búguò le③.
Lìshā:	Yúnnán zài nǎli? ...Wǒ zhǎo dào le, zài zhèr, shì yí ge shěng, zài xīnánbù④. Nàr dōngtiān bù lěng ma?
Zhāng Tiānmíng:	Tīngshuō Yúnnán yǒu xiē dìfang sìjì rú chūn, yì nián sìjì dōu bù lěng bú rè.
Lìshā:	Wǒ jìde diànshì li shuō guo④, Yúnnán fēngjǐng hǎo, shǎoshù mínzú⑤ duō, shì ge lǚyóu de hǎo dìfang.
Zhāng Tiānmíng:	Hǎo, Yúnnán, juédìng le, jiù qù Yúnnán.
Lìshā:	Zhāng jiàoshòu, xièxie nǐ jīntiān gěi wǒ shàng de Zhōngguó dìlǐ kè.
Zhāng Tiānmíng:	Xíng, xíng, xíng, bié pín le.

English Text

Soon it'll be winter break. Zhang Tianming has been thinking about his travel plans the last couple days. His parents hope that he'll go visit their hometown Nanjing. Zhang Tianming also very much wants to be Lisa's tour guide and take her to a few places in China. Beside Nanjing, where should they go? In order to decide on the itinerary he takes out a map of China and begins to study it.

Zhang Tianming:	Lisa, come take a look at this map of China and see where we want to go.
Lisa:	Look at the map? Great idea. I want to learn about Chinese geography. I know so little about Chinese geography.
Zhang Tianming:	We'll go to Nanjing, my parents' hometown first. ... Here, in southeastern China. Where do you want to go next?
Lisa:	This is Harbin, isn't it? Let's go to Harbin.
Zhang Tianming:	How come you want to go from the Southeast all the way to the extreme North?
Lisa:	Yesterday on TV there was a program about Harbin's ice lanterns. They were really beautiful.
Zhang Tianming:	Ice lanterns are nice, but it's winter now. It's really cold there. Let's go in the summer.
Lisa:	OK. We won't go to the North. Then let's take a train to the West. I hear that Xinjiang is a very special place.
Zhang Tianming:	Xinjiang is in the Northwest. It starts to get cold in October. Now is not a good time to go. Besides, trains take too long. Let's go next time.
Lisa:	You say trains take too long. Then boats are out, right? Otherwise I'd really like to take a boat from east to west to look at the landscape along the Yangtze or the Yellow River.
Zhang Tianming:	Most of China's rivers flow from the west to the east. If you take a boat from east to west, it'll take an even longer time.
Lisa:	Why do most of China's rivers flow from the west to the east?
Zhang Tianming:	Because China's western part is a plateau. The world's tallest mountain is there. In the eastern part there are plains and oceans.
Lisa:	It seems that all the big cities are by the sea or not too far away from it. See, in the North are Beijing and Tianjin. In the Southeast are Shanghai and Nanjing. In the South are Guangzhou and Shenzhen.
Zhang Tianming:	What you say is correct. China's population is concentrated along the coast. In the Southwest there are many tall mountains and plateaus. In the Northwest there are many deserts. The natural conditions are not very good. Therefore, the population is sparse.
Lisa:	I think China's topography is a little like America's.
Zhang Tianming:	What you said makes sense. Also, the latitude is almost the same and so is the land area, but China's population is more than four times

that of America's. I hear that during holidays or school breaks there
are huge crowds in all the scenic areas.

Lisa: Really?

Zhang Tianming: Luckily, when we go, students will still be in school and it won't be
around any major holidays.

Lisa: China is so big. Our break is so short. Where should we go?

Zhang Tianming: I think Yunnan is the best place to go.

Lisa: Where is Yunnan? Oh, I found it. It's here. It's a province in the
Southwest. Is it cold in winter?

Zhang Tianming: Some places in Yunnan are spring-like year round. No matter when
you go, it's not too cold or too hot.

Lisa: I heard on TV that Yunnan has beautiful scenery and many ethnic
minorities. It's a great place to visit.

Zhang Tianming: It's decided then. We'll go to Yunnan.

Lisa: Professor Zhang, thank you for today's geography lesson.

Zhang Tianming: OK, OK. Stop being so glib.

SELF-ASSESSMENT

How well can you do these things? Check (✔) the boxes to evaluate your progress
and see which areas you may need to practice more.

I can	Very Well	OK	A Little
Name some Chinese cities located in the North, Southeast, and South of China	☐	☐	☐
Give a brief account of the geographic features of China	☐	☐	☐
Describe the similarities and differences between China and the United States in terms of territorial size, population, and terrain	☐	☐	☐
Talk about the factors that help me select a travel destination	☐	☐	☐
Plan a trip to China, keeping in mind factors such as geography, climate, time, and budget	☐	☐	☐

Let's Review! (Lessons 6-10)

I. Chinese Character Crossword Puzzles

You have learned many vocabulary items from Lessons 6–10. You may have noticed that some words/phrases share the same characters. Let's see whether you can recall these characters. The common character is positioned in the center of the cluster of rings. The block arrows indicate which way you should read the words. Work with a partner and see how many association rings you can complete. Of course, you may add more rings if you can think of additional words/phrases sharing the same characters or you may create your own clusters of rings.

EXAMPLE:

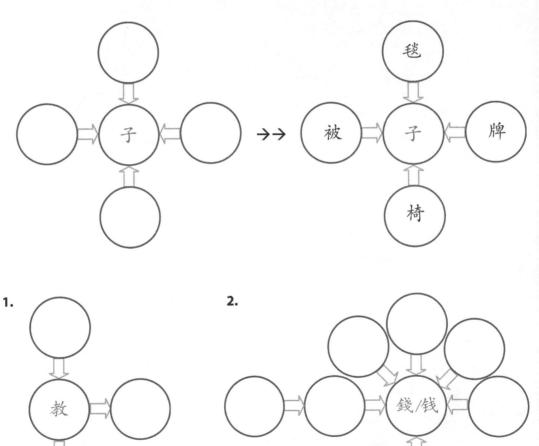

3.

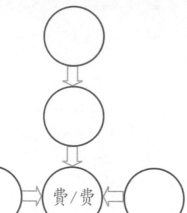

費/费

4.

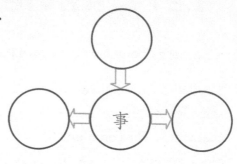

事

5.

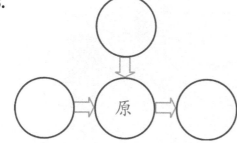

原

6.

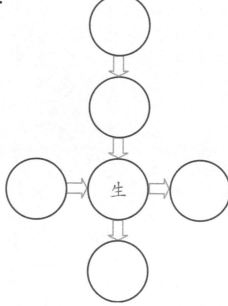

生

7.

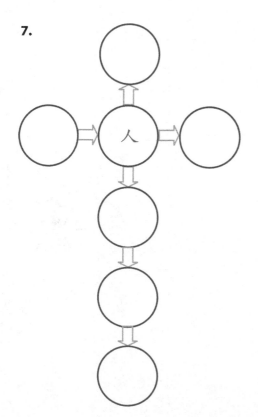

人

8. Create Your Own

II. Matching Words

Draw a line connecting the verb with its proper object.

交	玩笑
安排	資料/资料
解決/解决	看法
受(到)	經驗/经验
減輕/减轻	彆扭/别扭
取得	學費/学费
查	軟件/软件
鬧/闹	負擔/负担
下載/下载	教育
同意	問題/问题
開/开	時間/时间

III. Make a Word List

A. Brainstorm with a partner and ask each other what words come to mind when you want to

1. describe a compatible girlfriend/ boyfriend:

2. talk about the role that the internet plays in your daily life:

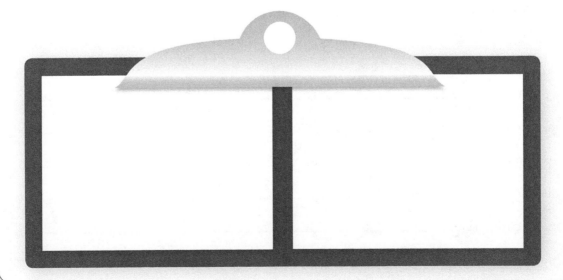

3. discuss how to be financially
responsible:

4. debate how to strike a balance
between study and play:

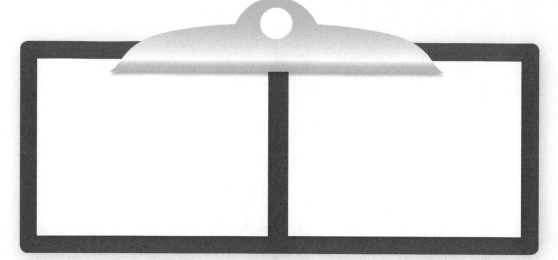

5. plan a trip to China:

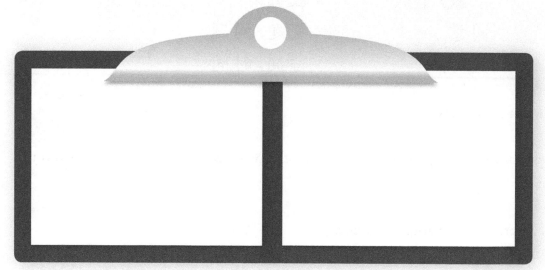

B. Brainstorm with a partner and ask each other what words or phrases will help if you wish
to

1. agree or disagree: _____

2. inquire if everything is OK: _____

3. apologize for your language or behavior: _____

4. discuss the pros and cons of something: _____

5. make comparisons: _____

6. make suggestions: _____

IV. Organize Your Thoughts

Select a topic from the four listed in III A. Discuss with your partner

a. what you want to say;

b. what words or phrases from III B will help your express your opinion;

c. what should be said first, next, and last;

d. what transitions may be needed; and

e. what cohesive devices should be used to connect your sentences.

It may be a good idea to jot down sentences that you wish to say, then number them in the order you think they should be presented, and finally consider how to make your sentences a coherent discourse. Then present your work to the class.

V. Are you a Fluent Speaker?

How would you make the following flow better in a paragraph? Don't forget to pay attention to time words, place expressions, and pronouns.

1. 昨天是星期六，我去同學家給他過生日

2. 我開車去他家

3. 我看見了很多同學，有男同學，也有女同學

4. 我們唱卡拉OK

5. 我們吃生日蛋糕了

6. 我玩得很高興

7. 我很晚才回家

1. 昨天是星期六，我去同学家给他过生日

2. 我开车去他家

3. 我看见了很多同学，有男同学，也有女同学

4. 我们唱卡拉OK

5. 我们吃生日蛋糕了

6. 我玩得很高兴

7. 我很晚才回家

_____

_____

_____

Vocabulary Index (Chinese-English)

The Chinese-English index is alphabetized according to *pinyin*. Words containing the same Chinese characters are first grouped together. Homonyms appear in the order of their tonal pronunciation (i.e., first tones first, second tones second, third tones third, fourth tones fourth, and neutral tones last). Pinyin in parentheses shows pronunciation of the characters before tone change. Proper nouns are shown in green.

Traditional	Simplified	Pinyin	Part of Speech	English	Lesson
A					
哎呀	哎呀	āiyā	interj	(an exclamation to express surprise) gosh; ah	4
愛好	爱好	àihào	n/v	hobby; interest; to love (something)	6
安排		ānpái	v	to arrange	9
安全		ānquán	adj	safe	1
B					
擺	摆	bǎi	v	to put; to place	2
搬家		bān jiā	vo	to move (one's residence)	1
幫忙	帮忙	bāng máng	vo	to help	1
幫助	帮助	bāngzhù	v	to help	7
抱怨		bàoyuàn	v	to complain	9
倍		bèi	m	(measure word for times by which something is multiplied)	10
背景		bèijǐng	n	background	6
被子		bèizi	n	comforter; quilt	2
比較	比较	bǐjiào	adv/v	relatively; comparatively; rather; to compare	1
比如		bǐrú	v	for example	3
畢業	毕业	bì yè	vo	to graduate	5
標準	标准	biāozhǔn	n/adj	criterion; standard	4
冰燈	冰灯	bīngdēng	n	ice lantern	10
並	并	bìng	adv	actually	9
菠菜	菠菜	bōcài	n	spinach	3
博客		bókè	n	blog	7
博士		bóshì	n	Ph.D.; doctor [academic degree]	9
部		bù		part; section	10

Traditional	Simplified	Pinyin	Part of Speech	English	Lesson
不必		(bùbì) búbì	adv	need not; not have to	4
不斷	不断	(bùduàn) búduàn	adv	continuously	8
不見得	不见得	(bù jiàn de) bú jiàn de		not necessarily	1
不如		bùrú	v	not equal to; inferior to; to not measure up to	3
不是…而是…		(bùshì) búshì… érshì…		it's not…but…	9
不停		bùtíng	adv	continuously; incessantly	6
不同		bù tóng		different; not the same	6

C

Traditional	Simplified	Pinyin	Part of Speech	English	Lesson
菜單	菜单	càidān	n	menu	3
餐館兒	餐馆儿	cānguǎnr	n	restaurant	2
餐巾		cānjīn	n	napkin	3
層	层	céng	m	(measure word for stories of a building)	2
長	长	cháng	adj	long	1
長江	长江	Cháng Jiāng	pn	the Yangtze River	10
吵架		chǎo jià	vo	to quarrel	6
遲到	迟到	chídào	v	to arrive late	7
出版		chūbǎn	v	to publish	7
出生		chūshēng	v	to be born	1
船		chuán	n	boat; ship	10
吹		chuī	v	to end a relationship; (lit.) to blow	6
純棉	纯棉	chúnmián	adj	pure cotton; 100 percent cotton	4
存		cún	v	to save up; to deposit	8

D

Traditional	Simplified	Pinyin	Part of Speech	English	Lesson
答應	答应	dāying	v	to agree (to do something); to promise; to answer	6
打交道		dǎ jiāodào	vo	to deal with	5
大多		dàduō	adv	mostly; for the most part	10
大人		dàren	n	adult	8
待		dāi	v	to stay	7
貸款	贷款	dàikuǎn	n/v	loan; to provide a loan	8
到處	到处	dàochù	adv	all around; all over	10

Traditional	Simplified	Pinyin	Part of Speech	English	Lesson
到底		dàodǐ	adv	what on earth; what in the world; in the end	6
道理		dàoli	n	reason; sense	4
道歉		dào qiàn	vo	to apologize	6
低		dī	adj	low	8
地道		dìdao	adj	authentic; genuine; pure	2
地理		dìlǐ	n	geography	10
地形		dìxíng	n	terrain; topography	10
電影院	电影院	diànyǐngyuàn	n	movie theater	6
丟三拉四		diū sān là sì		scatterbrained; forgetful	6
棟	栋	dòng	m	(measure word for buildings)	2
讀書	读书	dú shū	vo	to attend school; to study; to read aloud	8
短		duǎn	adj	short	10
E					
而		ér	conj	(conjunction to connect two clauses)	10
兒童	儿童	értóng	n	children	9
F					
發生	发生	fāshēng	v	to happen; to occur; to take place	6
番		fān	m	(measure word for rounds; measure word for type or kind)	9
翻譯	翻译	fānyì	v/n	to translate; interpreter; translation	7
反對	反对	fǎnduì	v	to oppose	9
非…不可		fēi…bù kě		have to; nothing but…would do	4
分手		fēn shǒu	vo	to break up; to part company	6
風景	风景	fēngjǐng	n	scenic landscape; scenery	10
負擔	负担	fùdān	n	burden	8
G					
敢		gǎn	mv	to dare	7
感覺	感觉	gǎnjué	n/v	feeling; sense perception; to feel; to perceive	7
鋼琴	钢琴	gāngqín	n	piano	9

Traditional	Simplified	Pinyin	Part of Speech	English	Lesson
高原		gāoyuán	n	plateau	10
高中		gāozhōng	n	senior high school	6
各		gè	pr	each; every	3
根本		gēnběn	adv	at all; simply	6
弓		gōng	n	bow	1
供		gōng	v	to provide; to support financially	8
工學院	工学院	gōng xuéyuàn	n	school of engineering	5
工資	工资	gōngzī	n	wages; pay	8
購物	购物	gòuwù	v	to shop	4
掛	挂	guà	v	to hang; to hang up	2
乖		guāi	adj	(of children) obedient; well-behaved	8
管		guǎn	v	to control, manage; to mind, to care about	5
管理學院	管理学院	guǎnlǐ xuéyuàn	n	school of management	5
廣東	广东	Guǎngdōng	pn	Guangdong (a Chinese province)	3
廣州	广州	Guǎngzhōu	pn	Guangzhou	10
櫃子	柜子	guìzi	n	cabinet; cupboard	2
過幾天	过几天	guò jǐ tiān		in a few days	2
過節	过节	guò jié	vo	to celebrate a holiday	10

H

哈		hā	ono	(imitating laughter)	6
哈爾濱	哈尔滨	Hā'ěrbīn	pn	Harbin	10
海		hǎi	n	sea; ocean	10
害		hài	v	to cause trouble; to do harm to	7
好處	好处	hǎochu	n	advantage; benefit	1
好看		hǎokàn	adj	nice-looking; attractive	4
河流		héliú	n	river	10
烘乾機	烘干机	hōnggānjī	n	(clothes) dryer	2
湖南		Húnán	pn	Hunan (a Chinese province)	3
畫畫兒	画画儿	huà huàr	vo	to draw; to paint	9
化學	化学	huàxué	n	chemistry	5
黃河		Huáng Hé	pn	the Yellow River	10
回		huí	m	(measure word for frequency of an action)	6
火車	火车	huǒchē	n	train	10

Traditional	Simplified	Pinyin	Part of Speech	English	Lesson
J					
雞	鸡	jī	n	chicken	3
擠	挤	jǐ	adj/v	crowded; to push against; to squeeze	10
記仇	记仇	jì chóu	vo	to bear a grudge; to harbor resentment	6
加		jiā	v	to add	4
家教		jiājiào	n	tutor	8
家庭		jiātíng	n	family (unit); household	8
家鄉	家乡	jiāxiāng	n	hometown	10
家長	家长	jiāzhǎng	n	parents; guardian of a child	9
價格	价格	jiàgé	n	price	7
價錢	价钱	jiàqian	n	price	4
減輕	减轻	jiǎnqīng	v	to lessen	8
建議	建议	jiànyì	n/v	suggestion; to suggest	5
將來	将来	jiānglái	n	future	5
獎學金	奖学金	jiǎngxuéjīn	n	scholarship money	8
交		jiāo	v	to hand over	8
交朋友		jiāo péngyou	vo	to make friends	6
叫		jiào	v	to make (someone do something)	6
叫(菜)	叫(菜)	jiào (cài)	v(o)	to order (food)	3
教授		jiàoshòu	n	professor	5
教育		jiàoyù	n/v	education; to educate	8
接近		jiējìn	v	to be close to	10
結果	结果	jiéguǒ	conj/n	as a result; result	7
結婚	结婚	jié hūn	vo	to get married; to marry	9
解決	解决	jiějué	v	to solve; to resolve	5
借		jiè	v	to borrow; to lend	8
芥蘭	芥兰	jièlán	n	Chinese broccoli	3
幾乎	几乎	jīhū	adv	almost	7
急忙		jímáng	adv	hastily; in a hurry	7
集中		jízhōng	v	to concentrate; to be concentrated	10
金融		jīnróng	n	finance; banking	5
經常	经常	jīngcháng	adv	often; frequently	5
經濟	经济	jīngjì	n	economics; economy	5

Traditional	Simplified	Pinyin	Part of Speech	English	Lesson
經驗	经验	jīngyàn	n/v	experience; to experience	5
景點	景点	jǐngdiǎn	n	scenic spot; tourist spot	10
舊	旧	jiù	adj	(of things) old	2
句		jù	m	(measure word for sentences)	6
決定	决定	juédìng	v/n	to decide; decision	5
K					
卡拉OK		kǎlā-OK (ōukēi)		karaoke	7
開朗	开朗	kāilǎng	adj	extroverted; open and sunny in disposition	6
開玩笑	开玩笑	kāi wánxiào	vo	to crack a joke; to joke around	7
開學	开学	kāi xué	vo	to begin a new semester	1
看法		kànfǎ	n	point of view	9
考慮	考虑	kǎolǜ	v	to consider	3
科		kē	n	a branch of academic or vocational study	5
柯林		Kē Lín	pn	Ke Lin (a personal name)	1
可靠		kěkào	adj	dependable	7
肯定		kěndìng	adv	definitely	5
空		kōng	adj	empty	2
空調	空调	kōngtiáo	n	air conditioning	2
恐怕		kǒngpà	adv	I'm afraid that; I think perhaps; probably	2
口水		kǒushuǐ	n	saliva	3
口味		kǒuwèi	n	taste; dietary preference	3
L					
垃圾		lājī	n	garbage; trash	7
拉		là	v	to leave (something) behind	1
辣		là	adj	spicy	3
老是		lǎoshì	adv	always	7
李哲		Lǐ Zhé	pn	Li Zhe (a personal name)	5
理解		lǐjiě	v	to understand	9
厲害	厉害	lìhai	adj	terrible; formidable	9
麗莎	丽莎	Lìshā	pn	Lisa (a personal name)	3
歷史	历史	lìshǐ	n	history	5
良好		liánghǎo	adj	good	8

Traditional	Simplified	Pinyin	Part of Speech	English	Lesson
輛	辆	liàng	m	(measure word for vehicles)	1
了解		liǎojiě	v	to understand; to know about; to be informed	10
林雪梅		Lín Xuěméi	pn	Lin Xuemei (a personal name)	3
零用錢	零用钱	língyòngqián	n	allowance; spending money	8
流		liú	v	to flow	3
留學	留学	liú xué	vo	to study abroad	9
留學生	留学生	liúxuéshēng	n	student studying abroad	3
路綫	路线	lùxiàn	n	route; itinerary	10
旅遊	旅游	lǚyóu	v/n	to travel; travel	10
落伍	落伍	luòwǔ	v	to lag behind; to be outdated	7

M

Traditional	Simplified	Pinyin	Part of Speech	English	Lesson
馬虎	马虎	mǎhu	adj	careless; perfunctory; mediocre	6
馬路	马路	mǎlù	n	road	2
滿	满	mǎn	adj	full	9
毛巾		máojīn	n	towel	4
毛衣		máoyī	n	woolen sweater	4
美滿	美满	měimǎn	adj	happy and satisfying	9
門	门	mén	n	door	2
門	门	mén	m	(measure word for academic courses)	5
門口	门口	ménkǒu	n	doorway; entrance	3
迷		mí	n/v	fan; to be infatuated with	6
免費	免费	miǎnfèi	v	to be free of charge	7
面積	面积	miànjī	n	area	10
民族		mínzú	n	ethnic group; people; nationality	10
名牌(兒)	名牌(儿)	míngpái(r)	n	famous brand; name brand	4
墨西哥		Mòxīgē	pn	Mexico	9

N

Traditional	Simplified	Pinyin	Part of Speech	English	Lesson
難吃	难吃	nánchī	adj	not tasty	8
難道	难道	nándào	adv	Do you mean to say…	4
難怪	难怪	nánguài	adv	no wonder	6
南京		Nánjīng	pn	Nanjing	10
鬧彆扭	闹别扭	nào bièniu	vo	to have a small conflict; to be at odds (with someone)	6

Traditional	Simplified	Pinyin	Part of Speech	English	Lesson
嫩		nèn	adj	tender	3
牛仔褲	牛仔裤	niúzǎikù	n	jeans	4
農村	农村	nóngcūn	n	countryside; village; rural area	8
O					
噢	噢	ō	interj	oh!	6
P					
牌子		páizi	n	brand	4
陪		péi	v	to accompany	6
碰見	碰见	pèng jiàn	vc	to bump into; to run into	5
貧	贫	pín	adj	gabby; glib	4
平原		píngyuán	n	plain	10
Q					
其實	其实	qíshí	adv	actually	5
其他		qítā	pr	other; else	5
欠		qiàn	v	to owe	8
清淡		qīngdàn	adj	light in flavor	3
輕鬆	轻松	qīngsōng	adj	light; relaxed	5
清蒸	清蒸	qīngzhēng	v	to steam (food without heavy sauce)	3
取得		qǔdé	v	to obtain; to gain; to acquire	8
R					
人材		réncái	n	person of ability, integrity, and talent	9
人口		rénkǒu	n	population	10
人山人海		rén shān rén hǎi		huge crowds of people	10
認為	认为	rènwéi	v	to think; to consider	9
日用品		rìyòngpǐn	n	daily household necessities	2
軟件	软件	ruǎnjiàn	n	software	7
S					
嫂子		sǎozi	n	older brother's wife	9
沙漠	沙漠	shāmò	n	desert	10
山		shān	n	mountain; hill	10

Traditional	Simplified	Pinyin	Part of Speech	English	Lesson
上癮	上癮	shàng yǐn	vo	to become addicted	7
少數	少数	shǎoshù	n	small number; few; minority	10
社會	社会	shèhuì	n	society	9
設計	设计	shèjì	v/n	to design; design to design; design	9
申請	申请	shēnqǐng	v	to apply (to a school or job)	5
深圳		Shēnzhèn	pn	Shenzhen	10
甚至		shènzhì	adv	even	7
生		shēng	v	to give birth to; to be born	8
生活		shēnghuó	n/v	life; livelihood; to live	1
生氣	生气	shēng qì	vo	to get angry	6
省		shěng	n	province	10
省錢	省钱	shěng qián	vo	to save money; to economize	1
省下來	省下来	shěng xia lai	vc	to save (money, time)	5
時代	时代	shídài	n	cra; age	7
時髦	时髦	shímáo	adj	fashionable, stylish	4
十分		shífēn	adv	very	6
實際上	实际上	shíjìshang	adv	in fact; in reality; actually	6
適合	适合	shìhé	v	to suit	8
適應	适应	shìyìng	v	to adapt; to become accustomed to	1
世界		shìjiè	n	world	5
事情		shìqing	n	thing; matter	8
事業	事业	shìyè	n	career; undertaking	9
收入		shōurù	n	income	8
受不了		shòu bu liǎo	vc	cannot take it; unable to bear	5
受到		shòu dào	vc	to receive	8
書本	书本	shūběn	n	books	9
數字	数字	shùzì	n	numeral; figure; digit	5
稅		shuì	n	tax	4
說不定	说不定	shuōbudìng	adv	perhaps; maybe	6
碩士	硕士	shuòshì	n	master's degree	9
四川		Sìchuān	pn	Sichuan (a Chinese province)	3
四季如春		sìjì rú chūn		spring-like all year around	10

Traditional	Simplified	Pinyin	Part of Speech	English	Lesson
T					
台		tái	m	(measure word for machines)	2
態度	态度	tàidu	n	attitude	6
談	谈	tán	v	to talk; to discuss	5
毯子		tǎnzi	n	blanket	2
討論	讨论	tǎolùn	v	to discuss	5
T恤衫		tīxùshān	n	t-shirt	4
提		tí	v	to mention; to bring up	6
天津		Tiānjīn	pn	Tianjin	10
條件	条件	tiáojiàn	n	condition; requirement	10
童年		tóngnián	n	childhood	9
同屋		tóngwū	n	roommate	2
同意		tóngyì	v	to agree	4
W					
外賣	外卖	wàimài	n	takeout	7
完全		wánquán	adv/adj	completely; fully; complete; whole	9
網絡	网络	wǎngluò	n	network; internet	7
網站	网站	wǎngzhàn	n	website	7
望女成鳳	望女成凤	wàng nǚ chéng fèng		to hope that one's daughter will become a phoenix; to hope that one's daughter will become successful	9
望子成龍	望子成龙	wàng zǐ chéng lóng		to hope that one's son will become a dragon; to hope that one's son will become successful	9
緯度	纬度	wěidù	n	latitude	10
味道		wèidao	n	taste; flavor	3
衛生紙	卫生纸	wèishēngzhǐ	n	toilet paper	4
文具		wénjù	n	stationery; writing supplies	2
文學	文学	wénxué	n	literature	5
文章		wénzhāng	n	essay; article	5
屋子		wūzi	n	room	7
無論	无论	wúlùn	conj	regardless of...; whether it be...	4
物美價廉	物美价廉	wù měi jià lián		attractive goods at inexpensive prices	4

Traditional	Simplified	Pinyin	Part of Speech	English	Lesson
X					
洗		xǐ	v	to wash	2
洗衣粉		xǐyīfěn	n	laundry powder	4
洗衣機	洗衣机	xǐyījī	n	washing machine	2
系		xì	n	department (of a college or university)	5
下載	下载	xiàzài	v	to download	7
鹹	咸	xián	adj	salty	3
嫌		xián	v	to dislike; to mind; to complain of	8
現金	现金	xiànjīn	n	cash	4
香		xiāng	adj	fragrant; pleasant-smelling	3
相處	相处	xiāngchǔ	v	to get along	6
像		xiàng	v	such as	4
小學	小学	xiǎoxué	n	elementary school; grade school	9
校內		xiào nèi		on campus	1
校外		xiào wài		off campus	1
心		xīn	n	heart; mind	6
心情		xīnqíng	n	mood	6
心事		xīnshì	n	something weighing on one's mind	6
新疆		Xīnjiāng	pn	Xinjiang	10
新生		xīnshēng	n	new student	1
新聞	新闻	xīnwén	n	news	7
新鮮	新鲜	xīnxian	adj	fresh	3
性格		xìnggé	n	personality; character	6
需要		xūyào	v/n	to need; needs	4
選	选	xuǎn	v	to choose	5
選擇	选择	xuǎnzé	n/v	choice; to choose	9
學分	学分	xuéfēn	n	academic credit	5
學位	学位	xuéwèi	n	(academic) degree	5
Y					
壓力	压力	yālì	n	pressure	8
牙膏		yágāo	n	toothpaste	4
沿海		yánhǎi	n	along the coast	10
研究		yánjiū	v/n	to study; to look into; research	10

Traditional	Simplified	Pinyin	Part of Speech	English	Lesson
研究生		yánjiūshēng	n	graduate student	1
嚴重	严重	yánzhòng	adj	serious; grave	7
演唱會	演唱会	yǎnchànghuì	n	vocal concert	6
要麽…	要么…	yàome…	conj	if it's not…, it's…; either…or…	5
要麽…	要么…	yàome…			
鑰匙	钥匙	yàoshi	n	key	6
一般		(yībān) yìbān	adv	generally	2
一帶	一带	(yīdài) yídài	n	the area around a particular place; the neighboring area	10
一乾二淨	一干二净	(yī gān èr jìng) yì gān èr jìng		completely; thoroughly	6
一會兒	一会儿	(yīhuìr) yíhuìr	nm	in a moment; a little while	4
衣櫃	衣柜	yīguì	n	wardrobe	2
衣食住行		yī shí zhù xíng		food, clothing, shelter and transportation; basic necessities of life	7
移民		yímín	n/v	immigrant; to immigrate	9
意見	意见	yìjiàn	n	opinion	5
銀行	银行	yínháng	n	bank	8
英語	英语	Yīngyǔ	pn	English language	8
影響	影响	yǐngxiǎng	v/n	to influence; to have an impact; influence	8
油		yóu	n/adj	oil; oily	3
遊戲	游戏	yóuxì	n	game	7
有用		yǒuyòng	adj	useful	7
於是	于是	yúshì	conj	so; therefore; thereupon	4
原來	原来	yuánlái	adv/adj	as a matter of fact; original; former	6
雲南	云南	Yúnnán	pn	Yunnan	10

Z

雜誌	杂志	zázhì	n	magazine	7
在乎		zàihu	v	to mind; to care	4
咱們	咱们	zánmen	pr	we; us	4
張天明	张天明	Zhāng Tiānmíng	pn	Zhang Tianming (a personal name)	1
着急		zháojí	v	to worry	2

Traditional	Simplified	Pinyin	Part of Speech	English	Lesson
哲學	哲学	zhéxué	n	philosophy	5
真的		zhēn de		really; truly	2
真心		zhēnxīn	n	sincere; wholehearted	6
整天		zhěng tiān		all day long	5
政府		zhèngfǔ	n	government	8
正好		zhènghǎo	adv	coincidentally	3
正式		zhèngshì	adj	formal	7
掙錢	挣钱	zhèng qián	vo	to earn money; to make money	8
之間	之间	zhī jiān		between; among	6
知識	知识	zhīshi	n	knowledge	9
知音		zhīyīn	n	someone who truly understands; soulmate	9
侄女		zhínǚ	n	brother's daughter	9
指導	指导	zhǐdǎo	v/n	to guide; guidance	5
只好		zhǐhǎo	adv	to be forced to; to have no choice but	4
質量	质量	zhìliàng	n	quality	4
至於	至于	zhìyú	prep	as for; as to	5
重要		zhòngyào	adj	important	7
主意		zhúyi	n	idea	3
主要		zhǔyào	adj	main; principal	10
賺錢	赚钱	zhuàn qián	vo	make money	5
資料	资料	zīliào	n	material	7
自然		zìrán	n/adj	nature; natural	10
自由		zìyóu	adj	free; unconstrained	1
總之	总之	zǒngzhī	conj	in short; in brief	7
尊重		zūnzhòng	v	to respect	9
做法		zuòfǎ	n	way of doing things; course of action	9

Vocabulary Index (English-Chinese)

Proper nouns are shown in green.

English	Traditional	Simplified	Pinyin	Part of Speech	Lesson
A					
academic credit	學分	学分	xuéfēn	n	5
(academic) degree	學位	学位	xuéwèi	n	5
accompany	陪		péi	v	6
actually	其實	其实	qíshí	adv	5
actually	並	并	bìng	adv	9
adapt; become accustomed to	適應	适应	shìyìng	v	1
add	加		jiā	v	4
adult	大人		dàren	n	8
advantage; benefit	好處	好处	hǎochu	n	1
agree	同意		tóngyì	v	4
agree (to do something); promise; answer	答應	答应	dāying	v	6
air conditioning	空調	空调	kōngtiáo	n	2
all around; all over	到處	到处	dàochù	adv	10
all day long	整天		zhěng tiān		5
allowance; spending money	零用錢	零用钱	língyòngqián	n	8
almost	幾乎	几乎	jīhū	adv	7
along the coast	沿海		yánhǎi	n	10
always	老是		lǎoshì	adv	7
apologize	道歉		dào qiàn	vo	6
apply (to a school or job)	申請	申请	shēnqǐng	v	5
area	面積	面积	miànjī	n	10
area around a particular place; neighboring area	一帶	一带	yídài	n	10
arrange	安排		ānpái	v	9
arrive late	遲到	迟到	chídào	v	7
as a matter of fact; original; former	原來	原来	yuánlái	adv/adj	6
as a result; result	結果	结果	jiéguǒ	conj/n	7
as for; as to	至於	至于	zhìyú	prep	5

English	Traditional	Simplified	Pinyin	Part of Speech	Lesson
at all; simply	根本		gēnběn	adv	6
attend school; study; read aloud	讀書	读书	dú shū	vo	8
attitude	態度	态度	tàidu	n	6
attractive goods at inexpensive prices	物美價廉	物美价廉	wù měi jià lián		4
authentic; genuine; pure	地道		dìdao	adj	2

B

English	Traditional	Simplified	Pinyin	Part of Speech	Lesson
background	背景		bèijǐng	n	6
bank	銀行	银行	yínháng	n	8
bear a grudge; harbor resentment	記仇	记仇	jì chóu	vo	6
become addicted	上癮	上瘾	shàng yǐn	vo	7
begin a new semester	開學	开学	kāi xué	vo	1
between; among	之間	之间	zhī jiān		6
blanket	毯子		tǎnzi	n	2
blog	博客		bókè	n	7
boat; ship	船		chuán	n	10
books	書本	书本	shūběn	n	9
(to be) born	出生			v	1
borrow; lend	借		jiè	v	8
bow	弓		gōng	n	1
branch of academic or vocational study	科		kē	n	5
brand	牌子		páizi	n	4
break up; part company	分手		fēn shǒu	vo	6
brother's daughter	侄女		zhínǚ	n	9
bump into; run into	碰見	碰见	pèng jiàn	vc	5
burden	負擔	负担	fùdān	n	8

C

English	Traditional	Simplified	Pinyin	Part of Speech	Lesson
cabinet; cupboard	櫃子	柜子	guìzi	n	2
cannot take it; unable bear	受不了		shòu bu liǎo	vc	5
career; undertaking	事業	事业	shìyè	n	9
careless; perfunctory; mediocre	馬虎	马虎	mǎhu	adj	6
cash	現金	现金	xiànjīn	n	4

English	Traditional	Simplified	Pinyin	Part of Speech	Lesson
cause trouble; do harm to	害		hài	v	7
celebrate a holiday	過節	过节	guò jié	vo	10
chemistry	化學	化学	huàxué	n	5
chicken	雞	鸡	jī	n	3
childhood	童年		tóngnián	n	9
children	兒童	儿童	értóng	n	9
Chinese broccoli	芥蘭	芥兰	jièlán	n	3
choice; choose	選擇	选择	xuǎnzé	n/v	9
choose	選	选	xuǎn	v	5
(to be) close to	接近		jiējìn	v	10
coincidentally	正好		zhènghǎo	adv	3
comforter; quilt	被子		bèizi	n	2
complain	抱怨		bàoyuàn	v	9
completely; fully; complete; whole	完全		wánquán	adv/adj	9
completely; thoroughly	一乾二淨	一干二净	yì gān èr jìng		6
concentrate; be concentrated	集中		jízhōng	v	10
condition; requirement	條件	条件	tiáojiàn	n	10
(conjunction to connect two clauses)	而		ér	conj	10
consider	考慮	考虑	kǎolǜ	v	3
continuously	不斷	不断	búduàn	adv	8
continuously; incessantly	不停		bùtíng	adv	6
control, manage; mind, care about	管		guǎn	v	5
countryside; village; rural area	農村	农村	nóngcūn	n	8
crack a joke; joke around	開玩笑	开玩笑	kāi wánxiào	vo	7
criterion; standard	標準	标准	biāozhǔn	n/adj	4
crowded; push against; squeeze	擠	挤	jǐ	adj/v	10

D

daily necessities	日用品		rìyòngpǐn	n	2
dare	敢		gǎn	mv	7
deal with	打交道		dǎ jiāodào	vo	5
decide; decision	決定	决定	juédìng	v/n	5
definitely	肯定		kěndìng	adv	5

English	Traditional	Simplified	Pinyin	Part of Speech	Lesson
department (of a college or university)	系		xì	n	5
dependable	可靠		kěkào	adj	7
desert	沙漠	沙漠	shāmò	n	10
design; design	設計	设计	shèjì	v/n	9
different; not the same	不同		bù tóng	adj	6
discuss	討論	讨论	tǎolùn	v	5
dislike; mind; complain of	嫌		xián	v	8
Do you mean to say...	難道	难道	nándào	adv	4
door	門	门	mén	n	2
doorway; entrance	門口	门口	ménkǒu	n	3
download	下載	下载	xiàzài	v	7
draw; paint	畫畫兒	画画儿	huà huàr	vo	9
(clothes) dryer	烘乾機	烘干机	hōnggānjī	n	2

E

English	Traditional	Simplified	Pinyin	Part of Speech	Lesson
each; every	各		gè	pr	3
earn money; make money	掙錢	挣钱	zhèng qián	vo	8
economics; economy	經濟	经济	jīngjì	n	5
education; educate	教育		jiàoyù	n/v	8
elementary school; grade school	小學	小学	xiǎoxué	n	9
empty	空		kōng	adj	2
end a relationship; (lit.) blow	吹		chuī	v	6
English language	英語	英语	Yīngyǔ	pn	8
era; age	時代	时代	shídài	n	7
essay; article	文章		wénzhāng	n	5
ethnic group; people; nationality	民族		mínzú	n	10
even	甚至		shènzhì	adv	7
experience; experience	經驗	经验	jīngyàn	n/v	5
extroverted; open and sunny in disposition	開朗	开朗	kāilǎng	adj	6

F

English	Traditional	Simplified	Pinyin	Part of Speech	Lesson
family (unit); household	家庭		jiātíng	n	8
famous brand; name brand	名牌(兒)	名牌(儿)	míngpái(r)	n	4
fan; be infatuated with	迷		mí	n/v	6

English	Traditional	Simplified	Pinyin	Part of Speech	Lesson
fashionable, stylish	時髦	时髦	shímáo	adj	4
feeling; sense perception; feel; perceive	感覺	感觉	gǎnjué	n/v	7
finance; banking	金融		jīnróng	n	5
flow	流		liú	v	3
food, clothing, shelter and transportation; basic necessities of life	衣食住行		yī shí zhù xíng		7
for example	比如		bǐrú	v	3
(to be) forced to; have no choice but	只好		zhǐhǎo	adv	4
formal	正式		zhèngshì	adj	7
fragrant; pleasant-smelling	香		xiāng	adj	3
free; unconstrained	自由		zìyóu	adj	1
(to be) free of charge	免費	免费	miǎnfèi	v	7
fresh	新鮮	新鲜	xīnxian	adj	3
full	滿	满	mǎn	adj	9
future	將來	将来	jiānglái	n	5

G

English	Traditional	Simplified	Pinyin	Part of Speech	Lesson
gabby; glib	貧	贫	pín	adj	4
game	遊戲	游戏	yóuxì	n	7
garbage; trash	垃圾		lājī	n	7
gosh; ah (an exclamation to express surprise)	哎呀	哎呀	āiyā	interj	4
generally	一般		yìbān	adv	2
geography	地理		dìlǐ	n	10
get along	相處	相处	xiāngchǔ	v	6
get angry	生氣	生气	shēng qì	vo	6
get married; marry	結婚	结婚	jié hūn	vo	9
give birth to; be born	生		shēng	v	8
good	良好		liánghǎo	adj	8
government	政府		zhèngfǔ	n	8
graduate	畢業	毕业	bì yè	vo	5
graduate student	研究生		yánjiūshēng	n	1
Guangdong (a Chinese province)	廣東	广东	Guǎngdōng	pn	3

English	Traditional	Simplified	Pinyin	Part of Speech	Lesson
Guangzhou	廣州	广州	Guǎngzhōu	pn	10
guide; guidance	指導	指导	zhǐdǎo	v/n	5

H

hand over	交		jiāo	v	8
hang; hang up	掛	挂	guà	v	2
happen; occur; take place	發生	发生	fāshēng	v	6
happy and satisfying	美滿	美满	měimǎn	adj	9
Harbin	哈爾濱	哈尔滨	Hā'ěrbīn	pn	10
hastily; in a hurry	急忙		jímáng	adv	7
have a small conflict; be at odds (with someone)	鬧彆扭	闹别扭	nào bièniu	vo	6
have to; nothing but…would do	非…不可		fēi…bù kě		4
heart; mind	心		xīn	n	6
help	幫忙	帮忙	bāng máng	vo	1
help	幫助	帮助	bāngzhù	v	7
history	歷史	历史	lìshǐ	n	5
hobby; interest; love (something)	愛好	爱好	àihào	n/v	6
hometown	家鄉	家乡	jiāxiāng	n	10
hope that one's daughter will become a phoenix; hope that one's daughter will become successful	望女成鳳	望女成凤	wàng nǚ chéng fèng		9
hope that one's son will become a dragon; hope that one's son will become successful	望子成龍	望子成龙	wàng zǐ chéng lóng		9
huge crowds of people	人山人海		rén shān rén hǎi		10
Hunan (a Chinese province)	湖南		Húnán	pn	3

I

I'm afraid that; I think perhaps; probably	恐怕		kǒngpà	adv	2
ice lantern	冰燈	冰灯	bīngdēng	n	10
idea	主意		zhúyi	n	3

English	Traditional	Simplified	Pinyin	Part of Speech	Lesson
if it's not..., it's...; either... or...	要麼… 要麼…	要么… 要么…	yàome... yàome...	conj	5
(imitating laughter)	哈		hā	ono	6
immigrant; immigrate	移民		yímín	n/v	9
important	重要		zhòngyào	adj	7
in a few days	過幾天	过几天	guò jǐ tiān		2
in a moment; a little while	一會兒	一会儿	yíhuìr	nm	4
in fact; in reality; actually	實際上	实际上	shíjìshang	adv	6
in short; in brief	總之	总之	zǒngzhī	conj	7
income	收入		shōurù	n	8
influence; have an impact; influence	影響	影响	yǐngxiǎng	v/n	8
it's not...but...	不是… 而是…		búshì...érshì...		9

J

| jeans | 牛仔褲 | 牛仔裤 | niúzǎikù | n | 4 |

K

karaoke	卡拉OK		kǎlā–OK (ōukēi)		7
Ke Lin	柯林		Kē Lín	pn	1
key	鑰匙	钥匙	yàoshi	n	6
knowledge	知識	知识	zhīshi	n	9

L

lag behind; be outdated	落伍	落伍	luòwǔ	v	7
latitude	緯度	纬度	wěidù	n	10
laundry powder	洗衣粉		xǐyīfěn	n	4
leave (something) behind	拉		là	v	1
lessen	減輕	减轻	jiǎnqīng	v	8
Li Zhe	李哲		Lǐ Zhé	pn	5
life; livelihood; live	生活		shēnghuó	n/v	1
light in flavor	清淡		qīngdàn	adj	3
light; relaxed	輕鬆	轻松	qīngsōng	adj	5
Lin Xuemei	林雪梅		Lín Xuěméi	pn	3
Lisa	麗莎	丽莎	Lìshā	pn	3
literature	文學	文学	wénxué	n	5

English	Traditional	Simplified	Pinyin	Part of Speech	Lesson
loan; provide a loan	貸款	贷款	dàikuǎn	n/v	8
long	長	长	cháng	adj	1
low	低		dī	adj	8

M

English	Traditional	Simplified	Pinyin	Part of Speech	Lesson
magazine	雜誌	杂志	zázhì	n	7
main; principal	主要		zhǔyào	adj	10
make (someone do something)	叫		jiào	v	6
make friends	交朋友		jiāo péngyou	vo	6
make money	賺錢	赚钱	zhuàn qián	vo	5
master's degree	碩士	硕士	shuòshì	n	9
material	資料	资料	zīliào	n	7
(measure word for academic courses)	門	门	mén	m	5
(measure word for buildings)	棟	栋	dòng	m	2
(measure word for frequency of an action)	回		huí	m	6
(measure word for machines)	台		tái	m	2
(measure word for rounds; measure word for type or kind)	番		fān	m	9
(measure word for sentences)	句		jù	m	6
(measure word for stories of a building)	層	层	céng	m	2
(measure word for times by which something is multiplied)	倍		bèi	m	10
(measure word for vehicles)	輛	辆	liàng	m	1
mention; bring up	提		tí	v	6
menu	菜單	菜单	càidān	n	3
Mexico	墨西哥		Mòxīgē	pn	9
mind; care	在乎		zàihu	v	4
mood	心情		xīnqíng	n	6
mostly; for the most part	大多		dàduō	adv	10
mountain; hill	山		shān	n	10
move (one's residence)	搬家		bān jiā	vo	1
movie theater	電影院	电影院	diànyǐngyuàn	n	6

English	Traditional	Simplified	Pinyin	Part of Speech	Lesson
N					
Nanjing	南京		Nánjīng	pn	10
napkin	餐巾		cānjīn	n	3
nature; natural	自然		zìrán	n/adj	10
need not; not have to	不必		búbì	adv	4
need; needs	需要		xūyào	v/n	4
network; internet	網絡	网络	wǎngluò	n	7
new student	新生		xīnshēng	n	1
news	新聞	新闻	xīnwén	n	7
nice-looking; attractive	好看		hǎokàn	adj	4
no wonder	難怪	难怪	nánguài	adv	6
not equal to; inferior to; not measure up to	不如		bùrú	v	3
not necessarily	不見得	不见得	bú jiàn de		1
not tasty	難吃	难吃	nánchī	adj	8
numeral; figure; digit	數字	数字	shùzì	n	5
O					
obedient; well-behaved (of children)	乖		guāi	adj	8
obtain; gain; acquire	取得		qǔdé	v	8
off campus	校外		xiào wài		1
often; frequently	經常	经常	jīngcháng	adv	5
oh!	噢	噢	ō	interj	6
oil; oily	油		yóu	n/adj	3
old (thing)	舊	旧	jiù	adj	2
older brother's wife	嫂子		sǎozi	n	9
on campus	校內		xiào nèi		1
opinion	意見	意见	yìjiàn	n	5
oppose	反對	反对	fǎnduì	v	9
order (food)	叫(菜)	叫(菜)	jiào (cài)	v(o)	3
other; else	其他		qítā	pr	5
owe	欠		qiàn	v	8

English	Traditional	Simplified	Pinyin	Part of Speech	Lesson
P					
parents; guardian of a child	家長	家长	jiāzhǎng	n	9
part; section	部		bù		10
perhaps; maybe	說不定	说不定	shuōbudìng	adv	6
person of ability, integrity, and talent	人材		réncái	n	9
personality; character	性格		xìnggé	n	6
Ph.D.; doctor [academic degree]	博士		bóshì	n	9
philosophy	哲學	哲学	zhéxué	n	5
piano	鋼琴	钢琴	gāngqín	n	9
plain	平原		píngyuán	n	10
plateau	高原		gāoyuán	n	10
point of view	看法		kànfǎ	n	9
population	人口		rénkǒu	n	10
pressure	壓力	压力	yālì	n	8
price	價錢	价钱	jiàqian	n	4
price	價格	价格	jiàgé	n	7
professor	教授		jiàoshòu	n	5
provide; support financially	供		gōng	v	8
province	省		shěng	n	10
publish	出版		chūbǎn	v	7
pure cotton; 100 percent cotton	純棉	纯棉	chúnmián	adj	4
put; place	擺	摆	bǎi	v	2
Q					
quality	質量	质量	zhìliàng	n	4
quarrel	吵架		chǎo jià	vo	6
R					
really; truly	真的		zhēn de		2
reason; sense	道理		dàoli	n	4
receive	受到		shòu dào	vc	8
regardless of...; whether it be...	無論	无论	wúlùn	conj	4

English	Traditional	Simplified	Pinyin	Part of Speech	Lesson
relatively; comparatively; rather; compare	比較	比较	bǐjiào	adv/v	1
respect	尊重		zūnzhòng	v	9
restaurant	餐館兒	餐馆儿	cānguǎnr	n	2
river	河流		héliú	n	10
road	馬路	马路	mǎlù	n	2
room	屋子		wūzi	n	7
roommate	同屋		tóngwū	n	2
route; itinerary	路綫	路线	lùxiàn	n	10

S

English	Traditional	Simplified	Pinyin	Part of Speech	Lesson
safe	安全		ānquán	adj	1
saliva	口水		kǒushuǐ	n	3
salty	鹹	咸	xián	adj	3
save (money, time)	省下來	省下来	shěng xia lai	vc	5
save money; economize	省錢	省钱	shěng qián	vo	1
save up; deposit	存		cún	v	8
scatterbrained; forgetful	丢三拉四		diū sān là sì		6
scenic landscape; scenery	風景	风景	fēngjǐng	n	10
scenic spot; tourist spot	景點	景点	jǐngdiǎn	n	10
scholarship money	獎學金	奖学金	jiǎngxuéjīn	n	8
school of engineering	工學院	工学院	gōng xuéyuàn	n	5
school of management	管理學院	管理学院	guǎnlǐ xuéyuàn	n	5
sea; ocean	海		hǎi	n	10
senior high school	高中		gāozhōng	n	6
serious; grave	嚴重	严重	yánzhòng	adj	7
Shenzhen	深圳		Shēnzhèn	pn	10
shop	購物	购物	gòuwù	v	4
short	短		duǎn	adj	10
Sichuan (a Chinese province)	四川		Sìchuān	pn	3
sincere; wholehearted	真心		zhēnxīn	n	6
small number; few; minority	少數	少数	shǎoshù	n	10
so; therefore; thereupon	於是	于是	yúshì	conj	4
society	社會	社会	shèhuì	n	9
software	軟件	软件	ruǎnjiàn	n	7
solve; resolve	解決	解决	jiějué	v	5

English	Traditional	Simplified	Pinyin	Part of Speech	Lesson
someone who truly understands; soulmate	知音		zhīyīn	n	9
something weighing on one's mind	心事		xīnshì	n	6
spicy	辣		là	adj	3
spinach	菠菜	菠菜	bōcài	n	3
spring-like all year around	四季如春		sìjì rú chūn		10
stationery; writing supplies	文具		wénjù	n	2
stay	待		dāi	v	7
steam (food without heavy sauce)	清蒸	清蒸	qīngzhēng	v	3
student studying abroad	留學生	留学生	liúxuéshēng	n	3
study; look into; research	研究		yánjiū	v/n	10
study abroad	留學	留学	liú xué	vo	9
such as	像		xiàng	v	4
suggestion; suggest	建議	建议	jiànyì	n/v	5
suit	適合	适合	shìhé	v	8

T

English	Traditional	Simplified	Pinyin	Part of Speech	Lesson
t-shirt	T恤衫		tīxùshān	n	4
takeout	外賣	外卖	wàimài	n	7
talk; discuss	談	谈	tán	v	5
taste; dietary preference	口味		kǒuwèi	n	3
taste; flavor	味道		wèidao	n	3
tax	稅		shuì	n	4
tender	嫩		nèn	adj	3
terrain; topography	地形		dìxíng	n	10
terrible; formidable	屬害	厉害	lìhai	adj	9
thing; matter	事情		shìqing	n	8
think; consider	認為	认为	rènwéi	v	9
Tianjin	天津		Tiānjīn	pn	10
toilet paper	衛生紙	卫生纸	wèishēngzhǐ	n	4
toothpaste	牙膏		yágāo	n	4
towel	毛巾		máojīn	n	4
train	火車	火车	huǒchē	n	10
translate; interpreter; translation	翻譯	翻译	fānyì	v/n	7

English	Traditional	Simplified	Pinyin	Part of Speech	Lesson
travel; travel	旅遊	旅游	lǚyóu	v/n	10
tutor	家教		jiājiào	n	8
U					
understand	理解		lǐjiě	v	9
understand; know about; be informed	了解		liǎojiě	v	10
useful	有用		yǒuyòng	adj	7
V					
very	十分		shífēn	adv	6
vocal concert	演唱會	演唱会	yǎnchànghuì	n	6
W					
wages; pay	工資	工资	gōngzī	n	8
wardrobe	衣櫃	衣柜	yīguì	n	2
wash	洗		xǐ	v	2
washing machine	洗衣機	洗衣机	xǐyījī	n	2
way of doing things; course of action	做法		zuòfǎ	n	9
we; us	咱們	咱们	zánmen	pr	4
website	網站	网站	wǎngzhàn	n	7
what on earth; what in the world; in the end	到底		dàodǐ	adv	6
woolen sweater	毛衣		máoyī	n	4
world	世界		shìjiè	n	5
worry	着急		zháojí	v	2
X					
Xinjiang	新疆		Xīnjiāng	pn	10
Y					
Yangtze River	長江	长江	Cháng Jiāng	pn	10
Yellow River	黃河		Huáng Hé	pn	10
Yunnan	雲南	云南	Yúnnán	pn	10
Z					
Zhang Tianming	張天明	张天明	Zhāng Tiānmíng	pn	1

Level 1 Vocabulary Index (Chinese-English)

The Chinese-English index is alphabetized according to *pinyin*. Words containing the same Chinese characters are first grouped together. Homonyms appear in the order of their tonal pronunciation (i.e., first tones first, second tones second, third tones third, fourth tones fourth, and neutral tones last). Proper nouns from the dialogues and readings are shown in green. Supplementary vocabulary from the "How About You?" section is shown in blue.

Traditional	Simplified	Pinyin	Part of Speech	English	Lesson
A					
啊	啊	a	p	(a sentence-final particle)	6
阿司匹林	阿司匹林	āsīpīlín	n	aspirin	19
阿姨	阿姨	āyí	n	aunt	20
哎	哎	āi	excl	(exclamatory particle to express surprise or dissatisfaction)	13
愛	爱	ài	v	to love; to like; to be fond of	14
安靜	安静	ānjìng	adj	quiet	17
B					
把	把	bǎ	m	(measure word for bunches of things, and chairs)	14
把	把	bǎ	prep	(indicating a thing is disposed of)	15
爸爸	爸爸	bàba	n	father, dad	2
吧	吧	ba	p	(a sentence-final particle)	5
白菜	白菜	báicài	n	bok choy	12
白英愛	白英爱	Bái Yīng'ài	pn	(a personal name)	2
百	百	bǎi	nu	hundred	9
百事可樂	百事可乐	Bǎishìkělè	pn	Pepsi-Cola	5
班	班	bān	n	class	14
搬	搬	bān	v	to move	16
斑馬線	斑马线	bānmǎxiàn	n	zebra crossing; pedestrian crosswalk	13
半	半	bàn	nu	half; half an hour	3
半天	半天	bàntiān		half a day; a long time	18
辦	办	bàn	v	to handle; to do	11
辦法	办法	bànfǎ	n	method; way (of doing something)	15

Traditional	Simplified	Pinyin	Part of Speech	English	Lesson
辦公室	办公室	bàngōngshì	n	office	6
幫	帮	bāng	v	to help	6
棒	棒	bàng	adj	fantastic; super [colloq.]	18
包	包	bāo	n	bag; sack; bundle; package	20
保險	保险	bǎoxiǎn	n	insurance	15
抱	抱	bào	v	to hold or carry in the arms	18
報紙	报纸	bàozhǐ	n	newspaper	17
杯	杯	bēi	m	(measure word for cup and glass)	5
北	北	běi	n	north	13
北京	北京	Běijīng	pn	Beijing	1
被	被	bèi	prep	by	18
本	本	běn	m	(measure word for books)	14
本子	本子	běnzi	n	notebook	7
鼻子	鼻子	bízi	n	nose	14
筆	笔	bǐ	n	pen	7
比	比	bǐ	prep/v	(comparison marker); to compare	11
比賽	比赛	bǐsài	n/v	game; match; competition; to compete	18
遍	遍	biàn	m	(measure word for complete courses of an action or instances of an action)	15
表姐	表姐	biǎojiě	n	older female cousin	14
別	别	bié	adv	don't	6
別人	别人	biérén	n	other people; another person	4
冰茶	冰茶	bīngchá	n	iced tea	12
冰箱	冰箱	bīngxiāng	n	refrigerator	15
餅乾	饼干	bǐnggān	n	cookies; crackers	14
病人	病人	bìngrén	n	patient	15
不	不	bù	adv	not; no	1
不錯	不错	(bùcuò) búcuò	adj	pretty good	4
不但…而且…	不但…而且…	(bùdàn) búdàn..., érqiě...	conj	not only..., but also...	11
不過	不过	(bùguò) búguò	conj	however; but	9
不好意思	不好意思	bù hǎoyìsi		to feel embarrassed	10
不用	不用	(bùyòng) búyòng		need not	9

Traditional	Simplified	Pinyin	Part of Speech	English	Lesson
C					
才	才	cái	adv	not until, only then	5
菜	菜	cài	n	dishes, cuisine	3
參觀博物館	参观博物馆	cānguān bówùguǎn	vo	to visit a museum	16
餐廳	餐厅	cāntīng	n	dining room, cafeteria	8
草莓	草莓	cǎoméi	n	strawberry	14
廁所	厕所	cèsuǒ	n	restroom, toilet	15
茶	茶	chá	n	tea	5
查	查	chá	v	to check; to look into	19
差不多	差不多	chàbuduō	adv/adj	almost; nearly; similar	17
常常	常常	chángcháng	adv	often	4
常老師	常老师	Cháng lǎoshī	pn	Teacher Chang	6
長城	长城	Chángchéng	pn	the Great Wall	19
長短	长短	chángduǎn	n	length	9
唱歌（兒）	唱歌（儿）	chàng gē(r)	vo	to sing (a song)	4
唱卡拉OK	唱卡拉OK	chàng kǎlā'ōukēi	vo	to sing karaoke	16
場	场	chǎng	n	field	13
超重	超重	chāozhòng	v	to be overweight (of luggage, freight, etc.)	20
潮濕	潮湿	cháoshī	adj	wet; humid	11
吵	吵	chǎo	v/adj	to quarrel; noisy	17
炒麵	炒面	chǎomiàn	n	stir-fried noodles	12
襯衫	衬衫	chènshān	n	shirt	9
成	成	chéng	v	to become	16
城市	城市	chéngshì	n	city	10
吃	吃	chī	v	to eat	3
吃壞	吃坏	chī huài	vc	to get sick because of bad food	15
寵物	宠物	chǒngwù	n	pet	17
初	初	chū	n	beginning	19
出去	出去	chū qu	vc	to go out	11
出租	出租	chūzū	v	to rent out	17
出租汽車	出租汽车	chūzū qìchē	n	taxi	10
廚房	厨房	chúfáng	n	kitchen	17

Traditional	Simplified	Pinyin	Part of Speech	English	Lesson
除了···以外	除了···以外	chúle...yǐwài	conj	in addition to; besides	8
春天	春天	chūntiān	n	spring	11
穿	穿	chuān	v	to wear; to put on	9
窗戶	窗户	chuānghu	n	window	19
次	次	cì	m	(measure word for frequency)	13
聰明	聪明	cōngming	adj	smart; bright; clever	14
從	从	cóng	prep	from	13
錯	错	cuò	adj	wrong	12

D

Traditional	Simplified	Pinyin	Part of Speech	English	Lesson
打棒球	打棒球	dǎ bàngqiú	vo	to play baseball	18
打車	打车	dǎ chē	vo	to take a taxi	10
打電話	打电话	dǎ diànhuà	vo	to make a phone call	6
打工	打工	dǎ gōng	vo	to work at a temporary job (often part time)	19
打噴嚏	打喷嚏	dǎ pēnti	vo	to sneeze	15
打乒乓球	打乒乓球	dǎ pīngpāngqiú	vo	to play table tennis	18
打球	打球	dǎ qiú	vo	to play ball	4
打掃	打扫	dǎsǎo	v	to clean up (a room, apartment or house)	16
打算	打算	dǎsuàn	v/n	to plan; plan	
打太極拳	打太极拳	dǎ tàijíquán	vo	to do Tai Chi (a kind of traditional Chinese shadow boxing)	
打折	打折	dǎ zhé	vo	to sell at a discount; to give a discount	19
打針	打针	dǎ zhēn	vo	to get an injection	15
大	大	dà	adj	big; old	3
大哥	大哥	dàgē	n	eldest brother	2
大家	大家	dàjiā	pr	everybody	7
大姐	大姐	dàjiě	n	eldest sister	2
大小	大小	dàxiǎo	n	size	9
大學生	大学生	dàxuéshēng	n	college student	2
大衣	大衣	dàyī	n	overcoat	9
帶	带	dài	v	to bring; to take; to carry; to come with	12

Traditional	Simplified	Pinyin	Part of Speech	English	Lesson
單程	单程	dānchéng	n	one-way trip	19
單行道	单行道	dānxíngdào	n	one-way street	13
擔心	担心	dān xīn	vo	to worry	18
蛋	蛋	dàn	n	egg	12
蛋糕	蛋糕	dàngāo	n	cake	14
蛋花湯	蛋花汤	dànhuātāng	n	egg drop soup	12
但是	但是	dànshì	conj	but	6
當	当	dāng	v	to serve as; to be	17
當然	当然	dāngrán	adv	of course	18
導遊	导游	dǎoyóu	n	tour guide	19
到	到	dào	v	to go to; to arrive	6
德國	德国	Déguó	pn	Germany	1
德文	德文	Déwén	pn	the German language	6
地	地	de	p	(particle to link adverbial and verb)	20
的	的	de	p	(a possessive or descriptive particle)	2
得	得	de	p	(a structural particle)	7
得	得	děi	mv	must; to have to	6
燈	灯	dēng	n	lamp; light	17
登機口	登机口	dēngjīkǒu	n	boarding gate	20
登機牌	登机牌	dēngjīpái	n	boarding pass	20
等	等	děng	v	to wait; to wait for	6
第	第	dì	prefix	(prefix for ordinal numbers)	7
弟弟	弟弟	dìdi	n	younger brother	2
地方	地方	dìfang	n	place	13
地鐵	地铁	dìtiě	n	subway	10
地圖	地图	dìtú	n	map	13
地下(通)道	地下(通)道	dìxià (tōng)dào	n	pedestrian underpass	13
點	点	diǎn	m	o'clock (lit. dot, point, thus "points on the clock")	3
點菜	点菜	diǎn cài	vo	to order food	12
點(兒)	点(儿)	diǎn(r)	m	a little, a bit; some	5
電	电	diàn	n	electricity	16
電腦	电脑	diànnǎo	n	computer	8

Traditional	Simplified	Pinyin	Part of Speech	English	Lesson
電視	电视	diànshì	n	television	4
電影	电影	diànyǐng	n	movie	4
電子郵件	电子邮件	diànzǐ yóujiàn	n	email	10
碟	碟	dié	n	disc; small plate, dish, saucer	11
訂	订	dìng	v	to reserve; to book (a ticket, a hotel room, etc.)	19
東	东	dōng	n	east	13
東京	东京	Dōngjīng	pn	Tokyo	13
東西	东西	dōngxi	n	things; objects	9
冬天	冬天	dōngtiān	n	winter	11
懂	懂	dǒng	v	to understand	7
都	都	dōu	adv	both; all	2
兜風	兜风	dōu fēng	vo	to go for a drive	16
豆腐	豆腐	dòufu	n	tofu; bean curd	12
肚子	肚子	dùzi	n	belly; abdomen	15
對	对	duì	adj	right; correct	4
對不起	对不起	duìbuqǐ	v	sorry	5
多	多	duō	adv	how many/much; to what extent	3
多	多	duō	adj	many; much	7
多少	多少	duōshao	qpr	how much/many	9

E

Traditional	Simplified	Pinyin	Part of Speech	English	Lesson
俄文	俄文	Éwén	pn	the Russian language	6
餓	饿	è	adj	hungry	12
兒子	儿子	érzi	n	son	2
二姐	二姐	èrji	n	second oldest sister	2

F

Traditional	Simplified	Pinyin	Part of Speech	English	Lesson
發短信	发短信	fā duǎnxìn	vo	to send a text message; (lit.) to send a short message	10
發燒	发烧	fā shāo	vo	to have a fever	15
發音	发音	fāyīn	n	pronunciation	8
法國	法国	Fǎguó	pn	France	1
法文	法文	Fǎwén	pn	the French language	6

Traditional	Simplified	Pinyin	Part of Speech	English	Lesson
飯	饭	fàn	n	meal; (cooked) rice	3
飯館(兒)	饭馆(儿)	fànguǎn(r)	n	restaurant	12
飯卡	饭卡	fànkǎ	n	meal card	12
飯桌	饭桌	fànzhuō	n	dining table	17
方便	方便	fāngbiàn	adj	convenient	6
房間	房间	fángjiān	n	room	16
房租	房租	fángzū	n	rent	17
放	放	fàng	v	to put; to place	12
放假	放假	fàng jià	vo	go on vacation; have time off	19
非常	非常	fēicháng	adv	very, extremely, exceedingly	11
飛機	飞机	feijī	n	airplane	10
(飛)機場	(飞)机场	(fēi)jīchǎng	n	airport	10
費	费	fèi	v	to spend; to take (effort)	16
費	费	fèi	n	fee; expenses	17
分	分	fēn	m	(measure word for 1/100 of a kuai, cent)	9
分鐘	分钟	fēnzhōng	n	minute	17
粉紅色	粉红色	fěnhóngsè	n	pink	9
份	份	fèn	m	(measure word for meal order, job)	19
風	风	fēng	n	wind	11
封	封	fēng	m	(measure word for letters)	8
服務員	服务员	fúwùyuán	n	waiter; attendant	12
附近	附近	fùjìn	n	vicinity; neighborhood; nearby area	17
父母	父母	fùmǔ	n	parents; father and mother	19
父親節	父亲节	Fùqīnjié	pn	Father's Day	3
付錢	付钱	fù qián	vo	to pay money	9
復習	复习	fùxí	v	to review	7

G

Traditional	Simplified	Pinyin	Part of Speech	English	Lesson
乾淨	干净	gānjìng	adj	clean	17
感恩節	感恩节	Gǎn'ēnjié	pn	Thanksgiving	3

Traditional	Simplified	Pinyin	Part of Speech	English	Lesson
感冒	感冒	gǎnmào	v	to have a cold	15
趕快	赶快	gǎnkuài	adv	right away; quickly; in a hurry	15
剛	刚	gāng	adv	just	12
剛才	刚才	gāngcái	t	just now; a moment ago	11
鋼筆	钢笔	gāngbǐ	n	fountain pen	7
高速公路	高速公路	gāosù gōnglù	n	highway	10
高文中	高文中	Gāo Wénzhōng	pn	(a personal name)	2
高小音	高小音	Gāo Xiǎoyīn	pn	(a personal name)	5
高興	高兴	gāoxìng	adj	happy, pleased	5
告訴	告诉	gàosu	v	to tell	8
哥哥	哥哥	gēge	n	older brother	2
個	个	gè/ge	m	(a measure word for many common everyday objects)	2
給	给	gěi	v	to give	5
給	给	gěi	prep	to; for	6
跟	跟	gēn	prep	with	6
更	更	gèng	adv	even more	11
宮保雞丁	宫保鸡丁	gōngbǎo jīdīng	n	Kung Pao chicken	12
工程師	工程师	gōngchéngshī	n	engineer	2
工人	工人	gōngrén	n	worker	2
工商管理	工商管理	gōngshāng guǎnlǐ	n	business management	8
工作	工作	gōngzuò	n/v	job; to work	2
公共汽車	公共汽车	gōnggòng qìchē	n	bus	10
公司	公司	gōngsī	n	company	19
公寓	公寓	gōngyù	n	apartment	17
公園	公园	gōngyuán	n	park	11
功課	功课	gōngkè	n	homework; schoolwork	7
狗	狗	gǒu	n	dog	14
夠	够	gòu	adj	enough	12
拐	拐	guǎi	v	to turn	13
廣告	广告	guǎnggào	n	advertisement	17
逛街	逛街	guàng jiē	vo	to windowshop	4
貴	贵	guì	adj	honorable; expensive	1
櫃子	柜子	guìzi	n	cabinet; cupboard	17
國際	国际	guójì	adj	international	18

Traditional	Simplified	Pinyin	Part of Speech	English	Lesson
果汁	果汁	guǒzhī	n	fruit juice	5
過	过	guò	v	to pass	13
過敏	过敏	guòmǐn	v	to be allergic to	15
過	过	guo	p	(particle used after a verb to indicate a past experience)	13

H

還	还	hái	adv	also; too; as well	3
還是	还是	háishi	conj	or	3
孩子	孩子	háizi	n	child	2
海報	海报	hǎibào	n	poster	17
海關	海关	hǎiguān	n	customs	20
海倫	海伦	Hǎilún	pn	Helen	14
韓國	韩国	Hánguó	pn	South Korea	1
韓文	韩文	Hánwén	pn	the Korean language	6
寒假	寒假	hánjià	n	winter vacation	10
漢字	汉字	Hànzì	n	Chinese characters	7
航班	航班	hángbān	n	scheduled flight	19
航空	航空	hángkōng	n	aviation	19
航站樓	航站楼	hángzhànlóu	n	concourse (of airport)	20
好	好	hǎo	adj	fine; good; nice; O.K.; it's settled	1
好吃	好吃	hǎochī	adj	delicious	12
好幾	好几	hǎo jǐ		quite a few	15
好久	好久	hǎo jiǔ		a long time	4
好玩兒	好玩儿	hǎowánr	adj	fun, amusing, interesting	11
好像	好像	hǎoxiàng	v	to seem; to be like	12
號	号	hào	m	(measure word for number in a series; day of the month)	3
號	号	hào	n	size	9
號碼	号码	hàomǎ	n	number	16
喝	喝	hē	v	to drink	5
和	和	hé	conj	and	2
合適	合适	héshì	adj	suitable	9
黑	黑	hēi	adj	black	9
很	很	hěn	adv	very	3
紅	红	hóng	adj	red	9

Traditional	Simplified	Pinyin	Part of Speech	English	Lesson
紅綠燈	红绿灯	hónglǜdēng	n	traffic light	13
紅燒	红烧	hóngshāo	v	to braise in soy sauce	12
後來	后来	hòulái	t	later	8
後天	后天	hòutiān	t	the day after tomorrow	16
胡蘿蔔	胡萝卜	húluóbo	n	carrot	12
護照	护照	hùzhào	n	passport	19
花	花	huā	v	to spend	10
花	花	huā	n	flower	14
花粉	花粉	huāfěn	n	pollen	15
花生	花生	huāshēng	n	peanuts	15
滑冰	滑冰	huá bīng	vo	to ice skate	11
畫畫兒	画画儿	huà huàr	vo	to draw; to paint	4
化學	化学	huàxué	n	chemistry	8
歡迎	欢迎	huānyíng	v	to welcome	20
還	还	huán	v	to return (something)	17
換	换	huàn	v	to exchange; to change	9
黃	黄	huáng	adj	yellow	9
黃瓜	黄瓜	huánggua	n	cucumber	12
灰塵	灰尘	huīchén	n	dust	15
灰色	灰色	huīsè	n	gray	9
回家	回家	huí jiā	vo	to go home	5
回來	回来	huí lai	vc	to come back	6
回去	回去	huí qu	vc	to go back; to return	11
會	会	huì	mv	can; know how to	8
會	会	huì	mv	will	11
活動	活动	huódòng	n	activity	13
或者	或者	huòzhě	conj	or	10
護士	护士	hùshi	n	nurse	2

J

Traditional	Simplified	Pinyin	Part of Speech	English	Lesson
雞	鸡	jī	n	chicken	12
極	极	jí	adv	extremely	12
幾	几	jǐ	nu	how many; some; a few	2
記得	记得	jìde	v	to remember	16

Traditional	Simplified	Pinyin	Part of Speech	English	Lesson
計劃	计划	jìhuà	n/v	plan; to plan	19
家	家	jiā	n	family; home	2
家常	家常	jiācháng	n	home-style	12
傢具	家具	jiājù	n	furniture	17
加拿大	加拿大	Jiā'nádà	pn	Canada	1
加州	加州	Jiāzhōu	pn	California	1, 11
夾克	夹克	jiákè	n	jacket	9
檢查	检查	jiǎnchá	v	to examine	15
簡單	简单	jiǎndān	adj	simple	18
件	件	jiàn	m	(measure word for shirts, dresses, jackets, coats, etc.)	9
見	见	jiàn	v	to see	3
見面	见面	jiàn miàn	vo	to meet up; to meet with	6
健康	健康	jiànkāng	adj/n	healthy; health	15
教	教	jiāo	v	to teach	7
腳	脚	jiǎo	n	foot	18
餃子	饺子	jiǎozi	n	dumplings (with vegetable and/or meat filling)	12
叫	叫	jiào	v	to be called; to call	1
教室	教室	jiàoshì	n	classroom	8
教授	教授	jiàoshòu	n	professor	2
接	接	jiē	v	to catch; to meet; to welcome	14
節	节	jié	m	(measure word for class periods)	6
姐姐	姐姐	jiějie	n	older sister	2
介紹	介绍	jièshào	v	to introduce	5
今年	今年	jīnnián	t	this year	3
今天	今天	jīntiān	t	today	3
緊張	紧张	jǐnzhāng	adj	nervous, anxious	10
近	近	jìn	adj	near	13
進	进	jìn	v	to enter	5
進來	进来	jìn lai	vc	to come in	5
經濟	经济	jīngjì	n	economics	8
經理	经理	jīnglǐ	n	manager	2
九月	九月	jiǔyuè	n	September	3
就	就	jiù	adv	precisely; exactly	6

Traditional	Simplified	Pinyin	Part of Speech	English	Lesson
就	就	jiù	adv	just; only (indicating a small number)	16
橘子	橘子	júzi	n	tangerine	14
橘紅色	橘红色	júhóngsè	n	orange (color)	9
覺得	觉得	juéde	v	to feel; to think	4
軍人	军人	jūnrén	n	soldier; military officer	2
K					
咖啡	咖啡	kāfēi	n	coffee	5
咖啡色	咖啡色	kāfēisè	n	brown; coffee color	9
卡片	卡片	kǎpiàn	n	card	14
開車	开车	kāi chē	vo	to drive a car	10
開會	开会	kāi huì	vo	to have a meeting	6
開始	开始	kāishǐ	v/n	to begin, to start; beginning	7
看	看	kàn	v	to watch; to look; to read	4
看病	看病	kàn bìng	vo	to see a doctor; (of a doctor) to see a patient	15
考試	考试	kǎo shì	vo/n	to give or take a test; test	6
烤鴨	烤鸭	kǎoyā	n	roast duck	20
靠	靠	kào	v	to lean on; to lean against; to be next to	19
咳嗽	咳嗽	késòu	v	to cough	15
渴	渴	kě	adj	thirsty	12
可愛	可爱	kě'ài	adj	cute; lovable	14
可口可樂	可口可乐	Kěkǒukělè	pn	Coca-Cola	5
可樂	可乐	kělè	n	[Coke or Pepsi] cola	5
可能	可能	kěnéng	adv/adj	maybe; possible	17
可是	可是	kěshì	conj	but	3
可以	可以	kěyǐ	mv	can; may	5
刻	刻	kè	m	quarter (of an hour)	3
課	课	kè	n	class; course; lesson	6
課本	课本	kèběn	n	textbook	7
課文	课文	kèwén	n	text of a lesson	7
客氣	客气	kèqi	adj	polite	6
客廳	客厅	kètīng	n	living room	17
空(兒)	空(儿)	kòng(r)	n	free time	6

Traditional	Simplified	Pinyin	Part of Speech	English	Lesson
口	口	kǒu	m	(measure word for number of family members)	2
哭	哭	kū	v	to cry; to weep	20
酷	酷	kù	adj	cool	7
褲子	裤子	kùzi	n	pants	9
快	快	kuài	adv/adj	quickly; fast, quick	5
快樂	快乐	kuàilè	adj	happy	10
塊	块	kuài	m	(measure word for the basic Chinese monetary unit)	9
礦泉水	矿泉水	kuàngquánshuǐ	n	mineral water	5

L

Traditional	Simplified	Pinyin	Part of Speech	English	Lesson
拉丁文	拉丁文	Lādīngwén	pn	the Latin language	6
來	来	lái	v	to come	5
藍	蓝	lán	adj	blue	10
籃球	篮球	lánqiú	n	basketball	18
懶	懒	lǎn	adj	lazy	15
老師	老师	lǎoshī	n	teacher	1
了	了	le	p	(a dynamic particle)	5
累	累	lèi	adj	tired	8
冷	冷	lěng	adj	cold	11
離	离	lí	prep	away from	13
梨	梨	lí	n	pear	14
裏邊	里边	lǐbian	n	inside	13
禮物	礼物	lǐwù	n	gift; present	14
李友	李友	Lǐ Yǒu	pn	(a personal name)	1
力氣	力气	lìqi	n	strength; effort	16
歷史	历史	lìshǐ	n	history	8
倆	俩	liǎ	nu+m	(coll.) two	16
連	连	lián	prep	even	17
臉	脸	liǎn	n	face	14
練習	练习	liànxí	v	to practice	6
練習本	练习本	liànxíběn	n	exercise book	7
涼拌	凉拌	liángbàn	v	(of food) cold "blended"; cold tossed	12

Traditional	Simplified	Pinyin	Part of Speech	English	Lesson
涼快	凉快	liángkuai	adj	pleasantly cool	11
兩	两	liǎng	nu	two; a couple of	2
聊天(兒)	聊天(儿)	liáo tiān(r)	vo	to chat	5
零食	零食	língshí	n	snacks	14
另外	另外	lìngwài	conj	furthermore; in addition	17
流鼻涕	流鼻涕	liú bítì	vo	to have a runny nose	15
樓	楼	lóu	n	multi-storied building; floor (of a multi-level building)	14
路口	路口	lùkǒu	n	intersection	13
錄音	录音	lùyīn	n/vo	sound recording; to record	7
旅館	旅馆	lǚguǎn	n	hotel	19
旅行	旅行	lǚxíng	v	to travel	16
旅行社	旅行社	lǚxíngshè	n	travel agency	19
綠	绿	lǜ	adj	green	10
律師	律师	lǜshī	n	lawyer	2
亂	乱	luàn	adv	randomly; arbitrarily; messily	15

M

媽媽	妈妈	māma	n	mother, mom	2
馬上	马上	mǎshàng	adv	immediately; right away	19
嗎	吗	ma	qp	(question particle)	1
麻煩	麻烦	máfan	adj	troublesome	10
麻婆豆腐	麻婆豆腐	mápó dòufu	n	Mapo tofu	12
買	买	mǎi	v	to buy	9
賣完	卖完	mài wán	vc	to be sold out	12
慢	慢	màn	adj	slow	7
慢跑	慢跑	mànpǎo	v/n	to jog; jogging	18
忙	忙	máng	adj	busy	3
貓	猫	māo	n	cats	15
毛	毛	máo	m	(measure word for 1/10 of a kuai, dime (for US money))	9
毛筆	毛笔	máobǐ	n	writing brush	7
毛衣	毛衣	máoyī	n	woolen sweater	9
帽子	帽子	màozi	n	hat; cap	9
沒	没	méi	adv	not	2
沒關係	没关系	méi guānxi		it doesn't matter	12

Traditional	Simplified	Pinyin	Part of Speech	English	Lesson
每	每	měi	pr	every; each	10
美國	美国	Měiguó	pn	America	1
美式	美式	Měishì	adj	American-style	18
美元	美元	Měiyuán	n	U.S. currency	17
妹妹	妹妹	mèimei	n	younger sister	2
悶熱	闷热	mēnrè	adj	hot and stifling	11
米飯	米饭	mǐfàn	n	cooked rice	12
免稅商店	免税商店	miǎn shuì shāngdiàn	n	duty-free shop	20
面試	面试	miànshì	v/n	to interview; interview	11
明天	明天	míngtiān	t	tomorrow	3
名勝古蹟	名胜古迹	míngshèng gǔjì		famous scenic spots and historic sites	19
名字	名字	míngzi	n	name	1
墨西哥	墨西哥	Mòxīgē	pn	Mexico	1
母親節	母亲节	Mǔqīnjié	pn	Mother's Day	3

N

Traditional	Simplified	Pinyin	Part of Speech	English	Lesson
拿	拿	ná	v	to take; to get	13
哪	哪	nǎ/něi	qpr	which	6
哪裏	哪里	nǎli	pr	where	7
哪兒	哪儿	nǎr	qpr	where	5
那	那	nà	pr	that	2
那	那	nà	conj	in that case; then	4
那裏	那里	nàli	pr	there	17
那麼	那么	nàme	pr	(indicating degree) so, such	11
那兒	那儿	nàr	pr	there	8
奶奶	奶奶	nǎinai	n	paternal grandmother	20
男	男	nán	adj	male	2
南	南	nán	n	south	13
難	难	nán	adj	difficult	7
難受	难受	nánshòu	adj	hard to bear; uncomfortable	18
呢	呢	ne	qp	(question particle)	1

Traditional	Simplified	Pinyin	Part of Speech	English	Lesson
能	能	néng	mv	can; to be able to	8
你	你	nǐ	pr	you	1
年級	年级	niánjí	n	grade in school	6
念	念	niàn	v	to read aloud	7
您	您	nín	pr	you (honorific for 你)	6
牛肉	牛肉	niúròu	n	beef	12
紐約	纽约	Niǔyuē	pn	New York	1
農民	农民	nóngmín	n	farmer; peasant	2
暖和	暖和	nuǎnhuo	adj	warm	11
女	女	nǚ	adj	female	2
女兒	女儿	nǚ'ér	n	daughter	2

P

Traditional	Simplified	Pinyin	Part of Speech	English	Lesson
怕	怕	pà	v	to fear; to be afraid of	18
拍	拍	pāi	n	racket	18
盤	盘	pán	n	plate; dish	12
旁邊	旁边	pángbiān	n	side	13
胖	胖	pàng	adj	fat	18
跑步	跑步	pǎo bù	vo	to jog	18
朋友	朋友	péngyou	n	friend	3
篇	篇	piān	m	(measure word for essays, articles, etc.)	8
便宜	便宜	piányi	adj	cheap; inexpensive	9
片	片	piàn	m	(measure word for tablet; slice)	15
票	票	piào	n	ticket	10
漂亮	漂亮	piàoliang	adj	pretty	5
瓶	瓶	píng	m/n	(measure word for bottles); bottle	5
平常	平常	píngcháng	adv	usually	7
蘋果	苹果	píngguǒ	n	apple	14
葡萄	葡萄	pútao	n	grape	14
葡萄牙文	葡萄牙文	Pútáoyáwén	pn	the Portuguese language	6

Q

Traditional	Simplified	Pinyin	Part of Speech	English	Lesson
騎摩托車	骑摩托车	qí mótuōchē	vo	to ride a motorcycle	10
騎自行車	骑自行车	qí zìxíngchē	vo	to ride a bicycle	10

Traditional	Simplified	Pinyin	Part of Speech	English	Lesson
起床	起床	qǐ chuáng	vo	to get up	8
起飛	起飞	qǐfēi	v	(of airplanes) to take off	20
氣球	气球	qìqiú	n	balloons	14
汽水(兒)	汽水(儿)	qìshuǐ(r)	n	soft drink; soda pop	5, 14
千	千	qiān	nu	thousand	19
鉛筆	铅笔	qiānbǐ	n	pencil	7
簽證	签证	qiānzhèng	n	visa	19
錢	钱	qián	n	money	9
前	前	qián	n	forward; ahead	13
前面	前面	qiánmian	n	ahead; in front of	13
青菜	青菜	qīngcài	n	green/leafy vegetable	12
清楚	清楚	qīngchu	adj	clear	12
情人節	情人节	Qíngrénjié	pn	Valentine's Day	3
晴天	晴天	qíngtiān	n	sunny day	11
請	请	qǐng	v	please (polite form of request); to treat or to invite (somebody)	1
請客	请客	qǐng kè	vo	to invite someone (to dinner, coffee, etc.); to play the host	4
秋天	秋天	qiūtiān	n	autumn; fall	11
去	去	qù	v	to go	4
去年	去年	qùnián	t	last year	14
裙子	裙子	qúnzi	n	skirt	9

R

Traditional	Simplified	Pinyin	Part of Speech	English	Lesson
然後	然后	ránhòu	adv	then	10
讓	让	ràng	v	to allow or cause (somebody to do something)	10
熱	热	rè	adj	hot	11
人	人	rén	n	people; person	1
人民幣	人民币	rénmínbì	n	renminbi (RMB, Chinese currency)	17
認識	认识	rènshi	v	to be acquainted with; recognize	3
日本	日本	Rìběn	pn	Japan	1, 13
日記	日记	rìjì	n	diary	8
日文	日文	Rìwén	pn	the Japanese language	6, 13
容易	容易	róngyì	adj	easy	7

Traditional	Simplified	Pinyin	Part of Speech	English	Lesson
肉	肉	ròu	n	meat	12
如果…的話	如果…的话	rúguǒ… de huà	conj	if	9

S

Traditional	Simplified	Pinyin	Part of Speech	English	Lesson
沙發	沙发	shāfā	n	sofa	17
商店	商店	shāngdiàn	n	store; shop	9
商人	商人	shāngrén	n	merchant; businessperson	2
商務艙	商务舱	shāngwùcāng	n	business class	19
上	上	shàng	v	to go [colloq.]	13
上菜	上菜	shàng cài	vo	to serve food	12
上次	上次	shàng cì		last time	15
上大學	上大学	shàng dàxué	vo	to attend college/university	18
上個	上个	shàng ge		the previous one	7
上海	上海	Shànghǎi	pn	Shanghai	1, 12
上課	上课	shàng kè	vo	to go to a class; to start a class; to be in class	7
上網	上网	shàng wǎng	vo	to go online; to surf the internet	8
上午	上午	shàngwǔ	t	morning	6
上衣	上衣	shàngyī	n	upper garment	9
誰	谁	shéi	qpr	who	2
身體	身体	shēntǐ	n	body; health	15
什麼	什么	shénme	qpr	what	1
生病	生病	shēng bìng	vo	to get sick	15
生詞	生词	shēngcí	n	new words; vocabulary	7
生日	生日	shēngrì	n	birthday	3
師傅	师傅	shīfu	n	master worker	12
十八	十八	shíbā	nu	eighteen	3
十二	十二	shí'èr	nu	twelve	3
時候	时候	shíhou	n	(a point in) time; moment; (a duration of) time	4
時間	时间	shíjiān	n	time	6
實習	实习	shíxí	v	to intern	19
試	试	shì	v	to try	9
是	是	shì	v	to be	1
事(兒)	事(儿)	shì(r)	n	matter; affair; event	3

Traditional	Simplified	Pinyin	Part of Speech	English	Lesson
收	收	shōu	v	to receive; to accept	9
手	手	shǒu	n	hand	18
手機	手机	shǒujī	n	cell phone	10
首都	首都	shǒudū	n	capital city	19
首都機場	首都机场	Shǒudū Jīchǎng	pn	the Capital Airport (in Beijing)	20
瘦	瘦	shòu	adj	thin, slim (usually of a person or animal); lean	20
售貨員	售货员	shòuhuòyuán	n	shop assistant; salesclerk	9
書	书	shū	n	book	4
書店	书店	shūdiàn	n	bookstore	13
書架	书架	shūjià	n	bookcase; bookshelf	17
書桌	书桌	shūzhuō	n	dcsk	17
舒服	舒服	shūfu	adj	comfortable	11
叔叔	叔叔	shūshu	n	uncle	20
屬	属	shǔ	v	to belong to	14
暑假	暑假	shǔjià	n	summer vacation	19
暑期	暑期	shǔqī	n	summer term	14
數學	数学	shùxué	n	mathematics	8
刷卡	刷卡	shuā kǎ	vo	to pay with a credit card	9
帥	帅	shuài	adj	handsome	7
雙	双	shuāng	m	(measure word for a pair)	9
水	水	shuǐ	n	water	5
水果	水果	shuǐguǒ	n	fruit	14
水平	水平	shuǐpíng	n	level; standard	18
睡覺	睡觉	shuì jiào	vo	to sleep	4
說	说	shuō	v	to say; to speak	6
說話	说话	shuō huà	vo	to talk	7
送	送	sòng	v	to see off or out; to take (someone somewhere)	10
送	送	sòng	v	to give as a gift	14
素	素	sù	adj	vegetarian; made from vegetables	12
素餐	素餐	sùcān	n	vegetarian meal	19
宿舍	宿舍	sùshè	n	dormitory	8
酸	酸	suān	adj	sour	12
酸辣湯	酸辣汤	suānlàtāng	n	hot and sour soup	12
算了	算了	suàn le		forget it; never mind	4

Traditional	Simplified	Pinyin	Part of Speech	English	Lesson
雖然	虽然	suīrán	conj	although	9
歲	岁	suì	n	year (of age)	3
所以	所以	suǒyǐ	conj	so	4

T

Traditional	Simplified	Pinyin	Part of Speech	English	Lesson
T恤衫	T恤衫	T-xùshān	n	T-shirt	9
他	他	tā	pr	he; him	2
她	她	tā	pr	she; her	2
它	它	tā	pr	it	9
台北	台北	Táiběi	pn	Taipei	19
太…了	太…了	tài…le		too; extremely	3
毯子	毯子	tǎnzi	n	blanket	19
湯姆	汤姆	Tāngmǔ	pn	Tom	14
糖醋魚	糖醋鱼	tángcùyú	n	fish in sweet and sour sauce	12
糖（果）	糖（果）	táng (guǒ)	n	candy	14
躺下	躺下	tǎng xia	vc	to lie down	15
桃兒	桃儿	táor	n	peach	14
套	套	tào	m	(measure word for suite or set)	17
特別	特別	tèbié	adv	especially	10
疼死	疼死	téng sǐ	adj+c	really painful	15
踢	踢	tī	v	to kick	18
提高	提高	tígāo	v	to improve; to raise; to heighten	18
天	天	tiān	n	day	3
天氣	天气	tiānqì	n	weather	11
天橋	天桥	tiānqiáo	n	pedestrian overpass	13
甜	甜	tián	adj	sweet	12
條	条	tiáo	m	(measure word for pants and long, thin objects)	9
跳舞	跳舞	tiào wǔ	vo	to dance	4
聽	听	tīng	v	to listen	4
聽說	听说	tīngshuō	v	to be told; to hear of	13
聽音樂會	听音乐会	tīng yīnyuèhuì	vo	to go to a concert	16
挺	挺	tǐng	adv	very; rather	9
同	同	tóng	adj	same; alike	16
同學	同学	tóngxué	n	classmate	3

Traditional	Simplified	Pinyin	Part of Speech	English	Lesson
頭等艙	头等舱	tóuděngcāng	n	first class	19
頭疼	头疼	tóu téng		to have a headache	15
圖書館	图书馆	túshūguǎn	n	library	5
托運	托运	tuōyùn	v	to check (luggage)	20

W

Traditional	Simplified	Pinyin	Part of Speech	English	Lesson
襪子	袜子	wàzi	n	socks	9
外國	外国	wàiguó	n	foreign country	4
外套	外套	wàitào	n	outer garment; coat; jacket	9
玩(兒)	玩(儿)	wán(r)	v	to have fun; to play	5
玩遊戲機	玩游戏机	wán yóuxìjī	vo	to play videogames	4
碗	碗	wǎn	n	bowl	12
晚	晚	wǎn	adj	late	7
晚飯	晚饭	wǎnfàn	n	dinner; supper	3
晚上	晚上	wǎnshang	t/n	evening; night	3
王紅	王红	Wáng Hóng	pn	(a personal name)	14
王朋	王朋	Wáng Péng	pn	(a personal name)	1
往	往	wǎng	prep	towards	13
往返	往返	wǎngfǎn	v	make a round trip; go there and back	19
網球	网球	wǎngqiú	n	tennis	18
網上	网上	wǎng shang		on the internet	11
忘	忘	wàng	v	to forget	12
危險	危险	wēixiǎn	adj	dangerous	18
喂	喂	wéi/wèi	interj	(on telephone) Hello!; Hey!	6
位	位	wèi	m	(polite measure word for people)	6
位子	位子	wèizi	n	seat	12
味精	味精	wèijīng	n	monosodium glutamate (MSG)	12
為了	为了	wèile	prep	for the sake of	18
為什麼	为什么	wèishénme	qpr	why	3
衛生間	卫生间	wèishēngjiān	n	bathroom	17
文化	文化	wénhuà	n	culture	19
問	问	wèn	v	to ask (a question)	1
問題	问题	wèntí	n	question; problem	6
我	我	wǒ	pr	I; me	1

Traditional	Simplified	Pinyin	Part of Speech	English	Lesson
我們	我们	wǒmen	pr	we	3
臥室	卧室	wòshì	n	bedroom	17
午飯	午饭	wǔfàn	n	lunch, midday meal	8
舞會	舞会	wǔhuì	n	dance party; ball	14
物理	物理	wùlǐ	n	physics	8

X

Traditional	Simplified	Pinyin	Part of Speech	English	Lesson
西	西	xī	n	west	13
西班牙文	西班牙文	Xībānyáwén	pn	the Spanish language	6
西北航空公司	西北航空公司	Xīběi Hángkōng Gōngsī	pn	Northwest Airlines	19
西瓜	西瓜	xīgua	n	watermelon	14
西裝	西装	xīzhuāng	n	(western-style) suit	9
希臘文	希腊文	Xīlàwén	pn	the Greek language	6
希望	希望	xīwàng	v/n	to hope; hope	8
喜歡	喜欢	xǐhuan	v	to like	3
洗澡	洗澡	xǐ zǎo	vo	to take a bath/shower	8
蝦	虾	xiā	n	shrimp	12
下車	下车	xià chē	vo	to get off (a bus, train, etc.)	10
下個	下个	xià ge		next one	6
下棋	下棋	xià qí	vo	to play chess	4
下午	下午	xiàwǔ	t	afternoon	6
下雪	下雪	xià xuě	vo	to snow	11
下雨	下雨	xià yǔ	vo	to rain	11
夏天	夏天	xiàtiān	n	summer	11
夏威夷	夏威夷	Xiàwēiyí	pn	Hawaii	1
先	先	xiān	adv	first	10
先生	先生	xiānsheng	n	Mr.; husband; teacher	1
線	线	xiàn	n	line	10
現金	现金	xiànjīn	n	cash	19
現在	现在	xiànzài	t	now	3
香港	香港	Xiānggǎng	pn	Hong Kong	19
香蕉	香蕉	xiāngjiāo	n	banana	14
箱子	箱子	xiāngzi	n	suitcase; box	20
想	想	xiǎng	mv	to want to; would like to; to think	4

Traditional	Simplified	Pinyin	Part of Speech	English	Lesson
想起來	想起来	xiǎng qi lai	vc	to remember; to recall	16
像	像	xiàng	v	to be like; to look like; to take after	14
小	小	xiǎo	adj	small; little	4
小姐	小姐	xiǎojiě	n	Miss; young lady	1
小時	小时	xiǎoshí	n	hour	15
小心	小心	xiǎoxīn	v	to be careful	20
笑	笑	xiào	v	to laugh at; to laugh; to smile	8
些	些	xiē	m	(measure word for an indefinite amount); some	12
鞋	鞋	xié	n	shoes	9
寫	写	xiě	v	to write	7
謝謝	谢谢	xièxie	v	to thank	3
新	新	xīn	adj	new	8
新年	新年	xīnnián	n	new year	10
信	信	xìn	n	letter (correspondence)	8
信用卡	信用卡	xìnyòngkǎ	n	credit card	9
星期	星期	xīngqī	n	week	3
星期四	星期四	xīngqīsì	n	Thursday	3
行	行	xíng	v	all right; O.K.	6
行李	行李	xíngli	n	luggage	20
姓	姓	xìng	v/n	(one's) surname is...; to be surnamed; surname	1
興趣	兴趣	xìngqù	n	interest	17
休息	休息	xiūxi	v	to take a break; to rest	15
學	学	xué	v	to study; to learn	7
學期	学期	xuéqī	n	school term; semester/quarter	8
學生	学生	xuésheng	n	student	1
學習	学习	xuéxí	v	to study; to learn	7
學校	学校	xuéxiào	n	school	5
雪碧	雪碧	Xuěbì	pn	Sprite	5

Y

Traditional	Simplified	Pinyin	Part of Speech	English	Lesson
壓	压	yā	v	to press; to hold down; to weigh down	18
押金	押金	yājīn	n	security deposit	17
亞洲研究	亚洲研究	Yàzhōu yánjiū	n	Asian studies	8

Traditional	Simplified	Pinyin	Part of Speech	English	Lesson
呀	呀	ya	p	(interjectory particle used to soften a question)	5
淹死	淹死	yān sǐ	vc	to drown	18
鹽	盐	yán	n	salt	12
顏色	颜色	yánsè	n	color	9
演	演	yǎn	v	to show (a film); to perform	16
眼睛	眼睛	yǎnjing	n	eye	14
洋蔥	洋葱	yángcōng	n	onion	12
羊肉	羊肉	yángròu	n	lamb; mutton	12
養	养	yǎng	v	to raise	17
癢	痒	yǎng	adj	itchy	15
樣子	样子	yàngzi	n	style	9
藥	药	yào	n	medicine	15
藥店	药店	yàodiàn	n	pharmacy	15
要	要	yào	v	to want	5
要	要	yào	mv	will, to be going to; to want to, to have a desire to	6
要不然	要不然	yàobùrán	conj	otherwise	15
要是	要是	yàoshi	conj	if	6
爺爺	爷爷	yéye	n	paternal grandfather	20
也	也	yě	adv	too; also	1
野餐	野餐	yěcān	v	to picnic	16
夜裏	夜里	yèli	n	at night	15
一邊	一边	(yībiān) yìbiān	adv	simultaneously; at the same time	8
一定	一定	(yīdìng) yídìng	adj/adv	certain(ly); definite(ly)	14
一房一廳	一房一厅	(yī fáng yī tīng) yì fáng yì tīng		one bedroom and one living room	17
一共	一共	(yīgòng) yígòng	adv	altogether	9
一路平安	一路平安	(yī lù píng'ān) yí lù píng'ān		have a good trip; bon voyage	20
一起	一起	(yīqǐ) yìqǐ	adv	together	5
一下	一下	(yī xià) yí xià	n+m	once; a bit	5
一言為定	一言为定	(yī yán wéi dìng) yì yán wéi dìng		it's a deal, that settles it; it's decided	16
一樣	一样	(yīyàng) yíyàng	adj	same; alike	9
一直	一直	(yīzhí) yìzhí	adv	straight; continuously	13

Traditional	Simplified	Pinyin	Part of Speech	English	Lesson
衣服	衣服	yīfu	n	clothes	9
醫生	医生	yīshēng	n	doctor; physician	2
醫院	医院	yīyuàn	n	hospital	15
以後	以后	yǐhòu	t	after	6
以前	以前	yǐqián	t	before	8
以為	以为	yǐwéi	v	to assume erroneously	14
已經	已经	yǐjīng	adv	already	8
椅子	椅子	yǐzi	n	chair	17
意大利文	意大利文	Yìdàlìwén	pn	the Italian language	6
陰天	阴天	yīntiān	n	overcast day	11
因為	因为	yīnwèi	conj	because	3
音響	音响	yīnxiǎng	n	stereo system	17
音樂	音乐	yīnyuè	n	music	4
音樂會	音乐会	yīnyuèhuì	n	concert	8
飲料	饮料	yǐnliào	n	beverage	14
飲水器	饮水器	yǐnshuǐqì	n	water dispenser	20
印度	印度	Yìndù	pn	India	1
印象	印象	yìnxiàng	n	impression	16
應該	应该	yīnggāi	mv	should; ought to	18
英國	英国	Yīngguó	pn	Britain; England	3
英文	英文	Yīngwén	pn	English (language)	2
用	用	yòng	v	to use	8
用功	用功	yònggōng	adj	hard-working; diligent; studious	14
游泳	游泳	yóu yǒng	vo	to swim	18
有	有	yǒu	v	to have; to exist	2
有的	有的	yǒude	pr	some	4
有名	有名	yǒumíng	adj	famous; well-known	19
有意思	有意思	yǒu yìsi	adj	interesting	4
又	又	yòu	adv	again	11
右	右	yòu	n	right	13
魚	鱼	yú	n	fish	12
語法	语法	yǔfǎ	n	grammar	7
語言學	语言学	yǔyánxué	n	linguistics	8
預報	预报	yùbào	v	to forecast	11
預習	预习	yùxí	v	to preview	7

Traditional	Simplified	Pinyin	Part of Speech	English	Lesson
元	元	yuán	m	(measure word for the basic Chinese monetary unit); *yuan*	17
圓	圆	yuán	adj	round	14
圓珠筆	圆珠笔	yuánzhūbǐ	n	ballpoint pen	7
遠	远	yuǎn	adj	far	13
願意	愿意	yuànyì	av	to be willing	18
約	约	yuē	v	to make an appointment	11
月	月	yuè	n	month	3
越來越	越来越	yuè lái yuè	adv	more and more	15
越南	越南	Yuènán	pn	Vietnam	1
運動	运动	yùndòng	n	sports	13
運動服	运动服	yùndòngfú	n	sportswear; athletic clothing	18

Z

Traditional	Simplified	Pinyin	Part of Speech	English	Lesson
在	在	zài	prep	at; in; on	5
在	在	zài	v	to be present; to be at (a place)	6
再	再	zài	adv	again	9
再見	再见	zàijiàn	v	goodbye; see you again	3
再說	再说	zàishuō	conj	moreover	15
糟糕	糟糕	zāogāo	adj	in a terrible mess; how terrible	11
早	早	zǎo	adj	early	7
早飯	早饭	zǎofàn	n	breakfast	8
早上	早上	zǎoshang	t	morning	7
怎麼	怎么	zěnme	qpr	how; how come	7
怎麼樣	怎么样	zěnmeyàng	qpr	Is it O.K.? How is that? How does that sound?	3
站	站	zhàn	m	(measure word for stops of bus, train, etc.)	
張	张	zhāng	m	(measure word for flat objects, paper, pictures, etc.)	7
長	长	zhǎng	v	to grow; to appear	14
長大	长大	zhǎng dà	vc	to grow up	14
找	找	zhǎo	v	to look for	4
找(錢)	找(钱)	zhǎo (qián)	v(o)	to give change	9
照顧	照顾	zhàogu	v	to look after; to care for; to attend to	20

Traditional	Simplified	Pinyin	Part of Speech	English	Lesson
照片	照片	zhàopiàn	n	picture; photo	2
照相機	照相机	zhàoxiàngjī	n	camera	19
這	这	zhè	pr	this	2
這麼	这么	zhème	pr	so; such	7
這兒	这儿	zhèr	pr	here	9
真	真	zhēn	adv	really	7
枕頭	枕头	zhěntou	n	pillow	19
整理	整理	zhěnglǐ	v	to put in order	16
證件	证件	zhèngjiàn	n	ID; document	19
正在	正在	zhèngzài	adv	in the middle of (doing something)	8
政治	政治	zhèngzhì	n	politics	19
枝	枝	zhī	m	(measure word for long, thin, inflexible objects, pens, rifles, etc.)	7
知道	知道	zhīdào	v	to know	8
直飛	直飞	zhí fēi		fly directly	19
植物	植物	zhíwù	n	plant	17
只	只	zhǐ	adv	only	4
紙	纸	zhǐ	n	paper	7
中	中	zhōng	adj	medium; middle	9
中國	中国	Zhōngguó	pn	China	1
中國城	中国城	Zhōngguóchéng	n	Chinatown	13
中國國際航空公司	中国国际航空公司	Zhōngguó Guójì Hángkōng Gōngsī	pn	Air China	19
中間	中间	zhōngjiān	n	middle	13
中文	中文	Zhōngwén	pn	Chinese (language)	6
中午	中午	zhōngwǔ	n	noon	8
中心	中心	zhōngxīn	n	center	13
中學	中学	zhōngxué	n	middle school ; secondary school	14
鐘頭	钟头	zhōngtóu	n	hour	14
種	种	zhǒng	m	(measure word for kinds, sorts, types)	9
重	重	zhòng	adj	heavy; serious	14
週末	周末	zhōumò	n	weekend	4

Traditional	Simplified	Pinyin	Part of Speech	English	Lesson
豬肉	猪肉	zhūròu	n	pork	12
住	住	zhù	v	to live (in a certain place)	14
祝	祝	zhù	v	to wish (well)	8
專業	专业	zhuānyè	n	major (in college); specialty	8
轉機	转机	zhuǎn jī	vo	change planes	19
准	准	zhǔn	v	to allow; to be allowed	17
準備	准备	zhǔnbèi	v	to prepare	6
桌子	桌子	zhuōzi	n	table	12
紫色	紫色	zǐsè	n	purple	9
字	字	zì	n	character	7
字典	字典	zìdiǎn	n	dictionary	7
自己	自己	zìjǐ	pr	oneself	10
走	走	zǒu	v	to go by way of; to walk	10
走道	走道	zǒudào	n	aisle	19
走路	走路	zǒu lù	vo	to walk	10, 17
租	租	zū	v	to rent	19
足球	足球	zúqiú	n	soccer; football	18
嘴	嘴	zuǐ	n	mouth	14
最	最	zuì	adv	most, (of superlative degree) -est	14
最好	最好	zuìhǎo	adv	had better	15
最後	最后	zuìhòu		final; last	10
最近	最近	zuìjìn	t	recently	8
昨天	昨天	zuótiān	t	yesterday	4
左	左	zuǒ	n	left	13
做	做	zuò	v	to do	2
做飯	做饭	zuò fàn	vo	to cook; to prepare a meal	17
做瑜伽	做瑜伽	zuò yújiā	vo	to do yoga	18
坐	坐	zuò	v	to sit	5
坐	坐	zuò	v	to travel by	10
坐船	坐船	zuò chuán	vo	to travel by ship; to take a boat	10
坐電車	坐电车	zuò diànchē	vo	to take a cable car, trolley bus, or tram	10
坐火車	坐火车	zuò huǒchē	vo	to travel by train	10
坐計程車	坐计程车	zuò jìchéngchē	vo	to take a taxi (in Taiwan)	10